D1632099

History and Heritage
Consuming the Past in Contemporary Culture

History and Heritage

Consuming the Past in Contemporary Culture

Edited by

John Arnold

Kate Davies

and Simon Ditchfield

Papers presented at the conference Consuming the Past,
University of York, 29 November – 1 December 1996

DONHEAD

© Donhead Publishing Ltd 1998
All rights reserved.

No part of this book may be reproduced or transmitted in any form or by any
means electronic, mechanical or otherwise without prior permission from the
publisher, Donhead Publishing Ltd.

First published in the United Kingdom
in 1998 by
Donhead Publishing Ltd
Lower Coombe
Donhead St Mary
Shaftesbury
Dorset SP7 9LY
Tel: 01747 828422

4303

ISBN 1 873394 28 4

A CIP catalogue for this book is available from the British Library.

Printed in Great Britain by T J International Ltd, Padstow

This book is produced using camera copy provided
by the editors and contributors.

Contents

THE PERSONAL PAST

THE POLITICAL PAST

THE PROFESSIONAL PAST

Foreword

Heritage studies as applied history

Although initially planned as an independent initiative by the editors of this volume, the conference from which these contributions have been selected came to occupy a prominent place in the launching of an exciting new project: *Heritage studies as applied history*. Entirely supported by the Higher Education Funding Council for England (HEFCE) as part of their Fund for the Development of Teaching and Learning (FDTL) programme, this project aims to encourage the engagement of History departments throughout the Higher Education sector with the manifold ways in which the past is consumed outside academe.

By so doing, it is hoped that both academic historians and their students will come to reflect constructively on their working practices and to consider how different they are from 'non-academic' history. Simultaneously, it is the intention of the project to encourage a more thoroughgoing historicization of heritage itself. What are its roots? What continuities/discontinuities are to be discovered between the world of the *wunderkammer* and the world of Walt Disney? How far are the working practices of heritage providers different from those of academic historians?

In parallel to such dialectical reflections on history and heritage, which are carried out in conferences such as that from which the following papers were selected, *Heritage studies as applied history* is concerned to design and develop both undergraduate and postgraduate courses in the field of Heritage, which are then piloted in suitably adapted forms in other HE institutions.

The extensive scope Heritage studies offers for the development of teaching and learning methods is unusual for the humanities. These include: group, project, field, and at postgraduate level, placement work; all of which promote the development of core transferable skills for history students in practical ways within a demanding academic programme. Any enquiries from institutions or individuals interested in the project should get in touch via the address below.

The following essays are intended, *inter alia*, to provide material for reflection in the furtherance of this enterprise and the editors would like to acknowledge HEFCE for its financial support of two of us from the editorial team and for its contribution towards the dissemination costs of this volume.

Simon Ditchfield
Project Director
Heritage studies as applied history
Department of History
UNIVERSITY OF YORK
King's Manor
YORK YO1 2EP

Acknowledgements

The scale of the conference out of which this volume emerged, combined with the relative inexperience of its organizers, ensured that its successful outcome was very much the result of a team effort. We would, first of all, like to thank our former colleague Peter Knight, who was in at the beginning and made significant contributions to our initial and subsequent planning stages before a British Academy Postdoctoral fellowship took him away from York.

Institutionally, we could not have done without the support of Allen Warren, Head of History together with that of Felicity Riddy and Mark Ormrod from the Centre for Medieval Studies. We would also like to record our appreciation of the interest shown in our project by our colleagues Chris Clark and Jim Walvin. Here at King's Manor, the facilities manager, Richard Goodacre, ensured that everything was in place for the conference. However, the smooth running of the actual proceedings was due in substantial part to the cheerful efficiency of Kate Giles, Jonathan Clark and Leigh Symonds who manned the conference office and supervised our (considerable) audiovisual requirements with patience and good humour.

The quality of debate generated by the papers was greatly facilitated by our session chairs who ably helped to draw together the multifarious strands of discussion resulting from such an interdisciplinary meeting of minds. We would particularly like to thank in this regard: Titus Bicknell, Geoff Cubitt, Colin Divall, Jane Grenville, Clare Hemmings, Edward James, Mark Jenner, Nichola Johnson, Ludmilla Jordanova, Paul Keen, Peter Knight, Mark Ormrod, Jane Rendall, Felicity Riddy and Michael Stratton. We also owe a considerable debt to David Lowenthal and Alex Werner for their sage advice whilst we attempted to orientate ourselves in the wide (and sometimes weird) world of heritage providers. To Peter Brown, curator of York's best-kept Heritage secret – the eighteenth-century Fairfax House – we are indebted both for his contribution to the conference programme of activities and for having generously given permission to reproduce a photograph taken from his set-piece re-creation of the sweetmeats laid out on Lord Fairfax's dining room table for our front cover.

We would like to thank *all* those who gave papers at *Consuming the past* and put it on record that the following selection was made in an effort, within the confines of a manageable single volume, to give a representative (rather than a comprehensive) picture of the issues and subjects discussed to those who were not there. We hope that the resulting volume communicates to the reader something of the excitement which accompanied the conference itself.

Finally, we are extremely grateful to Jill Pearce of Donhead for her invitation to publish these proceedings. A special debt of gratitude is owed to Sue Vincent for her herculean labours at the formatting stage when things threatened to go wrong and deadlines loomed.

John Arnold
Kate Davies
Simon Ditchfield   December 1997

Introduction

In 1989, Uppark House burnt down. Uppark was – or is – a late seventeenth-century house on the Sussex Downs, owned by the National Trust. The fire almost completely destroyed the upper floors so that even at ground-floor level, where much of the decorative plasterwork and woodwork had survived, all the ceilings had collapsed and the rooms were filled with wet smoking debris. However, in 1995, Uppark was reopened to visitors; indeed, more came after the fire than had ever visited it before. The house was reopened restored as if 'new' – that is, as the seventeenth-century original. Numerous craftsmen and contractors laboured to rebuild and restore the structure and its interior as it had been before. The end product is, apparently, highly convincing.

In a curious way, this volume was a product of the Uppark fire. A conversation between two of the editors (the relative of one editor worked as a volunteer at the house) revolved around the decision to restore the property, and the motives of the visitors to the new–old house. If the National Trust is now able to build a seventeenth-century house almost from scratch, does it matter if we let some or all of the existing ones fall down? Could we put up seventeenth-century houses wherever they were desired? Is history now, as it were, on tap? If there is some essential difference between the new Uppark and the old Uppark, what is that difference exactly? What is it about that difference that makes more people come to visit it now than before the conflagration? How do they see the house in its present form? Just what is it that we want from the past?

Of course, it is not just Uppark that raises these kinds of questions. History, heritage and the past are ever-present in contemporary culture. They are present in large and obvious ways: in documentaries and educational programmes, in the National Trust and English, Scottish and

Welsh Heritage, in a vast and expanding variety of sites, houses, museums, visitor centres, landscapes, parks, shops, services, pen-sets, tea-towels, coach tours, advertisements, and websites. But the past is also with us in more implicit ways, deliberately invoked or inescapably immanent: in arguments over devolution, nationality, identity; in the rhetoric of politicians in the media; in film, novels, fashion, town-planning, everyday conversation. If Uppark raises particular questions about our relationship to the past, do these other invocations of history and heritage not also deserve examination? What are the politics of invoking the past? Is it always (as some commentators suspect) reactionary and conservative? How does the past function in different discourses? How do we make use of – consume – the past? Do we choose to consume the past, or is it unavoidably present to us? What demands do we make of it, and it of us?

Interested by these questions – in part, perhaps, in an attempt to discover what the right question should be – we held a conference at the University of York from 29 November to 1 December 1996, under the title *Consuming the Past*. Over fifty papers were delivered, on a wide variety of topics; in an attempt to uncover the boundaries of our enquiry, we encouraged the most heterogeneous collection of disciplines and topics one could imagine. Historians, cultural critics, anthropologists, museum directors, heritage providers, archaeologists, postmodernists, practitioners, and other interested parties gathered together and talked to one another; sometimes stridently, sometimes at cross-purposes, but always with interest.

This present volume came out of that conference. Although the articles collected here present less than one third of the conference proceedings, they reflect the intellectual diversity of that weekend, and something of the multiplicity of ways in which we consume, represent, and make use of 'the past'. A war memorial in a Welsh village; an anthology of Irish writing; a Walt Disney comic-book; the faked remains of a pre-historic man; a steam locomotive; a celebrated royal icon; the speech of a British prime minister. The objects under scrutiny in this volume are as diverse as their author's disciplinary preoccupations. What all the essays in this collection share, however, is their concern with the appropriation of historical narratives and historical identities; with the politics of appropriation in the present – who is consuming what past and why?

From their various and often conflictual critical positions, the contributors to this volume address the ways we endorse and contest the meanings of images, stories, objects and memories, exploring both their cogency and contingency. Many of the essays are concerned with questions surrounding the representation, preservation and interpretation of history and heritage by professionals and for a public. Colin Divall and Keith

Emerick both examine the politics of conservation and display. The professional meanings of monuments and museums are also addressed in Christine Johnstone's and Angela Gaffney's contributions. They both examine how the agenda of specialists and institutions inflect or conflict with the more personal aspects of heritage as an occasion for commemoration and remembering. Gaffney considers how civic memorials provided "an essential focus for individual and collective grief" in Welsh communities following the First World War, while Johnstone explores how the historical narratives of museum visitors are often at odds with those of curators and institutions. All four chapters provide accounts of how audiences or heritage professionals use, consume and transform the past through objects and public spaces, through personal and cultural memory.

Some rather different questions concerning history, heritage and cultural memory are raised by Jude Davis's chapter. He considers how the media's construction of a celebrated public figure – Diana, Princess of Wales – works to define and redefine the meanings of history in the popular imagination. Diana has, he notes, been appropriated symbolically in the service of a range of narratives, such as those on the family, femininity, the status of the monarchy and national identity. 'Diana is', writes Davis, 'a potent but highly overdetermined sign; a sign whose meaning is not determined by its content but instead serves to crystallize debates over a range of "hot" cultural and political issues.' Fiona Watson similarly assesses the multiple meanings of popular signs in her examination of viewers' interpretations of Mel Gibson's *Braveheart*.

The past's problematic status as entertainment is a central theme of John Arnold's chapter. Arnold explores the relationship between the representation of violence and the representation of history in popular cinema with particular reference to David Fincher's recent film *Se7en*. *Se7en* powerfully illustrates how history operates as a distancing mechanism from or narrative containment for violence – sometimes sensitizing the viewer to the disjunction between past and present, sometimes precluding interrogation or censure. 'We use the past in many ways within our narratives: for authority, for identity, for distance,' writes Arnold, 'There is a politics and ethics to these uses which we would do well to recognize.'

The concerns Arnold voices – the politics and ethics of consuming the past – became one of the most hotly contested issues of the conference. In the discussion following papers, during workshops and panels, debate frequently turned to the question of the ethical implications of historians', critics' and heritage professionals' relationship to their research and their objects of inquiry; to the past which they interpreted, endorsed and disseminated. How far, it was asked, might history be a necessary fiction in the service of those who create it? Whose past is complicit with which politics? The urgency and tension of this debate is reflected in a number of the papers we have included here. Dave Andress, for example, explores how historians' claims to impartiality and 'truth' impact upon teaching practices; Peter Crawley reviews the discursive divisions between amateur and professional in the fascinating story of the Piltdown hoax, and Allegra Madgwick considers the political significance of the interaction of psychoanalytic and marxist models in recent British historiography. Sophie Breese similarly addresses the implications of the ideological consumption of the past in her appraisal of the reveries of nationhood, the rhetorics of Englishness which permeate the language of contemporary party politics. The meanings of nationhood are also of central concern to Rob Phillips and Sydney Wood. Both their papers consider how the creation of separate history curricula, designed to reflect the differences of the nations within the United Kingdom, has affected the culture of the contemporary classroom. Phillips explores the tension between the desire to consolidate national identities through traditional teaching methods and the mobilization of more 'global' historical accounts through the popular media. In Wood's paper, the over-emphasis on celebrated Scots in the classroom has reduced the teaching of history to something akin to tourism.

The act of reading, many contributors noted, is a central force for the past's consumption. History is transformed, transmitted and legitimated through literary trends and traditions, through critical methodologies and through the desires and priorities of readers. Michael Glencross, Alex Service and Harry Ziegler all examine the function of history in a range of popular reading practices, while Antonia Ward and Cathy Cremin explore the impact of gender on the formation of literary canons. Ward's chapter reviews the legacy of nineteenth-century narratives of manliness whereas Cremin focuses on the tensions between discourses of gender and nationalism in a recent anthology of Irish writing.

The papers in this volume are linked in more ways than this introduction has hinted at and their printed order should not impose itself on readers whom we invite to dip in and out as they wish. Perhaps the paper which came closer than any to reflecting the sheer range of issues and topics implicit in our conference theme is that by David Lowenthal, which indeed opened proceedings. So it is to his paper, and its journey through the many ways in which we consume and transform the meanings of the past – from the Federal Eagle morgue, Denver, Colorado to the tomb of Tutankhamen – that we direct the undecided reader.

THE POPULAR PAST

1

Making Use of Prehistory

Narratives of Human Evolution and the Natural History Museum

Peter Crawley

This chapter is about an example both of making use of history and of making it up. It looks at a celebrated hoax in the search for human origins: the Piltdown man.[1] Thus, while other chapters consider the uses made of history, here I am concerned with how, in rural Sussex, during an Edwardian summer in the years before the First World War, professional, middle class men – most notably a local solicitor and an expert in fossil fish – came to piece together a plausible version of human prehistory.

The fascination associated with the Piltdown man hoax persists. There is little sign – more than forty years since its exposure in 1953 – of this interest abating. This suggests that the hoax carries meanings disproportionate to any real significance it may ever have had as an archaeological or scientific artefact. After all, while at one level it was either an unscrupulous attempt to subvert science, or an unfortunately mistaken attribution, at another it functioned on the larger stage of an international search for human origins.

While interest in Piltdown persists, the search for human origins has become an important subject for popular science books and TV documentaries. Individual palaeontologists – particularly those who work in the field and make significant discoveries – become celebrity scholars, producing books for an interested general public.[2] The field of human origins is covered in scientific journals and the serious press in the same way as the other big questions in science.

In just these ways, human prehistories continue to be made, and in the case of putative human ancestors, this usually takes a literal form as three-dimensional representation, displayed in the museum. So, what I want to do in this chapter is to consider two aspects of the hoax which seem to me to have been neglected. First, I want to see the Piltdown man as an example of the making of a particular (and now rejected) version of human prehistory, and so suggest a certain critical scepticism when we encounter more recent versions of this particular genre. One positive outcome of the hoax – and one reason it continues to figure prominently in histories of the search for human origins – is that its exposure helped define and validate a more scientific study of human origins. Piltdown man could then become reconfigured as the naïve aberration of knowledge-making practices which had not yet attained the self-correcting ability of mature sciences.

But secondly, I want to stress the interplay between popular and scientific versions of human origins: an interplay which continues to characterise our encounters with the distant past. To do this, I want to focus on the role of the Natural History Museum as it emerged both as the appropriate site for the displaying of human prehistory, and also as the centre of professional expertise in an emerging field: an authority to which future finds would be referred. Part of this expertise is contained in the activities of the technicians working behind the scenes at the museum, making ideas about human evolution concrete.

I conclude this chapter by looking at the most recent attempt to solve the Piltdown problem. This account suggests a reading of the hoax which foregrounds the role of the museum at the intersection of professional and lay understandings of human origins. It also gives proper attention to the role of the museum and of museum workers in making and maintaining the hoax.

Charles Dawson and the Piltdown Man

I will begin by recounting the story of the discoveries at Piltdown common in East Sussex. The cranial fragments, jaw, assorted mammal teeth, flint and bone artefacts which comprised the Piltdown common 'finds' were uncovered by Charles Dawson between 1907 and 1915. Dawson was a successful solicitor with a practice in nearby Uckfield. He had a lasting interest in archaeology and antiquities, with a special fondness for 'transitional forms'.[3] As a young man, he had ambitions to be an archaeologist, and had collected a number of undeniably genuine items which had been accepted for display by the Natural History Museum in South Kensington. At least one fossil bore his name.[4] Dawson's status as unofficial collector at the Museum meant that at least since the late 1890s, he had been acquainted with Arthur Smith Woodward, Keeper of Fossil Fish. Dawson was well known as a local collector; referred to, perhaps sarcastically, as the 'Wizard of Sussex'. He donated items to the nearby and newly-established Hastings Museum, of which he was a Trustee, and had written a two-volume history of Hasting's Castle in 1909. But his interests were not exclusively antiquarian and archaeological: he had a hand in the discovery, at nearby Heathfield, of a gas field which was later used for lighting the railway station. He was also a member of the Sussex Archaeological Society, one of the oldest such societies in the country, and he associated with the Ingham circle, a group of local amateurs who collected early flint tools (eoliths) from Sussex and Kent gravel beds. The correspondence between these beds and those at similar levels in France and Belgium where celebrated hominid remains had recently been found, persuaded them that these beds represented the uplands of a vast and fertile plain which united Britain and Europe during the Ice Ages.

In the course of his duties, Dawson routinely visited Barkham Manor. On one occasion, perhaps as early as 1907, he noticed estate workers digging for road-gravel at the side of the drive. To Dawson, the iron-rich gravel revealed by their digging was clearly part of the ancient uplands. Accordingly, he asked the workmen to keep their eyes open; perhaps indicating what he wanted them to keep their eyes open *for*. Some time later, Dawson was presented with the broken fragments of what they had at first taken to be a 'coconut', but which Dawson immediately recognised as an unusually thick human-like skull.

For some years, Dawson took no more interest in the gravel diggings. According to some accounts, he showed the skull fragments, wrapped in newspaper, to any of his acquaintances who expressed an interest in seeing them. In a letter to Woodward, he looked forward to making a significant find, and in 1911, Dawson took the cranial fragments up to the Natural History Museum.[5] He put them on Woodward's desk with a flourish and the exclamation 'How's that for Heidelberg!'. They agreed to dig at weekends throughout the summer. No proper records were kept. At the same site, and at least one other nearby, there were later finds by Dawson, Smith Woodward and the young Teilhard de Chardin.[6] There was a great excitement when Dawson dislodged one side of a very ape-like lower jaw, but a jaw which still had two human-looking molars attached.

The Piltdown finds were publicly displayed for the first time at the December 1912 meeting of the Royal Geological Society; Woodward described the finds, but the subsequent paper was published jointly by him and Dawson.[7] At the meeting, a reproduction of the full skull, with jaw, was presented. Woodward had entrusted Barlow, a technician at the Musem with the task of making the representation. Barlow's skills have been universally commented upon; nevertheless, he was obliged to make a number of versions before Woodward was satisfied. The resulting skull is remarkable for containing so much plaster work (supplied by Barlow) supporting so little in the way of bone. But it clearly showed an unlikely combination of a fully modern skull and an ape-like jaw. This combination seemed an uncomfortably crude version of a 'missing link'; a too-literal representation of part-man, part-animal. However, whatever suspicions there may have been about the authenticity of the find were to be allayed by Teilhard's fortuitous discovery of a suitably ape-like canine tooth in the summer of 1913, and this settled the matter. The accumulating number of artefacts at one place could only mean a genuine archaeological site or a dumping ground for assorted precious relics. This last possibility was considered so bizarre as to be discounted.

Barlow's reconstruction of the skull was challenged by Arthur Keith, Curator of the Hunterian Museum at the Royal College of Surgeons. Woodward enlisted Grafton Elliot Smith to argue for his reconstruction, and throughout 1912 a debate between the two was carried on in the pages of *Nature*.[8] Keith's theory of human evolution stressed the role of early encephalisation: here was a hominid skull exhibiting the domed forehead associated with fully human skulls, found at a site dated well before more recent, but more brutal-looking French finds. In fact, Keith's main objection to the Woodward/Barlow reconstruction was its failure to emphasise the human-looking forehead enough. Consequently, he made his own reconstruction, a more modern-looking skull, which Woodward went some way to accept. Barlow's second official reconstruction of the skull reflected this. For Keith, the ape-like canine always remained a disturbing anomaly, and the embossed illustration of the skull on the cover of his *Antiquity of Man*, published in 1915, omitted it by accident or design.

The debate about human origins and a correct chronology for the 'earliest Englishman' was thus carried on by professional scientists and articulated through reconstructions made in the museum workshops.[9] As in the case of the Neanderthals, and quite commonly in human evolution debates, here the arguments themselves became embodied in the very reconstructions. [10] Elliot Smith had his own reasons to dispute versions of human evolution with Keith, but at least part of Keith's dispute with Woodward rested on a double question of attribution: which was the appropriate home for Piltdown – human anatomy or natural history?

Between 1912 and 1953, the Piltdown skull and its associated artefacts remained in the museum, but new discoveries at Taung in South Africa in 1924 and at Swanscombe in Kent in 1935 made its place in a coherent human genealogy increasingly untenable. Nevertheless, throughout the 1920s and 30s, popular science accounts, school textbooks and museum displays still included Piltdown man.[11] Clearly within an increasingly self-confident, academic speciality called palaeontology there were rumours and suspicions about its authenticity. By the late 1940s when it came under final attack, by a new group of scientific anthropologists, Dawson was dead (unexpectedly in 1916), Keith had retired and Woodward, now blind, was dictating his last work, an account of the Piltdown man called, sadly and ironically, *The Earliest Englishman.* It was published in 1948, two years before Kenneth Oakley's flourine analysis began the process of undermining Piltdown man's status by revealing that while the skull had been stained by contact with iron-rich soil, the jaw had been artificially coloured with dark umber paint to match. What is more, the mammalian fossils had come from a variety of sites around the world; they had been 'planted' to add authenticity. The jaw, was that of a medieval, female orang-utan which had originally come from Tunisia. Oakley suggested it may even have come from the stocks of the Natural History Museum itself.

J.S. Weiners' account of the hoax has remained the authoritative version.[12] It implied that an honest and trusting scientific community had been the victim of Dawson, a devious confidence trickster. Accusations of plagiarism in regard to his history of Hasting's Castle, and allegedly shady dealings in his acquisition of the Lodge at Lewes Castle were invoked to discredit him. By making the Piltdown man fraud, Dawson had clearly revealed himself to be a fraud, and his reputation as collector and antiquarian was ruined.[13] However, Weiner always left open the possibility that Dawson might himself have been the accomplice or even dupe of another, as yet unrevealed, and it is this possibility which has allowed scope for the steady stream of publications on the subject since 1953.

Narratives of Human Evolution and the Museum

What we are considering here, in this briefest of outlines, is a dual narrative; both of archaeological discovery and of a possible course of human evolution. In other words, the Piltdown story tells us something about the knowledge, but also much about the knowledge-making practices which produced it. All recent writings on the subject of human origins has taken this reflexive turn.[14] Any consideration of the Piltdown man hoax must now situate it clearly within its historical, cultural and social context. We expect to find its success explained in terms of pressures imposed by national and scientific rivalries, or of an emergent and unstable disciplinary field, or quite simply of a fraudulent amateur exploiting a system of knowledge-making which depended on a system of mutual trust.[15]

Such accounts necessarily play down the uncomfortable fact that frauds, hoaxes, or just plain mistakes are always inherent to knowledge-making activities. Schliemann's fraudulent discovery of the site of Troy has many parallels with Piltdown: an important excavation coming as the culmination of a long-held ambition, almost indefinitely postponed during a lifetime of business and commerce.[16] Similarly, in the field of human prehistory, there is a long tradition of fraudulent fossils, 'touched-up' or fake cave paintings, and stone age flints made to satisfy amateur collectors.[17] Stories of finds which seem to bear a more direct relationship to Piltdown can be found in Dubois' Java Man and the Moulin-Quignon Jaw.[18]

Amateur collectors like Charles Dawson were typical of a certain type of the professional middle classes who responded to the re-enchanting of nature which was one of the effects of the impact of Darwin's evolutionary ideas. Evidence for this is widespread; in Darwin's writing itself, as well as in more obvious fictional forms.[19] The concrete representations of dinosaurs were an undeniable hit of the 1851 Great Exhibition, and the discoveries of dinosaur fossils and dinosaur footprints by Gideon Mantell in Sussex itself must have allowed Dawson to go on country rambles with newly-opened eyes and imagination. Certainly, the depictions of Piltdown man striding through a primeval Sussex of swamp, jungle and wild hippopotamus suggest this interpretation.[20]

What is perhaps more difficult to explain is why the Natural History Museum and museum professionals should have been involved and effectively – if Dawson was the hoaxer – themselves dupes. To understand this, we need to look in more detail at the concept of a natural history museum as an institution and at the internal organisation of the Natural History Museum in South Kensington in particular.

The Natural History Museum

As it evolved since the renaissance, natural history collections shifted between a number of discourses and represented a number of different epistemes.[21] Analyses of the nineteenth-century disciplinary museum, along the lines which Tony Bennett adopts, probably take too little account of the Natural History Museum's immediate precursors.[22] Museums have always embodied both entertainment and pedagogy, and the modern science/natural history museum began with Charles Wilson Peale.[23] It was always part cabinet of curiosities, part collection of Nature's oddities and part Barnum and Bailey sideshow. The kind of straightforward narrative of progress which Bennett imposes on the Natural History Museum display, was, I would suppose, always only partial and held in place with difficulty.[24] For example, during the late nineteenth and early twentieth centuries, displays of supposed 'missing links' were presented in fairground settings, alongside their more pedagogic representations in national museums.[25] The opportunity to display a reconstructed two-million-year-old primitive Englishman would have been irresistible.

Museum Organisation and Another Possible Solution to the Piltdown Problem

For the institutional aspects of Piltdown man's acceptance, we must look at the museum as organisation. For a long time after the publication of Weiner's book, it was almost universally accepted that Dawson had acted alone. Isolating and blaming the only non-scientist involved (who had in any case died in 1916 having not been rewarded with the public recognition which election to the Royal Society would have entailed) was clearly convenient. Many have been suggested as perpetrators. One of the most recent attempts to expose the perpetrator has even implicated Keith.[26]

The role of the museum and the different categories of possible perpetrator (what one might call 'insiders' and 'outsiders') suggests a more profitable approach. Grigson, by consulting the records of the Hunterian Museum, has suggested that there 'were two classes of baddie involved with Piltdown'; that is, those that did it and knew or suspected.[27] Out of fear of ridicule or dismissal, or simply enjoying the spectacle, they kept quiet. So, for Grigson, the key to the acceptance of Piltdown lies in the 'rivalry between two of the greatest museums in London at that time: the Museum of the Royal College of Surgeons and the Natural History Museum.'[28]

There may be a way of thinking about the Piltdown man hoax which can move across the insider/outsider, professional/amateur divisions. Perhaps the Piltdown man was a youthful practical joke which got out of hand, and its perpetuation was largely the unintended outcome of institutional practices within the museum.

The most recent name to consider as a perpetrator has been provided by Brian Gardiner, who makes a case against Martin Hinton, an assistant working in the Natural History Museum at the time of the hoax.[29] Like Gould's case against Teilhard de Chardin, it raises the intriguing possibility that the Piltdown hoax was a practical joke which circumstances prevented from being exposed at the correct time.[30] In Gardiner's case against Hinton, the key clue turns out to be a canvas travelling trunk with the initials of Martin Hinton inscribed on it, found in the roof space at the

9

Natural History Museum during renovations in the 1970s.

Hinton's name had already been suggested.[31] However, previous attempts to explain his involvement suggested that after Dawson perpetrated the fraud, Hinton spotted it immediately. But:

> Because Hinton was afraid of exposing his boss, Smith Woodward, to ridicule, he sought to expose the hoax by planting increasingly ridiculous fossils, such as the 'cricket bat' at the site in order to scare Dawson and expose him as a fraud in the eyes of Smith Woodward.[32]

Gardiner claims that the evidence from the travelling trunk disproves this explanation. All the Piltdown remains had been stained with the same chemical recipe, one invented by Hinton alone: Dawson becomes Hinton's unwitting dupe. Hinton was 'the sole author of the fraud...well known for his elaborate practical jokes.' He cites further evidence provided by a letter from Hinton to Gavin de Beer (from 1954, after the exposure of the fraud):

> The temptation to invent such a 'discovery' of an ape-like man associated with late Pliocene mammals in a Wealdon gravel might have proved irresistible to some unbalanced member of old Ben Harrison's circle at Ightham.[33]

It has been noted that Hinton himself was a member of this circle.

That Dawson was the victim of a hoax rather than its perpetrator has been a common belief amongst the amateur circles in which he moved. Costello has suggested the active involvement of members of Dawson's circle, including the Uckfield Public Analyst and Principal of the Agricultural College, Samuel Woodhead. According to Costello, he was in league with Dr. John Hewitt and 'one other'. Here the object of the hoax was to ridicule not Smith Woodward but Dawson, and the motive Hewitt's professional pique at Dawson's earlier intervention over the Heathfield gas field.

Once Dawson's innocence is accepted, the 'coconut' story of the first find need not be the malicious invention which accounts hostile to Dawson have suggested. Tests in 1959 showed the skull pieces to be genuine, medieval human bone. Fragments of medieval pottery were also found in this later dig; presumably they had been there in 1912 but overlooked as irrelevant to the narrative of a prehistoric site. The field on the other side of the hedge was known as 'Church Field', the place of local burials following an outbreak of the black death in 1348-9. A medieval human skull might well have found its way into the gravel workings.

After Dawson retrieved other pieces of the skull, and before involving Smith Woodward or finding the jaw, he took them to Woodhead. It was Woodhead who suggested to Dawson that he might 'harden' them by soaking them in potassium dichromate, a practice which also had the effect of altering their colour. Not until the following summer, in company with Woodward, did Dawson find the ape-like jaw, which was also of a dark colour – the same as the 'hardened' pieces. Costello adds:

> The skull, as we have seen, was a genuine find. The Piltdown hoax began with the discovery of the jawbone.[34]

Costello admits there 'has been much speculation in the past that someone at the Natural History Museum in South Kensington was involved in the hoax.' Woodhead may have acted as the 'man on the spot', but clearly at least one accomplice and co-conspirator was required. If Hinton was implicated in this role, there is no assumption that he and Woodhead intended the hoax to last; rather, they wished it to be exposed so as to make a fool of Dawson. As it came to be widely accepted, they deliberately circulated rumours that it was a hoax.[35]

This most recent version of events at least has the merit of offering a plausible explanation for the last artefact found at Piltdown, the so-called 'cricket bat'. No satisfactory explanation has ever been offered to account for this object's possible use. One of the last finds at the site, Dawson uncovered it in 1914. It had clearly been cut and shaped for use as a tool, but was quite unlike any other prehistoric tool, found before or since. Now we may interpret this as Hinton's final attempt to push the joke so far that someone must notice. But the fact was that so much personal, professional and national capital had by then been invested on Piltdown, that there was no retreat.

There remains one intriguing question: why didn't Hinton admit his part in the hoax. Part of the attraction of a practical joke lies in its exposure and the discomfort of the victim, be that victim Woodward or Dawson. The answer lies in the course of Hinton's career within the Museum. Like his contemporary Dawson, Hinton was something of an outsider. In 1905 he had been a clerk in a London Law office and like Dawson, a regular visitor with research privileges in the zoology department. In 1921, he joined the museum in a technician's role, but by 1927 had become Deputy Keeper of Zoology and then Keeper until 1936. He retired in 1945, on the eve of Piltdown's exposure, and was probably the last museum professional who had been involved in 1912. As a young man, he was well-known as a practical joker, and the hoax seems plausible as either (Gardiner's case) perpetrated against the pompous Woodward or (Costello's) in combination with other members of the Ightham circle against the equally pompous Dawson.

However, as Hinton progressed through his museum career, we can surmise that the possibility of uncovering the hoax and revealing his part in it must have receded. In a letter to *The Times*, 4 December 1953, Hinton was still dropping hints:

> I have no knowledge of Kennard's suspicion of a hoax and no names were ever mentioned by him to me. I never suspected a hoax myself, but I have never handled the original material. Had I done that I am pretty sure the recent bones would not have deceived me. But from the beginning I was sure a false association had been made by Smith Woodward – he had lined up the jaw of a chimpanzee (I still regard it as that and not Gorilla) with a human skull and 'Eoanthropus' was a vile compound...

And in a later passage from the same letter:

> I think the original discovery of the skull by the workmen was very likely genuine – but the rest was a practical joke which succeeded only too well.[36]

Some Conclusions

In this chapter I have tried to illustrate how it might have been possible for the Piltdown man to pass as a plausible human ancestor for a period of more than forty years. I have suggested that attempts to explain the Piltdown hoax which fail to take account of the role of the Natural History Museum, and of professionals working within the museum in making and reaintaining it must only be partial. Contrary to these writers who see the museum as a straightforward instantiating of a dominant ideology, I want to argue that it is the result of a number of complex, and often contingent factors. That the kinds of knowledge(s) on display are often, as in this case study of searching for our own human origins, usually rather less substantial than the material form of their representation invites us to believe.

The Author

Peter Crawley is a researcher in the Department of Sociology and Social Anthropology at Keele University. He is currently completing a PhD examining the cultural context of the Piltdown man hoax. His thesis focuses on the role of the twentieth-century science/natural history museum in constructing and communicating versions of human evolution to an interested and educated public.

References

1   The literature on Piltdown is now large. F. Spencer, *Piltdown: A Scientific Forgery*, Oxford University Press, Oxford, 1990. This book stimulated the most recent wave of interest. The latest book on the subject is J.E. Walsh, *Unravelling Piltdown*, Random House, New York, 1996.
2   Numerous popular science books by Richard Leakey, Roger Lewin, Chris Stringer and Clive Gamble, for example.
3   Walsh, *Unravelling Piltdown*, p. 178. Dawson had an abiding interest in 'transitional forms' like, for example, an ancient boat halfway between coracle and canoe; a transitional horsehoe, flint weapons with wooden hafts.
4   Walsh, *Unravelling Piltdown*, p. 182-3.
5   F. Spencer, *The Piltdown Papers*, Oxford University Press, Oxford, 1990, pp. 4ff.
6   Teilhard de Chardin was at a seminary in Hastings, and had met Dawson at a local quarry, where they were both looking for fossils.
7   *Quarterly Journal of the Geological Society of London*, vol. 69, 1913, pp. 117-151.
8   A leading neuro-anatomist and advocate of diffusion theory of human evolution, which claimed Europeans descended from waves of immigration from Egypt and the east.
9   The description of the Piltdown man which Smith Woodward used in his 1948 autobiography.
10   The role of representation and reconstructions in arguments about human origins have been examined by C. Stringer and C. Gamble, *In Search of Neanderthals*, Thames and Hudson, London, 1994 and S. Moser, 'Visual Representations in Archaeology', in B. Baigrie ed., *Picturing Knowledge*, University of Toronto Press, Toronto, 1996.
11   For example in Keith's own popular texts on human evolution such as *The Antiquity of Man* (Williams & Norgate, London, 1915) and *New Discoveries Relating to the Antiquity of Man* (Williams & Norgate, London, 1931).
12   J.S. Weiner, *The Piltdown Forgery*, Oxford University Press, Oxford, 1955.
13   Following the public revelations about the Piltdown man in 1953, all the

artefacts donated to the Hastings museum by Dawson were withdrawn from display and stored.

14   See, for example, R. Lewin, *Bones of Contention*, Penguin, Harmondsworth, 1989 and M. Landau, *Narratives of Human Evolution*, Yale University Press, New Haven, 1991.

15   See S. Shapin, *A Social History of Truth*, University of Chicago Press, Chicago, 1994.

16   See D. Traill, *Schliemann of Troy: Treasure and Deceit*, Penguin, Harmondsworth, 1996.

17   See A. Reith, *Archaeological Fakes*, Barrie and Jenkins, London, 1970.

18   In nineteenth-century Britain, 'Flint Jack' was the best-known exponent. See R. Millar, *The Piltdown Men*, Gollancz, London, 1972.

19   As it has been analysed by G. Beer, *Darwin's Plots,* Ark, London, 1985. J. Verne, *Journey to the Centre of the Earth*, Penguin, Harmondsworth, [1864] 1965; see also the more recent (and relevant to Piltdown) A. Conan Doyle, *The Lost World*, Oxford University Press, Oxford, [1912] 1995.

20   Reproduced in Spencer, *Piltdown Papers,* pp. 52-3.

21   To use the Foucauldian analysis employed by E. Hooper-Greenhill, *Museums and the Shaping of Knowledge*, Routledge, London, 1992.

22   Tony Bennett, *The Birth of the Museum: History, Theory, Politics*, Routledge, London, 1995.

23   C.C. Sellers, *Mr. Peale's Museum*, Norton and Co, New York, 1980.

24   Bennett, *Birth of the Museum*, pp. 177ff.

25   See W. Rydell, *All the World's a Fair: Visions of Empire at American International Expositions*, Chicago University Press, Chicago, 1984, for the uses made of 'savages' in display, as well as displays of human evolution as sideshow.

26   Spencer considers the cases against eight of the 'usual suspects' before deciding it was Keith. Spencer, *Piltdown*, pp. 159-187.

27   C. Grigson, 'Missing Links in the Piltdown Fraud', *New Scientist*, 13 Jan. 1990, pp. 55-58.

28   Grigson, 'Missing Links', p.56

29   B. Gardiner and A. Currant, *The Piltdown Hoax: Who Done It?*, The Linean Society, London, n.d.

30   S. J. Gould, *Hen's Teeth and Horse's Toes*, Penguin, Harmondsworth, 1984.

31   P. Costello, 'The Piltdown Hoax Reconsidered', *Antiquity*, vol. 59, 1985, pp. 167-173 and 'The Piltdown Hoax: Beyond the Hewitt Connection', *Antiquity*, vol. 60, 1986, pp. 145-7 . S. Zuckermann, 'A Phony Ancestor', *The New York Review of Books*, 8 November, 1990, pp. 12-16.

32   H. Gee, 'Box of Bones Clinches Identity of Piltdown Palaeontology Hoaxer', *Nature*, vol. 381, 23 May 1996, pp. 261-62.

33   Spencer, *Piltdown Papers*, p. 243.

34   Costello, 'The Piltdown Hoax Reconsidered', p. 170.

35   Spencer, *The Piltdown Papers*, p. 137. From a handwritten letter in 1916 from Hinton to G.S. Miller, the American palaeontologist who was always

convinced that the jaw was that of an ape: 'Hearty congratulations on the dissolution of Eoanthropus. You have stirred our friends in the basement some. I gather from Andrews that Woodward is not inclined to reply and I think the only reply will be on the 'improbability' score. From a purely geological and prehistoric standpoint, Eoanthropus as originally constructed was impossible as the 'human' of the one hundred foot terrace. But now that Keith builds and expands the brain case to modern dimensions and you knock away the mandible as *pan vetus* the poor geologist stands some chance of recovering his balance and realising that Eoanthropus was only a bad dream.'

36   Spencer, *Piltdown Papers*, p. 227.

2

Vikings and Donald Duck

Alex Service

Adventure – the kind of rip-snorting fun those old Vikings must have had!

[Donald Duck and the Golden Helmet]

This paper consists of three parts. I will be focusing on a particular Donald Duck comic book, *Donald Duck and the Golden Helmet*. In the first section I will discuss the comic book itself, and look briefly at contemporary political factors which I think may have influenced the story's content. The second portion examines ways in which the comic presents the Vikings. Finally, in the third portion, I will look at how this comic book approaches attitudes to the past.

Donald Duck and the Golden Helmet, number 408 of Walt Disney Productions' bi-monthly Donald Duck series, was published in 1952. It is the work of writer and illustrator Carl Barks, who was the main artist on the series from 1943 to 1966.[1] It is appropriate to look on Barks as the main creator of these comic books, rather than Walt Disney himself. While it has often been asserted that Disney tried to maintain control over every aspect of his vast production empire, he seems to have focused primarily on the films. At least in the first decade or so of Barks's work, the comic book artists were left largely to their own devices. In addition, Barks lived and worked in Northern California, away from the Los Angeles Disney headquarters.[2] The comic book artists were never allowed to sign their names to their work, so officially at least the comics remained Disney's creation. But it has long been maintained by students of the Disney comics that Barks alone should be seen as the guiding force behind the directions taken in the Donald Duck series.[3]

Barks has been described as a man whose political attitudes were conservative, 'bordering on reactionary'.[4] There is, however, debate over the

17

forms Barks's outlook took in his comics. Although some analyses present the Disney comics, and particularly Donald Duck, as straightforward agents of American cultural imperialism, [5] other studies suggest that Barks's work took a more satirical and irreverent approach to the sacred cows of the American Way of Life. According to David Kunzle, in his introduction to Dorfman and Mattelart's celebrated Marxist analysis *How to Read Donald Duck: Imperialist Ideology in the Disney Comic,*

> [t]he picture which emerges from the U.S. perspective ... is that Barks, while in the main clearly conservative in his political philosophy, also reveals himself at times as a liberal, and represents with clarity and considerable wit, the contradictions and perhaps, even some of the anguish, from which U.S. society is suffering. [6]

Martin Barker, in his study *Comics: Ideology, Power and the Critics*, argues that Barks's Donald Duck stories reveal the tension between 'two typical poles of American middle class ideology: a self-congratulatory but humorous desire for wealth, and an obsessive fear of power-politics'. [7]

At the time *Donald Duck and the Golden Helmet* was published, the Communist threat and McCarthyism were ever-present issues in American politics and the media. Senator Joseph McCarthy had launched his anti-Communist crusade in early 1950, with the investigation of supposed Communists in the State Department. By 1952, the year of *Donald Duck and the Golden Helmet,* 'McCarthyism' had become a household word, as can be seen from a favourable McCarthy biography, also published in 1952, entitled *McCarthy: The Man, the Senator, The "Ism".* [8] 1952 was a presidential election year, and McCarthy and his viewpoints were an inescapable part of the campaign rhetoric of both political parties. McCarthy's own party, the Republicans, were torn between those who whole-heartedly supported his Communist-hunting agenda, and the more moderate Republicans, such as presidential nominee and future president General Eisenhower, who attempted to distance themselves from McCarthy's extreme standpoint. The Democrat party line, meanwhile, tended to portray McCarthy as the great enemy, accusing him of introducing the beginnings of a fascist movement into American politics. McCarthy, one prominent Democrat stated during the campaign, had done 'more harm to our country than any other individual'. [9] *Donald Duck and the Golden Helmet* does not overtly address issues of McCarthyism and anti-Communism, but the story clearly shows Barks's sensitivity to the idea that the American way of life is under threat from the spectre of totalitarian control. Whether that control is envisioned as communist or fascist must depend on the perspective of the reader.

The comic's plot concerns Donald Duck's race to save America from being enslaved. On one side are ranged Donald, his three nephews, and a kindly old museum curator, while on the other are the unscrupulous Azure Blue, who schemes to become 'owner of North America', and Blue's crooked lawyer. In his moment of apparent victory, Blue gloats:

> From now on, the people of America are my slaves! They'll work for me every day of their lives – with no Sundays off! Their homes belong to me! Their autos! Their dishes and pots and pans! I own everything, and I'll take everything![10]

Against this terrible threat, Donald and his nephews Huey, Dewey and Louie stand as representatives of the American everyman, fighting against the odds to protect American citizens' rights, property and independence. But the conflict between the Ducks and Azure Blue is not one of straightforward good against evil. Instead, the story develops into a parable of the corrupting influences of power, as one by one the characters fall under its spell, and try in turn to claim America for themselves.

When *Donald Duck and the Golden Helmet* opens, Donald is employed as assistant guard in the Duckburg museum. He is bored to tears. A Viking ship in the museum sets Donald daydreaming. He longs for 'adventure – the kind of rip-snorting fun those old Vikings must have had!'[11] Donald's wish is about to be granted, for that day he discovers a trespasser on the Viking ship. This is the sinister Azure Blue, a dog with a wispy goatee and a bowler hat. Having chased Blue away, Donald then finds the treasure that Blue had been searching for: an ancient map written on a roll of deerskin, which had been hidden in the hold of the ship. Donald takes his discovery to the museum Curator. It turns out that the map is the ship's log of Viking commander Olaf the Blue, who, according to the log, discovered America in 902 A.D. The log further states that 'to prove that he'd been there, ... [Olaf] buried a golden helmet at about latitude 59 degrees, on the coast of Labrador'. Donald and the Curator rejoice, the Curator telling Donald that this is 'one of the great discoveries of history', and that 'You'll be famous! The museum will be famous! Millions of people will come here to see Olaf's ship and the golden helmet!'[12]

Immediately, however, the plot thickens. Azure Blue enters the room with his lawyer, who claims that Azure is 'the eldest descendant of Olaf, the Blue'.[13] Not only does this make him rightful owner of the map and the helmet, it makes him the owner of America as well. For, as the comic informs us: 'it seems that during the reign of Charlemagne, in 792 A.D., the rulers of all the nations gathered in Rome and drafted a law which read: "any man who discovers a new land beyond the seas shall be the owner of that land, unless he claims it for his king"'.[14] Since Olaf the Blue claimed America for his own, Azure, as his legal heir, has inherited North America. Naturally, our heroes are not going to sit back and let Blue enslave them. The plot follows the race for the golden helmet, with Donald and the Curator vowing that they will destroy the helmet rather than let it fall into Azure's hands. Without the helmet, Azure will have no proof supporting his claim to America.

The Curator sets out to reach Labrador by land, while Donald and his three nephews set forth by sea. The Ducks undergo storm and shipwreck, perils which Donald at first welcomes, exclaiming enthusiastically, 'if we're going to be like Vikings, we'll sail like Vikings – through anything the seas can throw at us!'[15] Eventually, the parties of Donald, the Curator, and Azure Blue reach the golden helmet simultaneously. There follows an extended sequence in which one character after another manages to seize the helmet, and America, for himself, until one of Donald's nephews finally saves the day by flinging the map and the golden helmet into the sea.

It was the Viking connection which first caused me to look at *Donald Duck and the Golden Helmet*. Since my research is on modern popular perceptions of the Vikings, my initial interest in the comic lay in determining how the Vikings are represented and used in it. A useful opening question on this subject is, why Vikings in the first place? What was it about Vikings which led Barks to develop a Donald Duck adventure around them?

Barks clearly did some research on the Vikings. His Olaf the Blue is a recognisable nod in the direction of Erik the Red, saga-extolled founder of the Greenland Colony. Olaf the Blue's ship is based on the vessel from the Oseberg ship burial in Norway, which was excavated in 1904. Parenthetically, there is a fair amount of prophetic accuracy in Barks's choice of Labrador as the resting place of the golden helmet, since Labrador is the next-door neighbour to Newfoundland, where the one authenticated Viking settlement in North America was to be excavated in the 1960s. However, Barks did not need to be an expert in medieval archaeology or history to have encountered the idea of the Vikings. In the early 1950s, Viking presence in America had become a hot topic.

Debate over whether the Vikings ever reached America, and particularly the regions which are now part of the United States, had been a feature of both popular and scholarly discussion since the mid-nineteenth century. The debate, however, was largely confined to mid-western communities which were dominated by settlers of Scandinavian origin.[16] To the country as a whole, Vikings in America did not become a focus of major popular interest until the opening of the Kensington runestone exhibition at the Smithsonian museum, which ran from February 17, 1948 to February 25, 1949.[17]

The Kensington stone is an apparent Viking runestone, allegedly discovered in 1899 by a Swedish immigrant farmer in Minnesota. The stone was the focus of rancorous argument from the time of its discovery on, with supporters hailing it as proof positive that the Vikings had reached the American mid-west, and detractors dismissing it as an audacious, but obvious, hoax. While the Smithsonian's representatives apparently never stated that the Kensington stone was unquestionably genuine, the fact that the nation's most respected museum had exhibited the stone bolstered the runestone's supporters. In glowing phrases similar to those of the Curator in *Donald Duck and the Golden Helmet*, the director of the Smithsonian's Bureau of American Ethnology stated in a March 1949 *Washington Times-Herald* interview that the stone was 'probably the most important archaeological object yet found in North America'.[18]

Such enthusiastic appraisals have proved to be wishful thinking. The Kensington stone, though still a focus of local pride in Douglas County, Minnesota, has been thoroughly debunked, joining the ranks of other supposed Viking proofs such as the Viking tower in Rhode Island which has been shown to be a seventeenth-century windmill, and the Viking spears which are in fact nineteenth-century farm implements.[19] In *Donald Duck and the Golden Helmet*, Barks provides what none of these would-be proofs were able to give: water-tight evidence for Viking presence, along with a conveniently detailed documentary source that any Viking period scholar would envy. It seems very likely that the publicity surrounding the Kensington Stone provided Barks's initial inspiration for Olaf the Blue and his golden helmet. But how does Barks see Olaf and his shipmates? What sort of Vikings are they?

The Vikings never appear in person in this comic. Their visual manifestations are limited to their Oseberg-inspired ship, and the golden helmet itself, an improbably elaborate creation reminiscent of the illustrations found in nineteenth-century Viking-themed children's novels. But while they make no physical appearance, the character of the Vikings is emphasised throughout the comic book. In American popular culture, the Viking image tends follow one of two basic patterns. Either Vikings are portrayed as villains, rampaging barbarians *par excellence*, or they are great heroes, celebrated for their courage and skill. Often they are presented as a combination of both, men of deplorable violence who are nonetheless redeemed by their devil-may-care bravery, their loyalty to each other, and their remarkable skill as 'the greatest sailors of their day'.

In *Donald Duck and the Golden Helmet*, Barks depicts only one side of the Viking equation. His Vikings are heroes. They are, at least apparently, representative of everything a man should live up to. The Vikings are described as 'brave', and 'rugged', they are valiant fighters and 'as strong as horses'.[20] They are linked with those other great heroes of American mythology, the cowboys and outlaws of the Wild West, in Donald's proclamation of himself as 'King Donald, the Viking Kid!'[21] In the Duckburg museum, Donald reflects wistfully that, unlike the degenerate humankind of his own era, Vikings were 'real he-men'.[22] He longs to follow in their footsteps, to be 'Donald, the Terror of the Northern Seas', and experience 'the salt spray in my teeth, and the howl of the gale in the rigging'.[23] Donald's enthusiasm for the Viking lifestyle seems to survive the perils of the sea, although his nephews are less enamoured of the experience.

Barks's emphasis is on Vikings as sailors and explorers. He gives barely any hint of the raiding and pillaging aspects of the Viking image. Apart from the reference to Donald as the would-be Terror of the Northern Seas, the only other suggestion of Viking cruelty is in Barks's observation, during the sequence in which Donald claims both the golden helmet and America, that Donald has 'become as mean as the Vikings of old'.[24] It is possible that Viking rapaciousness is meant to be reflected in the ruthlessness displayed by each character who seizes the helmet in turn, but if so, this is implied only with the greatest obliqueness. By contrast, the Vikings' qualities as great seafarers are emphasised. Gazing at Olaf's ship, Donald muses: 'Think of it! Men crossed the ocean in that old tub with nothing to guide them but the sun and the stars! They sailed to Iceland and Greenland and maybe even America hundreds of years before the Queen Mary!'[25]

Barks's treatment of the Vikings illustrates one strand of his approach to mankind's (or duck-kind's) interactions with the past. Here, perhaps, is one key to why Barks opts for so predominantly positive an interpretation of the Vikings. To be useful to Barks, the Vikings must appear as an ideal, figures worthy of emulation. For the first half of the comic book, Barks depicts the past as superior to the present, a focus of intense and desperate nostalgic longing. Donald despairs when he considers how low the human race has fallen, when compared with the rugged adventurers of old. And when presented with the chance to follow his heroes' example, Donald, despite his initial nervousness, does not falter. When Donald quails at the idea of going 'up there to Labrador – among the icebergs and polar bears', the Curator's defiant response is: 'Olaf, the Blue, did it! Are we less of men than he was?'[26] Of course Donald accepts that challenge, and throws himself into the struggle to live up to the Viking image.

In some aspects, Donald and the Curator embody two rival visions of the past, representing the same divide which is often seen today between those who favour history as a strictly academic discipline, and those who lean more toward the heritage/re-enactment side of things. To Donald, the past is most meaningful when he seeks to live it. He wants to be like a Viking, to sail like a Viking, to truly be Donald, Terror of the Northern Seas. In contrast, the Curator's version of the past, represented by his beloved museum, is 'musty', as Donald declares with disdain.[27]

Meanwhile, in Barks's characterisation of the Curator there can be seen another aspect of the debate that has recently dogged Britain's 'heritage industry'. In this sense, the Curator personifies the worst nightmare of commentators who fear that devotion to the past is causing Britain to stagnate, turning the UK into a nation of museums. A nation of museums is precisely what the Curator wants, as Barks reveals when the Curator takes his turn at claiming the helmet and North America. The Curator does not wish to enslave Americans as Azure does, but his plans are presented as being nearly as appalling. When *he* rules America, the curator will 'run the country for the benefit of the museums! Everybody will have to go to a museum twice a day! ... Every Sunday there will be a museum party! People will bring their lunches and study ancient bric-a-brac! And when they're not doing that, they'll be building more museums ...'. To this announcement, one of the nephews emphatically declares 'Gak! I think I liked Azure's deal better!'[28] The Curator and his museum may at first appear harmless, but Barks is making the point that claiming the past can be dangerous, no matter who is doing the claiming. As the comic progresses, Barks moves steadily toward a far grimmer version of the past and its relations with the present. From focusing on the past as nostalgic ideal, as Donald sees it, Barks turns to increasingly present the past as a threat.

Throughout the comic book, different characters attempt to claim the past for different reasons. For Donald, the past is an adventurous paradise, which at least temporarily provides him fulfilment while he seeks to immerse himself in it. Azure Blue, meanwhile, has more materialistic designs on the past. Azure claims the past in order to seize control of a continent. He is an embodiment of the fact that control of the past, and of its material relics, often imparts material and political control of the present. The museum Curator, while seemingly more benign than Azure Blue, has his own agenda for the past. To him, ownership of the golden helmet is important for the fame and glory it will bring to his museum. When he discovers the helmet's existence, the Curator conjures up grandiose visions of a proto-Jorvik Viking Centre. The helmet and the map are of course important in a purely historical sense, because they prove who really discovered America, at least as far as Europeans are concerned. But what most elates the Curator is the image of millions of people thronging to *his* suddenly famous museum. At the comic's darkest point, when Donald attempts to seize control of the helmet and of America, Barks depicts the past as a curse. It possesses an evil charm which has taken control of Donald, turning him from a mild-mannered duck and loving uncle into a power-hungry manipulator who cheerfully maroons his nephews on an iceberg.

However, Barks seems to imply that the real danger is not in the past itself, but in people's uses of it. This is the message of the story's semi-mystical climax. Human abuses of the past are what turn it into a curse, and one cannot expect to get away with manipulating the past without being punished for it. After marooning his nephews, the Curator and Azure Blue, and setting off with the crooked Lawyer to take command of America, Donald finds himself lost in the North Sea and starving. One of the nephews had pocketed the ship's compass before being marooned, and a polar bear devours all of the provisions. After days of aimless drifting, Donald comes to realise that this is his punishment for 'trying to get something for nothing'.[29] He had no right to claim Olaf the Blue's golden helmet, and now Olaf has arrived to claim his revenge. Through the mist, Donald sees the grim, dark form of a dragon-headed Viking ship, sail billowing proudly, gunwales lined with Viking shields. The past is tired of being manipulated, and it has come to reclaim its own. Of course, this terrifying vision is not in fact Olaf the Blue, back from the dead. Rather, it is a 'hot rod iceberg',[30] which Huey, Dewey and Louie have carved in the shape of a Viking ship in order to make it more streamlined and speed its progress in drifting south! Thus past and future, the Vikings and the next generation of Ducks, work together, to chastise Donald for his manipulations.

At the close of the comic book, Donald Duck is back at his job as assistant guard in the Duckburg museum. He is musing, 'that rugged life had its points – but I don't know ...' when he is interrupted by a man asking where to find the embroidered lamp shades. Rather than being moved to despair, as he would have been at the beginning of the story, in the last frame of the comic Donald greets this inquiry with 'I'll take you there! Darned if I ain't getting interested in embroidered lampshades myself!'[31]

Donald Duck and the Golden Helmet seems to fit well with the analysis quoted near the beginning of this paper, that Barks's Donald Duck stories focus on the tension between the desire for wealth and power, and 'an obsessive fear of power-politics'. Barks warns his readers of the disastrous consequences when one goes too far in the search for power, and manipulation of the past is part of that quest. The past can be glorious, as it is in Donald's nostalgic visions, but it must be kept in its place. When people try to claim it, bringing its influence into the present, it becomes an instrument of destruction. The rugged, adventurous past has its good points, but one must remain loyal to one's present – even to its embroidered lampshades.

24

The Author

Alex Service researches the representation of Vikings in popular culture, at the Centre for Medieval Studies, University of York.

References

1   M. Barker, *Comics: Ideology, Power and the Critics*, Manchester, Manchester University Press, 1989, pp. 290-1.
2   A. Dorfman and A. Mattelart, *How to Read Donald Duck: Imperialist Ideology in the Disney Comic*, trans. David Kunzle, International General, New York, 1975, p. 16.
3   Dorfman and Mattelart, *How to Read Donald Duck*, p. 16.
4   Barker, *Comics*, p. 291.
5   Barker, *Comics*, p. 279.
6   Dorfman and Mattelart, *How to Read Donald Duck*, p. 17.
7   Barker, *Comics*, p. 298.
8   J. Anderson and R. W. May, *McCarthy: The Man, the Senator, the "Ism"*, Beacon Press, Boston, 1952.
9   R. M. Fried, *Men Against McCarthy*, Columbia University Press, New York, p. 225.
10   C. Barks, *Walt Disney's Donald Duck and the Golden Helmet*, Donald Duck no. 408, Dell Publishing Co., New York, July-August 1952, p. 23.
11   *Ibid.*, p. 1.
12   *Ibid.*, pp. 5-6.
13   *Ibid.*, p. 6.
14   *Ibid.*, p. 7.
15   *Ibid.*, p. 13.
16   E. Wahlgren, *The Kensington Stone: A Mystery Solved*, University of Wisconsin Press, Madison, 1958, pp. 121-2.
17   Wahlgren, *Kensington Stone*, p. 4.
18   Wahlgren, *Kensington Stone*, p. 5.
19   B. Linderoth Wallace, 'The Vikings in North America', in R. Samson, ed, *Social Approaches to Viking Studies*, Cruithne Press, Glasgow, pp. 208-19.
20   Barks, *Donald Duck and the Golden Helmet*, pp. 3, 17.
21   *Ibid.*, p. 27.
22   *Ibid.*, p. 2.
23   *Ibid.*, p. 11.
24   *Ibi d.*, p. 28.
25   *Ibid.*, p. 2.
26   *Ibid.*, p. 9.

27   *Ibid.*, p. 11.
28   *Ibid.*, p. 26.
29   *Ibid.*, p. 30.
30   *Ibid.*, p. 31.
31   *Ibid.*, p. 32.

3

Anarchy and Order

Re-inventing the Medieval in Contemporary Popular Narrative

Harry Ziegler

In her analysis of action-adventure stories, Marchetti argues that particular genres

> tend to be popular at certain points in time, because they somehow embody and work through those social contradictions the culture needs to come to grips with and may not be able to deal with except in the realm of fantasy.[1]

If this is considered in relation to the popularity of the medieval setting in contemporary fiction then the question of why so many writers have been attracted to different aspects of the Middle Ages becomes extremely pertinent. One response can be found in the introduction to what may be seen as the first bestseller set in the Middle Ages, Tuchmann's *A Distant Mirror*. Tuchmann writes there that France in the 14th century was a 'violent, tormented, bewildered, suffering and *disintegrating* age', which she found 'consoling in *a period of similar disarray*', because 'it is reassuring to know that the human species has lived through worse before'. Furthermore, she writes that 'qualities of conduct that we recognise as familiar amid the alien surroundings [of the Middle Ages] are revealed as *permanent in human nature*'.[2] This sense of repetition, continuity and constancy is deeply ideological.

Tuchmann's feeling of consolation and familiarity is not isolated. In popular journalism of the 1970s, and into the 1980s and 90s, this connection between the bewildering present and the medieval past has often been made. Take for example the following quote from *The Sunday Times* of 4 March 1973:

> Headlines notwithstanding, most observers feel that the Mafia's great spoils are trivial in the context of New York's total lawlessness, just as gang rub-outs comprised a trifling percentage of its 1346 murders ... in the first nine months of last year. It is a new kind of crime which beleaguers the city – more accurately, an ancient, crudely simple kind: *an atavism perceived as a return to the dark ages*.[3]

On the basis that there is some permanent human nature (a common assumption as expressed by Tuchmann), the Middle Ages of these popular narratives thus draw upon, and negotiate, a feeling that an established order was breaking down, and that the consequence would be the return to a state of lawlessness. In journalese, this is called anarchy, but correctly should be called 'anomie', the breakdown of a consensual standard of social and ethical behaviour. It was thus the perceived parallels between the contemporary and the Middle Ages which fuelled the interest in all things medieval. According to Walkerdine's research on audiences, setting narrative in other temporal or spacial locations is a means by which 'stories can be held at a distance, as fantasy, and thus work out displaced emotions and desires'.[4] This suggests an active reader rather than the passive one which is so often postulated in connection with popular fiction.

In his essay 'Living in the New Middle Ages', Umberto Eco systematises this impression of a return to an insecure, lawless and violent age which superseded earlier depictions of the future as bright.[5] He relates this feeling to a certain degree of permissiveness which led to the breakdown of supposedly common values through the import of others which were alien to our societies, and to the ongoing fragmentation of the cities.[6] An important feature he did not mention was the dismantling of the welfare state and the role of women in society, both of which we will investigate in some more detail below. By and large, the context shows, however, why the romantic view of the Middle Ages as a golden age was replaced by an image of the medieval as a Dark Age. In Romanticism, the Middle Ages were conceived of as a *counter*-image to the social changes created through the Industrial Revolution, a mainly rural and pastoral country with clear (and accepted) social boundaries. The Middle Ages of Scott and others had the golden sheen of nostalgia (and helped to re-define the social role of the 'gentle-man'),[7] whereas the Middle Ages of contemporary popular narrative were rather the *mirror* image of wide-spread social anxieties.

The feeling that the Dark Ages were returning was also mirrored in those films set in a 'Dark Future'. A number of great box office successes sported images of a barbarian future: in *Robocop* (1987), we can see the knight in shining armour, defender of the weak, upholder of the law;[8] the cityscape of *Highlander II* (1991), and of *Bladerunner* (1981), reflected anomie and fear of violence.[9] Moreover, there have also been a whole array of less well known releases, mainly on video, which have a post-catastrophe setting where humanity has, by and large, returned to a state of barbarity. Apart from the popular *Mad Max* films (1981, 1985),[10] there were also the medieval fantasy films such as *The Beastmaster* (1982),[11] the *Conan* (1981) films starring Arnold Schwarzenegger,[12] and a further range of less known ones. The fact that the Middle Ages were ubiquitous in popular narrative reinforced their powerfulness, but also demonstrated that there was a growing market for this fare. Ellis Peters, for example, had started her *Brother Cadfael* novels before Eco's *The Name of the Rose*, but it was only in the wake of the latter that she became widely known and marketed.[13] The general perception of the pattern of social development probably found its complete expression in the plot of *Excalibur* (1981), where we travel full cycle from an age of violence, to an age of order, which then disintegrates once more into new violence.[14]

We are thus confronted with an essentially conservative, Hobbesian world view which sees civilisation as a thin veneer over bubbling primal instincts, ready to break loose if left unchecked. This in itself would not necessarily have been remarkable. What did make the narratives remarkable was how they located the reason for this 'descent into anomie' within the societies they depict. Generally, those in power are held responsible. Films like *Mad Max* and others set after some sort of catastrophe (be this nuclear or ecological), may not have made this particularly explicit, but others, like *Robocop* (for example), located the blame squarely in the board room of the big corporations. In *Robocop*, the big corporation is making profit on both sides: they develop (and sell) law enforcement equipment to the police, and drugs to the criminals at the same time. One market thus reinforces the other. This scenario is not quite borne out in Follett's *The Pillars of the Earth*,[15] but there too disruption of the social order, and the continuation of the state of lawlessness and civil war, is definitely pinned on the aristocracy and the clergy who all hope to enrich themselves from this turmoil.

To some degree we can see this is as the expression of middle-class resentment and anxiety. As Martin Jacques argues in 'Caste Down',[16] the middle classes, thinking themselves safe in suburbia, were much more affected by the deregulated market of the 1980s than they had anticipated. In particular, the post-war perception of job security was lost, which led to a threatening loss of status, when confronted first by 'yuppies', and then by 'fat cats' in top management. Not by accident then are the good guys in Follett's *The Pillars of the Earth* all sensible middle managers or small business people: a builder, the prior, the daughter of a nobleman turned wool merchant, and so on. Order in that novel is finally restored when the incompetent, selfish and greedy social risers have finally been removed.[17]

The pull of the medieval as a setting proved so popular in the Eighties that writers from other genres moved in as well (Ken Follett from thrillers, Willis and Holland from science fiction). Marion Zimmer Bradley, for example, who was originally better known for the feminist science fiction of the Darkover cycle, published in 1983 *The Mists of Avalon* which retold the Arthurian legend from the point of view of a heathen priestess.[18] The book was an immediate success and widely translated across Europe. Popular fiction is still predominantly written by women, and for a female audience, and even where men write mainstream fiction, they will have to cater for this female audience. Therefore, the role of women in these narratives is one of the more interesting points to examine. This will now be done through examining four opposing texts: Eco's *The Name of the Rose*, Follett's *The Pillars of the Earth*, Holland's *The Lords of Vaumartin*,[19] and Willis' *The Doomsday Book*.[20]

In *The Myth of Superwoman*, Dudovitz specifically investigates how the role and image of women in popular fiction has changed in the 1980s. She makes the following observation:

> The social mythology of woman as wife and mother which previously structured women's fiction has given way to a stronger female image which not only challenges the myth of female weakness but also denies the too familiar woman-as-victim syndrome.[21]

In *The Name of the Rose*, the only female character in the story is literally a character created by a male writer, but even within the plot this 'male representation' has a double sense: Eco's monks represent her as they feel fit for their own purposes. For the novice who enjoys her (freely offered) sexual favours, she is the epitome of beauty and innocence. For others, she is an incarnation of the devil, and a witch; but the reader realises that she is just a pawn in a game she does not understand. As she does not speak the language of the men (that is, the language of power), she is unable to represent herself and thus becomes a victim in a power game between men. She appears so inconsequential as a person that we never even learn her name.

Follett, writing ten years later, conforms to the changed paradigm of 'super woman'. One of the main characters in his book is a young noble woman with the name of Aliena. As her father is imprisoned for treason and loses his fief, she loses her social rank; the consequences of this loss of protection are rape and destitution. However, she has made a promise to her dying father that she would look after her younger brother. This entails providing him with an education which befitted his former social rank, and to do whatever she could to get the lost earldom back. The superwoman thus picks herself up and reconstructs herself as a wool merchant, only to lose her flourishing business through a second attack from the knight who raped her and became Earl in her father's place. The woman may be a victim, but she does not take it lying down. At the end of the novel, her brother has been restored to his social rank, the enemy is humiliated and defeated, and she is in effect (but not in name), the new Earl of Shiring. The novel can be thus be classified as melodrama in Cawelti's definition. He writes:

> [T]he social melodrama ... synthesizes the archetype of melodrama with a carefully and elaborately developed social setting in such a way as to combine the emotional satisfactions of melodrama with the interest inherent in a detailed, intimate, and realistic analysis of major social ... phenomena. [...] [T]he social setting is often treated rather critically with a good deal of anatomizing of the hidden motives, secret corruption, and human folly ...; yet the main plot works out in proper melodramatic fashion to affirm ... that God is in Heaven and all's right with the world.[22]

On the other hand, a change has nevertheless to be noted. Dudovitz writes:

> Some critics have praised the erotic historical romances as furthering strong independent female characters. In her study of the genre, Carol Thurston writes that "rather than the abductions, rapes and betrayals common to the subgenre, *it is the overcoming of these misadventures that is the central focus of the stories*".[23]

It is probably no accident that the male writers form the two major extremes in the representation of women. The two female writers have slightly different agendas. Holland contrasts three women characters: Isobel, who is the aunt of the future lord of Vaumartin; Jeanne, the dutiful wife of the heir; and the wilful, adopted daughter Silviane. Isobel, the noblewoman, is a powerful character who uses her sexuality to achieve her ends. One of her major aims is to prevent her nephew Everard, whom she deems unmanly and unfit to be a knight, to come into his birthright. Her husband, eventually won over by her sexual allure, leaves Everard for dead on the battle field of Agincourt. Isobel's strategy initially appears to achieve her goal. However, this superficial success is in the long run her undoing since her husband feels that in obeying his wife's advice, he has lost his honour.

On reaching this conclusion, he leaves his wife, who in the end also loses the castle she so wrongfully wanted to keep. The disinherited Everard resembles Follett's character of Aliena inasmuch that both fall from their rightful social position and have to start from scratch. Both embark on what has been referred to as a postmodern career: Aliena as merchant, Everard as scholar and civil servant. The latter adopts the daughter of a family who died in the plague, and eventually marries a widow without children. Everard's struggle in the outside world is thus juxtaposed with the domestic struggle between adopted daughter and wife which the wife suffers (more or less) silently. In the end, the dutiful wife emerges as the victor over the sexually alluring woman: when her husband is offered his rightful heritage by a repentant Isobel, he turns it down because it would entail leaving his wife. This final crisis also resolves the domestic struggle: in the face of the threat to have the family fall apart, wife and adopted daughter, the two opposing parties unite against it. The conclusion of the narrative appears to be that in the long run, it pays to suffer silently and to stand by your man; the use of sexual power, albeit a successful short-term strategy for achieving a woman's goal, is portrayed in the final analysis as self-defeating and destructive. Women who thus exert their power conspicuously, make themselves vulnerable to male rejection which in turn may lead to loss of property and status.

All three authors presented so far stress the importance of education as a basis for survival in a changing social environment. The lack of education, represented in *The Name of the Rose* by the female character's inability to speak the language of power, puts her in a situation where she cannot defend herself against the allegations of witchcraft (although the defence might anyway have been useless). In both Follett and Holland, education is the means by which to build a new life whereby 'the University of Life' is just as important as a formal education. Crisis is thus not only cause for anxiety, it is also to be considered as an opportunity: it tests the mettle, and if you have got what it takes, you will restore yourself to an appropriate position. Everard is the postmodern middle class hero *par excellence*. Even without secure income, he can console himself in the concluding pages of the book with the thought that, '[i]f his life was uncertain and full of risk, that meant that he was living it well'.[24]

What we are offered through these stories then, is some criticism of those in power, but also the sense that social change is a time for opportunities. For those who are flexible and adaptable, and who are not set in the old ways, as well as for those who can pick the right husband, social and economic advance is possible. Female power does thus not appear to reside in the ability to make a living for oneself only, but to pick the right husband.

At the end of the Eighties, we get some backlash to the idea of the liberated, feminist female; this is also reflected in detective narratives, where the bestsellers no longer feature the hard-boiled female private eye, but career women in large organisations, such as in the novels of Cornwell or the *Prime Suspect* series. Tomc writes about this change that '*Prime Suspect* is one of a number of women's crime stories released or published in the early 1990s that bizarrely combine an aggressive critique of "patriarchy" with a narrative that highlights the virtues of submission and conformity'.[25] She argues that this contradiction 'works as a rather straightforward register of changes both in feminism and in middle-class women's work situations in the late 1980s'.[26] Thus, 'the stress ... on corporate over independent action and occupational over gender alliances seems to chronicle and champion women's entrenchment in corporate culture'.[27] Dudovitz would like to explain the change of emphasis within the narrative as responding to other elements of the cultural climate:

> The tendency towards the end of the 1980s ... has been a return to traditional values with an increasing emphasis on family, work and country. Any residual radicalism left over from the early 1970s has been channelled into assuring job security in face of continued economic crisis.[28]

The medieval diegesis is reflective of both arguments which are not mutually exclusive, but which both substantiate Albrecht's findings that popular fiction negotiates social values under strain.[29] Willis' novel *The Doomsday Book* can be said to carry its name rightfully, because neither future nor medieval past, linked through the ability to travel in time, are particularly uplifting: disease and death reign in both. The main character, a female history student, wants to travel back into the Middle Ages to carry out research. Although the period of time in question has been barred from such travel as it generally considered unsafe, the Deputy Head of History, wanting to assert his authority and claim to power, allows the research programme to go ahead. The Head of History who could override his deputy's decision, cannot be reached, however: he has disappeared for the duration of the vacation, and has not left an address because he does not want anyone to find out that he has a mistress. Through the mistake of a male technician, the female student does not land in Oxford 20 years before the plague of 1348 reached it, but virtually on the eve of it arriving. The Oxford of the twenty-first century, which she has just left, is ravaged by a flu epidemic. Women are again the carers, even though they may not be able to prevent suffering and death. However, they stand their ground where the men either shirk their responsibilities or make matters worse. The patterns of allegiance in the novel do not necessarily work along 'gender' lines, but rather those of probity and professionalism.

The backlash argued by Dudovitz can therefore also be seen to originate in another area: the dismantling of the welfare state which put the responsibility for caring back on the shoulders of wives and mothers. Women in the fictional medieval diegesis thus also have to cope with illness and birth without 'professional' help. By and large, the Middle Ages of contemporary popular narrative can thus be argued to negotiate the role of women in a hostile and uncertain environment, in which the individual is thrown back on their own resources (and resourcefulness) because there is no social support. The New Middle Ages are thus less concerned with the breakdown of an international order, but negotiate the changes arising from the conservative *tendenzwende*: there is no society, there are only individuals and families, and they struggle for survival in an essentially hostile environment.

The medieval diegesis, it has been argued, has served as a mirror image for social change. Its function, however, is not 'to record actual events but to demythify [sic] previous accounts and deny the traditional inferiority of women'.[30] Whereas Dudovitz is concerned mainly with the image of women, it has been argued here that the New Middle Ages have a far wider significance: they are the appropriate setting because they are remembered as a period when established social (rather than political) structures were dissolved from above. The class war 'from above' finds its expression in the fact that the disruption of the order is a consequence of those classes entrusted with the upkeep of that order (nobility and clergy). However, neither the narrative conventions nor the middle class view allow for a structural analysis: it is not the system that is at fault, but individuals; and as soon as they are defeated and removed from the positions of power, order is restored.

This new order is not, however, identical with the old one: the new people at the helm have achieved their position through merit and not through accident of birth or intrigue. The crisis emanating from the disruption of order is thus beneficial in the long run: it is an age of opportunity for those who confront the problems with initiative and resolution. Although critical of the social changes imposed from 'above', the New Middle Ages subscribe to an essentially Social Darwinist view: survival of the fittest. Despite the criticism inherent in the medieval diegesis then, there is a certain degree of Thatcherite/Reaganite populism with its ideal of a society of small, independent producers.

The Middle Ages of popular narrative can thus be taken to be a part in the negotiation of a larger hegemonic shift which started, not incidentally, in the late 1970s: the break-up of the post-war consensus on social responsibility and welfare. The new Middle Ages are thoroughly individualist and reflect what Heitmeyer called the 'risk society', the central characteristic of which is individualisation. It is marked furthermore by social and geographic mobility, 'artificial differentiation within classes' (i.e. individual orientation towards social upward mobility which does not change relations of inequality) and the dissolution of social 'milieus' through large urban resettlements.[31] Accordingly, the medieval setting does not have a 'society', but only families and individuals, and solutions to problems created by the powers-that-be are always individualistic.

It will appear, however, that the heyday of the New Middle Ages is over and that a new consensus has been reached. The narratives of the 1990s have now returned to the competitive individualism of the thriller.[32] The livelihood of the middle classes is still threatened, but this time by a darker force: the serial killer. As a corollary, it is no longer women's role in the family which is at the forefront of the narrative, but rather their trials and tribulations in the male hierarchy of corporations and law enforcement. The emphasis on the family and the community, still of prime importance for survival in the medieval diegesis, has been superseded by a 'community of professionals', a development which made its first appearance in the medieval diegesis. This new scenario of re-alignment of allegiances in a world of 'professionals' cannot, however, be accommodated through the medieval diegesis, so that, for the time being, it appears to have lost its popularity and appeal in popular narrative.

The Author

Harry Ziegler lectures in the department of humanities at the University of Lincoln and Humberside. His research is chiefly concerned with the links between popular fiction and the social and ideological context in which it is produced and consumed. He is editor of the forthcoming volume: *Transgression and control: essays in the history of the book and reading practices* (Peter Lang, Bern, 1998).

References

1   G. Marchetti, 'Action-Adventure as Ideology', in I. Angus & S. Jhally, eds., *Cultural Politics in Contemporary America*, Routledge, London, 1989, pp. 182–97, (p. 187).

2   B. Tuchmann, *A Distant Mirror; The Calamitous 14ᵗʰ Century*, Penguin, Harmondsworth, 1979, first published 1978, pp. xv, xvi (emphases added).

3   Quoted in S. Hall et al., *Policing the Crisis; Mugging, the State and Law and Order*, Macmillan, London, 1978, p. 25, (emphasis added).

4   Quoted in M. Barker, *Comics; Ideology, Power and the Critics*, Manchester University Press, Manchester, 1989, pp. 216–7.

5   U. Eco, 'Living in the New Middle Ages', in U. Eco, *Travels in Hyperreality*, Picador, London, 1987, pp. 73–85, (article first published 1976).

6   Eco, 'Living', pp. 74, 76–77.

7   See M. Girouard, *The Return to Camelot: Chivalry and the English Gentleman*, Yale U.P., New Haven, 1981.

8   *Robocop*, US 1987, dir. Paul Verhoeven.

9   *Highlander 2 – The Quickening*, US 1991, dir. Russell Mulcahy; *Blade Runner*, US 1982, dir. Ridley Scott.

10 For example, *Mad Max II – The Road Warrior*, Aus. 1981, dir. George Miller, and *Mad Max III – Beyond Thunderdome*, Aus. 1985, dirs. George Miller and George Ogilvie.

11 *The Beastmaster*, US 1982, dir. Don Coscarelli.

12 *Conan the Barbarian*, US 1981, dir. John Milius, and *Conan the Destroyer*, US 1984, dir. Richard Fleischer.

13 Peters's first novel was *A Morbid Taste For Bones*, published 1977; Eco's *The Name of the Rose*, was first published 1980. On Ellis's popularity, see N. Moody, 'Ellis Peters and English Place Names.', unpublished paper given at the International Medieval Congress at the University of Leeds, 1994.

14 *Excalibur*, US 1981, dir. John Boorman.

15 K. Follett, *The Pillars of the Earth*, Macmillan, London, 1989.

16 M. Jacques, 'Caste Down', *The Sunday Times*, Culture Supplement, June 12, 1994, pp. 12 – 14.

17 This casting of the professions and the middle classes as the true champions of order is also borne out by other contemporary fiction, e.g. that of John Grisham, Patricia Cornwell and others. Nick Hefferan argues for example that Grisham's novels are an attempt at saving the reputation of 'good professionalism' – see N. Heffernan, 'Law Crimes: The Legal Fictions of John Grisham and Scott Turow', in P. Messent, ed., *Criminal Proceedings. The Contemporary American Crime Novel*, Pluto Press, London, 1997.

18 M. Zimmer Bradley, *The Mists of Avalon*, Sphere, London, 1984, first published 1983.

19 C. Holland, *The Lords of Vaumartin*, Houghton Mifflin, Boston, 1988.

20 C. Willis, *The Doomsday Book*, Hodder & Stoughton, London, 1992.

21 R. L. Dudovitz, *The Myth of Superwoman; Women's Bestsellers in France and the United States*, Routledge, London, 1990, p. 164.

22 J. Cawelti, *Adventure, Mystery, and Romance; Formula Stories as Art and Popular Culture*, University of Chicago Press, London, 1976, p. 261.

23 Dudovitz, *Superwoman*, p. 111, (emphasis added).

24 Holland, *Vaumartin*, p. 361.

25 S. Tomc, 'Questioning Women: The Feminist Mystery after Feminism', in G. Irons, ed., *Feminism in Women's Detective Fiction*, University of Toronto Press, Toronto, 1995, p. 47.

26 Tomc, 'Questioning Women', p. 58.

27 Ibid.

28 Dudovitz, *Superwoman*, p. 157.

29 See J. Hall, *The Sociology of Literature*, Longman, London, 1979, p. 96.

30 Dudovitz, *Superwoman*, p. 114.

31 W. Heitmeyer, *Rechtsextremistische Orientierungen bei Jugend-lichen*, Juventa Verlag, Weinheim/München, 1987, p. 64.

32 See J. Palmer, *Thrillers. Genesis and Structure of Popular Genre*, Edward Arnold, London, 1978.

4

Nasty Histories

Medievalism and Horror

John Arnold

We have transformed the pierced body of Christ into gentle Jesus meek and mild. Yet it is our own 20th century that took the technology of the cinema, applied it to the medieval fascination with the dead, and used it to create the genre of the horror film.
[Linda Grant, *Guardian*, 28 September 1996, p.29]

For me, going to the movies is a religious experience.
[David Fincher, *Observer*, 7 January 1996, p.17]

Anyone who has read the newspapers recently will be aware that once again we have decided to declare a 'moral crisis' in this country; perhaps because we have a government hanging on to its majority of one by the skin of its teeth.[1] The crisis is enunciated through public discourse on the murders of Jamie Bulger and of the school teacher Philip Lawrence, concern over the possibility (and desirability) of censoring the Internet, debates about 'innate' or 'learned' elements in male aggression, and other related topics. The question of the representation of violence has, as usual, played a part in this moral crisis: the film *The Agony and the Ecstasy* has just been refused a certificate by the BBFC, the video games industry has initiated a self-administered system of age-certification, and David Cronenberg's film *Crash* has been banned by Westminster council. Implicit, and at times explicit, in these discourses is a desire that violence should be given meaning (most apparent in the aftermath of the Bulger case, in the coding and recoding of the young murderers) and that such meaning should be 'moral'. These should in fact be noted as two different, albeit interconnected, discursive drives. The desire that violence should *mean* something, should have valency, should be comprehensible, is the first drive. The crusades mounted by the surviving relatives of the victims of murders, accidents, unsuccessful medical treatments, all rest upon this desire for meaning: 'we don't want them to have died in vain'. To die in vain would be to have a death without meaning; by giving meaning to violence, we make it part of discourse and hope to control its representation if not its reality. The second stage of the process is the particular discourse within which that meaning is produced; in our present climate, usually right-wing and certainly ideological. Thus a concern for children's safety leads to increased video surveillance; thus Phillip Lawrence's widow appears on television and radio to valorize 'the family' and 'discipline'; thus another Home Secretary promises tougher prison regimes and that criminal culpability will be extended to infants.

This process of inscription frequently uses 'the past' as a hermeneutic framework; uses it, in fact, in two contradictory ways. On the one hand, 'the Past' functions as the nostalgic 'Golden Age', when society was free of such horrors: 'it was never like this in my day'. On the other, 'the past' is the necessary complement to a modernity of freedom, a past of violence and disorder against which we can set our 'right' to a civilised society .[2] One can see both hermeneutic codes at work simultaneously in the fascinating quote from Linda Grant's article which addresses the representation of violence: the simultaneous invocation and interweaving of (1) a violent medieval past, fascinated with death, that supplements a civilised (and slightly bloodless) present; and (2) a medieval past that had a solid, 'real' moral code, in contrast to a present that has warped its ethics into the splatterfest horror movie.

Given the apparent immanence of 'the past' to discourses surrounding violence and morality, it is interesting to note that historical films seem *per se* to operate outside this arena. As various people have noted, Cronenberg amongst them, concern about the representation of violence has ignored recent films that set their action in an historical context. A prime example is *Braveheart* (1995) which, although provoking debate in a number of ways about ethnicity, history and nationalism, has escaped censure for the level of violence it depicts. As Jim Shelley, interviewing Cronenberg, remarked, 'it's historical. They have costumes'.[3]

Costumes, strangely enough, seem to make a difference. Somehow 'history' can make violence safe; particularly, perhaps, medieval history. To examine the politics of this phenomenon, I want to look at medievalism and horror films, and in particular David Fincher's *Se7en* (1996). I am not claiming any particular link between the genre of 'horror' (which is, in any case, a highly problematic category) and the middle ages.[4] There are a few horror movies set in a generic 'medieval' period: one thinks of the not-very-scary Hammer horror films of the 60s, with their vaguely feudal (and regionally accented) peasant onlookers; of such curiosities as *Häxen* (1921) and *The Keep* (1983); and of *Army of Darkness – The Medieval Dead* (1992), the third and least-frightening of the *Evil Dead* films. The very paucity of these offerings, and the blandness of those I can summon, illustrates the main point: curiously, horror and the medieval do not fit well together. Or rather, in becoming 'medieval', horrific violence eludes the genre of horror. It is the politics of this elusion that interests me; how the medieval past functions within violent narratives.

I am also interested in how an historian might approach film, and in particular, film that does not seek to represent a 'factual' past, nor simply to invoke a psychoanalytic or Marxist idea of 'the past',[5] but places itself somewhere in between. Robert Rosenstone has described what he calls the 'Dragnet (just the facts, Ma'am)' approach of historians to historical films: the apparent desire felt by our profession to supply a check-list of accuracies and inaccuracies. This methodology fails to rise above the level of the necessary; it is remarkably unproductive, in terms of analysis, and unsurprisingly tedious.[6] Rosenstone's own approach – to read certain 'historical' films as challenges to historians' sense of project and textualisation – is more interesting, but still appears to be part of a project of representing history 'for its own sake'.[7] In any case, I am not concerned here with films which represent a specific, historical past, but in something more elusive. To return to my previous point, I am interested in the politics of one's invocation of 'the past', and more specifically of the medieval past.

Umberto Eco, in his essay 'Dreaming of the Middle Ages', notes that one 'medieval period' recognised by contemporary culture is the medievalism of brutishness and violence, the very 'Dark' middle ages: 'one is asked to celebrate, on this earth of virile, brute force, the glories of a new Aryanism. It is a shaggy medievalism and the shaggier its heroes, the more profoundly ideological its superficial naiveté'.[8] A recent example of this phenomenon is Michael Baldwin's novel *The Rape of Oc*, set during the Albigensian Crusade in the south of France in the early thirteenth century. This is a period familiar to me, and following the traditional method of a historian reading historical fiction, Baldwin scores quite highly: he is accurate about events, captures something of the social context, and is aware of the nuances of aspects of historical interpretation. However, *The Rape of Oc*, as the title promises, is also a bodice-ripper, with the emphasis on 'ripper'. A number of women get raped in the course of the narrative; a number of people are violently dismembered; some women are violently dismembered and then raped.[9] This left me uneasy, not because I am opposed to representations of the monstrous, but because Baldwin's representations of violence were, through their historical context, left uninterrogated. History, in his book, legitimates a kind of voyeurism, the voyeurism where the 'Dark Ages' are definitely 'other' than our own, and violence is simply 'how it was back then'. Nothing, I think, in

The Rape of Oc was any less shocking than in, say, Brett Easton Ellis's *American Psycho* or Will Self's *My Idea of Fun*; but unlike those contemporary novels, the work of historical fiction seems to elude public ethical interrogation.

So my first suggestion is that 'the past' can provide, unsurprisingly, a degree of distance in a narrative; that one way 'the past' can function in narrative is to buffer us from the force of that narrative. People did things differently back then, and so we are allowed to watch, fascinated, but not implicated. One might take this as a rough guide to when 'the past' begins: at what point do we stop caring? Would we allow archaeologists to dig up the recently deceased? [10]

This process of distancing seems problematic; to require, at least, some ethical consideration. Not, I should emphasize, because I think we should all be empathizing so strongly with every historical subject that we cry with their pain, but because in the tricky negotiation of the representation of violence, an appeal to the 'historical' setting of a narrative can elide questions which would otherwise be to the forefront of our minds. Principally, the question, 'what is the point of all this raping and dismemberment'? Although the historical setting thrusts the import of the violence into the 'otherness' of 'back then', by dressing it up in garters and broadswords, it also in some ways naturalizes violence. These tortures are in the past; therefore they have already happened, they cannot be changed, they must be accepted. But where does the past begin? At what point will 1939– 1945 become 'the past' – or is it already?

In contrast to the Baldwin or *Braveheart* use of history and violence, I want to discuss David Fincher's film *Se7en*. My argument, put most crudely, is that where I think *The Rape of Oc* is dubious, *Se7en* is rather good and certainly more interesting. The bones of the plot of *Se7en* are relatively simple. Two cops investigate a series of murders which are being carried out in the manner of the seven deadly sins: a model is disfigured by the killer and, unable to face the world without her beauty, kills herself, thus illustrating pride; a drug dealer is tied to a bed and starved to death over the course of a year, dying by sloth; and so on. The murderer turns himself in, but uses himself and one of the cops to 'perform' the last sins of envy and wrath. Everyone goes home unhappy. Reactions to the film have been mixed: everybody praised its style and visual flair; many critics noted its power to shock; the horror/thriller audience were glad that someone had come up with a relatively new plot. The fact that the movie was concerned with sin, and was self-consciously literate about its approach, was also noted. Amy Taubin, writing in *Sight and Sound*, felt that it displays 'revulsion against the body' and is 'as right-wing as Newt Gingrich's natterings about New York';[11] in fact, the framing narrative of 'sin' also prompted David Cronenberg to dismiss the film.[12] What I want to focus on is what might be called the 'historical' content of the film, the very knowing way it plays upon ideas of comprehensible narratives drawn from 'the Past'. Noting its use of history makes it harder, I think, to dismiss the film as 'right-wing' – but also suggests some rather interesting things about the use of 'the Past' in narrative logic, and in assigning 'meaning' to violence.

Se7en invokes and then undermines several narrative modes in order to confound audience expectation. It is a buddy movie, where an older cop, Somerset (Morgan Freeman), is seven days from retirement; he is assigned to teach the ropes to Mills (Brad Pitt). Somerset has had enough of the city whereas Mills is full of young idealism; however, the relationship between them is more like novice and monk than veteran and hotshot. It is initially a whodunnit movie, but as Ryan Gilbey remarks in *The Independent*, becomes more of a 'what the hell have we come to' movie.[13] It is a cop thriller, and knowingly reflects on that fact (Mills's wife calls him 'Serpico' at one point); but it is a thriller which lacks a car chase, and refuses to depict the acts of violence. The only chase – on foot – takes place in pouring rain and gloom, making it almost impossible to distinguish good guy from bad guy. Indeed, the movie is, until its apocalyptic ending, so dark and shadowy that one spends much of the time trying to figure out exactly what one is seeing on screen.[14]

It is this problem of interpreting visual signs that leads me to what my title promises: the medieval aspects of the film. The killer is never seen performing his acts of violence; all he leaves us are the bodies. And the bodies themselves are problematized as polysemic signs. The first victim we see is a hideously obese man, tied to a chair and forced at gun-point to eat until his stomach burst. We are shown his pale, marbled skin, the chair to which he is bound, the food heaped around him, but never the whole picture. Looking at his body the cops run through a number of possible interpretations: that he had a heart attack; that he was greedy; then, following the discovery that he had been trussed up, an autopsy scene, providing a scientific reading of the body; and finally the realisation that he is an 'illustration' of the sin of gluttony. Somerset remarks on the manner of his murder, 'you don't bother to do this unless the act itself has meaning'. At the same time, the luminous flesh of the victim, the grainy and precise camera work, have been offering to us throughout an aesthetic experience of the body.[15]

We are thus introduced to what might be seen as a very medieval preoccupation with the interpretation of the body as sign, an invitation to read the violence done to bodies as an indication of 'higher' meaning. [16] Researching the murder, Somerset uses a library; the first book he takes from the shelf is *The Canterbury Tales*, followed by Dante's *Inferno* and the

Dictionary of Catholicism. We see him studying, in the last tome, medieval pictures of tortured bodies. He quickly realises that the murders are parallels to medieval preaching tools ('these murders are his sermons to us'), and a kind of 'forced attrition'. Further into the film, Somerset and Mills come close to catching the killer by using the FBI computer to trace people who have borrowed library books on Purgatory, the Canterbury Tales, St Thomas Aquinas and so on. When the killer's apartment is discovered, it resembles a medieval reliquary, displaying glass jars containing a severed hand from one of his victims, and other significant trophies from his crimes. And there is a very strong suspicion that the city in which the film is set, a city which is never named but presented as an ocean of pain, is in fact Purgatory itself.

These 'historically aware' ways of reading the deaths in the film are centred on Somerset, the older cop, and are presented at first as privileged readings. Somerset's learning is emphasized, and contrasted to the less cerebral Mills, who tries to keep up by reading the Cliff's Notes versions of the medieval texts. Somerset, to return to the distorted 'buddy movie/novice–monk' narrative, is also Mills's instructor: 'I want you to look and I want you to listen' he says, again emphasizing the need to *read* the clues or signs. Mills's exasperation with the problems of interpreting the crimes is contrasted to Somerset's patient rationalism: Mills remarks, 'So many evil fuckers out there doing evil deeds. "Jesus made me do it. Jodie Foster made me do it"'. Somerset, in comparison, sets out the method of investigation: 'We are doing everything – taking pictures, writing things down, noting down the time'. In other words, looking for meaning, constructing a history.

As the film progresses, tension develops between Somerset's method of interpretation and Mills's crude psychological view; and this tension is slowly revealed to be not so much a right way versus a wrong way, but as a moral and philosophical problem relating back to what I have suggested is a medieval question – how to interpret the signs of violence on the flesh. Mills uses the idea of madness as a way of dismissing (and hence foreclosing and making safe) the riddle set by the killer: 'Right now he's probably dancing around in his Grandma's panties'. A 'commonsense' or pop-psychological reading is set against a historical, Old Testament scheme of interpretation. Mills remarks, 'We're talking about crazies'; Somerset responds, 'No, we're talking about everyday life'. The idea of Original Sin looms large: the killer's method of preaching suggests that these sins, and more disturbingly the desire to punish these sins, lurk within us all.

All of this might be seen to fit with Taubin's assessment of the film's politics: a neo-conservative, fundamentalist diatribe. However, the film also sets out to disrupt these narratives and interpretations. Fincher himself has said that, '[*Se7en*] builds and lulls you into thinking that there is some kind of order and sense to things. And then the final act of the movie is revealed to contain just as much chaos as everyday life'.[17] How does this renunciation of interpretation manifest itself? The opening titles of the movie show someone (we subsequently realise it is the killer) writing in a journal, cutting and pasting things into books. From the very beginning we are set up to expect the revelation of an explanatory narrative, a history which will make sense of what ensues. However, when the police discover the killer's apartment halfway through the film, and come across his notebooks and relics, this expectation is dashed. There are two thousand notebooks in the apartment; an invitation for a genre audience to expect a satisfying narrative of explanation. But the books are not arranged in any discernable order, and defy interpretation. They record the killer's thoughts and madness, the violence inside him, but they are not locatable within a chronological framework. There is no Oedipal narrative to uncover, à la *Psycho*; no 'descent into Madness'; no dancing around in Grandma's panties. The notebooks do not explain the violence, the meanings of the bodies. In the last act of the movie, the murderer defies all expectations by giving himself up (which is when things start to get *really* scary) and still confounds explanation. He is named 'John Doe' and has cut off the ends of his fingers to avoid leaving prints. There are no official records relating to him, no previous accounts of his existence. He is, in a sense, beyond explanation, beyond narrative.

In the final act of the film, the tension between sense and no-sense continues. Mills avers that there can be no meaning to his murderous acts, which for Mills means that he must be a psycho: 'All this work ... in two months from now no-one's going to remember, no-one's going to give a shit. You'll be a fucking T-shirt'. John Doe replies, 'People won't be able to comprehend, but they won't be able to deny ... It's more comfortable for you to label me insane'. Whereas *The Rape of Oc* bypasses the question of the meaning of violence by setting its narrative in a self-enclosed Past, *Se7en* highlights the *desire* for meaning in violence, and the tensions inherent within that desire, by playing on the gap between a violent, medieval and biblical past, and a rational present. Somerset has started to realise the problems of interpretation earlier in the film. In a key speech he points out the limits of interpretation, and the problems inherent in that present/past tension: 'You know, this isn't going to have a happy ending. If we catch John Doe and it turns out that he's the Devil, he's Satan himself, that *might* live up to our expectations... He's not the Devil, he's just a man'.

The film ends by trapping Mills in a hideous moral choice, a moral choice that invites him to enter fully into John Doe's narrative by embodying the last remaining sin of wrath, executing the murderer. It is an invitation to avenge Doe's crimes, and simultaneously to give meaning to his actions (the two, perhaps, being the same thing). However, we are left in no doubt that Mills is damned if he goes along with Doe's plan, and damned if he does not. The medieval, moral, Old Testament narrative wins out over the commonsense and psychoanalytic narratives, and all Somerset's learning cannot save his partner. It is this triumph of the medieval – that a moral interpretation of violence is the only one which finally makes sense – which presumably led Amy Taubin to condemn *Se7en* as right-wing. However, it is clear that the film does *not* endorse the Old Testament narrative; it does not say either, 'yes, the sin should be reflected onto the sinner' or, 'serial killers are indeed sent by God to do his dirty work'. It surely cannot be seen as solely right-wing: when Hell is understood as a deep-seated touchstone of cultural resonance, Satan transcends notions of political affiliation.[18]

What the film suggests is that 'the past' is a dangerous place. This is also the message of *The Rape of Oc*, but in that book the idea of the violent past is used as an excuse for relishing much mayhem and viciousness. In *Se7en*, we are shown firstly that explaining violence through medieval models still carries a great attraction; there is no catharsis in the film, but the closest one comes to closure is by accepting that we actually *want* to believe the killer's medieval narrative, simply because it makes the most sense. It speaks to us. And here *Se7en* does something rather interesting: it suggests that narratives which have recourse to 'the Past' carry with them a great momentum; and that this momentum can be dangerous. Mills is damned not because of his rejection of the moral, medieval interpretive framework, but *despite* that rejection; at the end, he too is bound into John Doe's preaching *exemplum*. There is no explanation comfortably left open for the audience; at the end of the film we are returned to the beginning position of trying to decide how to interpret the signs of violence. Perhaps in recognition of this, David Fincher disconcertingly has the closing credits running backwards. One can compare this representation of evil with Frederic Jameson's analysis of *Blue Velvet*. He suggests that Lynch's film seeks to code 'evil' as a 'simulacrum', produced through the complicated prism of 'the 50s' and 'the 60s' invoked by the film:

> The lesson implied by all this ... is that it is better to fight drugs by portraying them as vicious and silly, than by awakening the full tonal range of ethical judgements and indignations, and thereby endowing them with the otherwise glamorous prestige of genuine Evil, of the Transgressive in its most august religious majesty.[19]

Se7en, in contrast, adopts the 'wholly and transcendentally Evil' line – not in order to authorize it, but rather to show the *seduction* and danger of this viewpoint. The film is engaged with problematizing, not affirming, its 'historical' elements; but problematizing them precisely because of their cultural allure.

So where does this leave us? There are three points or questions I want to raise. Firstly, that the relationship between film and 'the past' may not simply be representational or misrepresentational, but a dialogue; *Se7en* uses recognisable elements of the past in order to prompt interrogation of the present – how do we interpret the signs of violence? What sense can we make of death and disfigurement? What role should we allow 'the past' in our explanatory narratives? There is a simple strength in reminding ourselves that current concerns have a long history, and that that history often unwittingly informs our contemporary fears. But *Se7en* does not hold out medieval morality as a preferred system of interpretation; rather, it challenges us, 'if we discover that we now would rather not think *that*, then what *shall* we think?' Some cinematic uses of the past are best approached not through the 'Dragnet' system of assessing 'accuracy', but by examining what they have to say about our relation to the past, about the intrusions the past makes into our present, about the ways in which we have to supplicate our own histories.[20]

Secondly, we are both distanced from and close to the Past. There is an ethical question of how we negotiate that mutable gap, and the example of the representation of violence provides a particularly illuminating case. Although in one sense the past is a foreign country, and they are not like us, there is a need to reflect upon that alterity. The past should not become a dumping ground for our psychoses, a playground for our voyeuristic impulses. This last point stretches wider than the arena of film-making: when we read, for example, Michel Foucault's description of the execution of the regicide Damiens, what is the ethical response to that past horror?[21] At what point does 'the past', or 'the other', begin? *At what point do we stop caring, and why?*

Finally, we use the past in many ways within our narratives: for authority, for identity, for distance. There is a politics and an ethics to these uses, which we would do well to recognise. However, *Se7en* also suggests that 'the past', as a narrative or interpretive framework, has a momentum of its own. The past is easily invoked; indeed, it seems that contemporary political and moral discourse is fixated on simultaneously demonizing and valorizing 'how things used to be'. The past offers obvious rewards as a hermeneutic code or narrative structure, through its familiarity and apparent weight of authority. But once invoked, does it remain within our control? Or is it possible that, in fact, it is we who are consumed by the past?[22]

The Author

John Arnold has studied and taught at the Centre for Medieval Studies, and the Department of History, at the University of York. He now lectures in the School of History at the University of East Anglia. His future projects include publications on medieval and contemporary topics, and the philosophy of history.

References

1   The situation has obviously changed since this paper was first written, but it seemed illustrative of my point to leave this statement as it stood. We now have a new government with a massive majority – and the moral crisis has returned once more to its slumber, no doubt ready to be reawakened when next required. Cronenberg's *Crash* is still banned by Westminster Council, and the arguments over its censorship are still reverberating (see, for example, *Sight and Sound*, August 1997, letter from Alexander Walker).
2   For more discussion of this latter kind of past and how it functions in the present, see the paper by Harry Ziegler in this volume.
3   *The Guardian*, 2 October 1996, p. 16.
4   For an interesting, if flawed, attempt to categorise 'horror', see N. Carroll, *The Philosophy of Horror; or, Paradoxes of the Heart*, Routledge, London and New York, 1990.
5   On these topics see the paper by Allegra Madgwick in this volume.
6   See, for example, the great, missed opportunity that is M. Carnes, ed., *Past Imperfect; History According to the Movies*, Cassell, London, 1996, which vacillates between a tepid worthiness, and an embarrassing condescension. The film reviews now appearing in *American Historical Review* have the same tendencies – unsurprisingly, since the stated brief for the reviews encourages a remarkable colonisation by academic history of other discourses (see *American Historical Review*, vol. 102, pp. xviii–xix).
7   R. Rosenstone, *Visions of the Past; The Challenge of Film to our Idea of History*, Harvard University Press, Cambridge MA, 1995. There is much to praise in Rosenstone's approach, but many problems, principally around his understanding of 'History', postmodernism, and his sometimes rather naïve reading of particular films.
8   U. Eco, 'Dreaming of the Middle Ages', in *Travels in Hyperreality*, Picador, London, 1987, pp. 61– 72, p. 69.
9   M. Baldwin, *The Rape of Oc*, Little, Brown & Co, London, 1993.
10 I may here be eliding the different ethical assumptions made within particular disciplines. The following passage from a book review gave me a shock, but

then, I am a virgin in such matters: 'this reviewer remembers the lure of old bones – the surprising pleasure felt by almost anyone who has hacked away at (archaeological) digs!' (H. Solterer, *Speculum*, vol.72, 1997, p. 505).

11   A. Taubin, 'The Allure of Decay', *Sight and Sound*, January 1996, pp. 23–24, p. 23.

12   *The Guardian*, 2-10-96, p. 17. Alex Cox, usually an enthusiast for extreme movies, has expressed similar feelings.

13   *Independent on Sunday,* 9 June 1996.

14   For commentary, see Taubin, 'Allure', p. 24; see also interview with Darius Khondji, the cinematographer, 'Inside the Light', *Sight and Sound*, April 1996, pp. 18–20.

15   Taubin's comments on 'body-horror' in *Se7en* appear particularly misplaced; the film is *fascinated* by bodies, and renders them with a terrible beauty.

16   Miri Rubin has noted in her book on the Eucharist that the body in medieval culture was 'a metaphor of metaphors'. The tortured body, whether that of the saint or the sinner, had meaning, and could impart information about God's higher plan. See M. Rubin, *Corpus Christi: The Eucharist in late Medieval Culture*, Cambridge University Press, Cambridge, 1991, p. 269. See also S. Kay & M. Rubin, 'Introduction', in *Framing Medieval Bodies*, Manchester University Press, Manchester, 1994, pp. 1–9. Note that I am not arguing that the idea of the body-as-sign is restricted to the medieval period but that it is coded as 'medieval' within the film.

17   Quoted by Adam Higginbotham, *The Observer,* 7 January 1996, p. 7.

18   It is interesting to contrast the apparent (though, as I argue, illusory) Old Testament narrative logic of *Se7en* with Jonathon Lake Crane's comments on the film *Friday the 13th*. Crane suggests that although one is sometimes tempted to see the killer Jason as a particularly stern moral avenger (and critics have interpreted him thus), the narrative of 'punishing sin' cannot be sustained by a careful reading of the film; 'Jason is a random event', a killer without motive. This concept of evil is precisely antithetical to those discourses that attempt to give meaning to violence. See J. L. Crane, *Terror and Everyday Life; Singular Moments in the History of the Horror Film,* Sage, London, 1994, pp. 146–47.

19   F. Jameson, 'Nostalgia for the Present', in *Postmodernism; or, the Cultural Logic of Late Capitalism*, Verso, London, 1991, pp. 279–96, p. 295.

20   Rosenstone helpfully points out that when cultural critics talk about 'history' in film, they do not usually mean what historians understand by that term, but are referring (usually) to the dramatic import of 'the Past' (and, one might add, usually working within a psychoanalytic or Marxist framework) (*Visions*, p. 10). I think that I am suggesting something else here again: not 'the Past' as the history of the Subject, but 'the Past' as one hermeneutic code.

21   M. Foucault, *Discipline and Punish; Birth of the Prison*, trans. A.M. Sheridan Smith, Penguin, London, 1979, pp. 3–6.

22   My thanks to Katherine Lewis, for her companionship and comments when watching *Se7en*; thanks also to Antonia Ward for encouraging me to address the topic.

5

The Media Iconicity of Diana, Princess of Wales, 1981-1996

Jude Davies

The Princess of Wales's honest confusion and soul-searching as she has tried to come to terms with her new status as a fallen idol has been watched by a worldwide audience, eager to reassess a woman who was, until her separation, seen as an exquisite enigma, an adored holy Madonna, whose elusive personality was a blank canvas on which we were invited to paint our fantasies and dreams.

[Andrew Morton, *Diana: Her New Life* [1]]

A vandalised icon, a betrayed innocent, a manipulative hysteric: Diana, Princess of Wales is many things to many people. The diverse Dianas who pour forth from biographers and newspaper columnists, 'sources close to' and other pub bores are all, in the end, mere reflections of their creators. Just as the British have an umbilical need for their monarchy, like a pricey national nanny or a golden dummy to suck, so every kitchen table in the land needs its own private Diana to perk up its own private soap opera. She's right, he's wrong; hate him, love her. The people's princess is pawn to K-4 in any conversational gambit.

[Anthony Holden, 'Diana: Monster or Martyr?[2]]

One of the principal arguments taken up in this book is that notions of 'Heritage' are politically unstable. Appropriations, validations, commemorations and other uses of the past constitute a variety of practices, working in the service of diverse and complexly related structures of power and identity. What I intend to do here is to relate an awareness of these complexities to current debates around identity and cultural studies. A fundamental point of contact between these sets of issues is the relationship between a politics of positive images, which takes iconicity at face value, and a politics of structural critique or deconstruction, which undertakes to understand the codes by which notions of the past are produced, disseminated, and consumed. Current tensions between different practices of academic and official history can be seen as exemplifying these binaric positions. On the one hand are the projects of producing and disseminating social histories previously marginalised; on the other hand is work stemming from a more theoretically self-conscious ontological critique of historical practices themselves. Tensions between these positions spilled over more than once into heated discussion at the conference which gave rise to this book. The debate bears ramifications of such weight and complexity that it would be foolish to attempt to resolve it here, although I hope that my argument underlines the urgent need to develop syntheses of these positions. Instead, I will trace an analogous and linked set of issues in the discourses of and about popular culture surrounding the British royal family, and in particular Diana, Princess of Wales.

The senses of ambiguity, polyvalence, and blankness attributed to Diana in the above quotations make the Princess of Wales a useful example for the study of uses of the past. Such comments as those of Morton and Holden draw attention to the proliferation of different readings of Diana and hint at the implications of privileging some readings over others. As I will show, different constructions of Diana have been explicitly identified with specific positionalities, of which the most obvious is the articulation of a pre-feminist notion of the wronged woman to a more overt feminist critique of patriarchal power. Thus within the field of popular culture Diana has become a focus of debates over gender, while also functioning iconically with respect to other codes of identity (for example in terms of race, nationality, ethnicity, and class). What is crucially important, I will argue, is to distinguish between mobilisations of Diana's iconicity in the service of particular politics, and a critique of the sign-system which constructs that iconicity.

Monster or martyr? Manipulator or pawn? Wronged woman or spoilt aristocrat? We are accustomed to seeing the media iconography of Diana, Princess of Wales structured as a series of binary oppositions. But at the same time that Diana is defined tightly in terms of one half of these binaries, her iconic meanings proliferate beyond the containment of mainstream discourses. The effect of this is to make *Diana* visible as a potent but highly overdetermined sign; a sign whose meaning, recognisably, is not determined by its content but instead which serves to crystallize debates over a range of "hot" cultural and political issues concerning, for example, gender roles, sexuality, and class. It is possible to discern a variety of responses to these developments in popular culture and mass culture, polarised between on one extreme postmodernist celebrations of Diana as floating signifier, and on the other extreme attempts to stabilise the iconicity of Diana according to a range of discourses of identity. These positions foreground one of the central debates in identity politics and contemporary cultural studies: the relative utility of the deconstruction of authoritive signs *versus* the struggle for control of iconic meaning according to a rhetoric of positive images. The sign *Diana* is a useful focus of this debate since it offers a means of mediating between the strategies of deconstruction (which have previously remained largely confined to the academy) and popular, populist and everyday contestations over identity on the basis of gender, class, race and ethnicity.

The key development which I will be arguing and examining here is the notion that the breakdown of the Wales's marriage has coincided with a 'popular deconstruction' of hegemonic codes and values associated with royalty. I will outline a history of the *Diana* sign whereby its transition from a magical synthesis of binary oppositions to a focus of argument and inspiration has opened up possibilities for unpacking the knot of meanings around royalty, patriarchy, class, imperialism and ethnicity. In addition, I will be arguing for this popular deconstruction over attempts to stabilise and to appropriate Diana's iconicity according to discourses of positive images.

Ever since the publication of Andrew Morton's *Diana: Her True Story* in 1992, constructions of *Diana* have increasingly taken the form of judgemental responses rather than definitive descriptions.[3] While these have come from all sectors of the political spectrum, some of the most surprising have been those associated with leftish feminists such as Suzanne Moore and Susie Orbach, as well as a more downmarket version by Anne Robinson in *The Sun,* headlined 'She has evened the score for every cheated wife and mother'.[4] They have argued for a specific and stable reading of Diana as a somewhat inspirational figure: a formerly exploited woman who has rehabilitated herself from the role of victim, and has now claimed popularity, financial and emotional independence, and retained some influence over the upbringing of her sons. Despite its overtly pro-Diana and anti-Windsor stance, this inspirational construction of Diana perpetuates a construction of celebrity identity that reproduces and naturalises dominant power relations. In privileging Diana as an archetype of female suffering, regeneration, and empowerment, the determination of Diana's narrative by gender is allowed to obscure totally other codes of identity. In particular, what is missing from such accounts is any sense of the ways in which economic class, social class, race and ethnicity have affected Diana's biography and image. Without a consciousness of these, any attempt to claim Diana for feminism remains at best severely compromised and at worst can serve to reinscribe deferential authority to the complex of patriarchy/royalty/aristocracy. Moore and Orbach are smart enough to avoid the latter, but I'm not sure how far their positions are from something like the *Daily Mirror's* campaign for 'justice' for Diana, whose sole aim was articulated in its title: 'Give Her HRH Back'. As an alternative to such readings, what I am interested in exploring here is a sense that the deterioration of Charles' and Diana's marriage, and their subsequent divorce, have highlighted, and, arguably, played a part in deconstructing for a popular readership the multiple and interlocking codes of dominant constructions of royalty, patriarchy, class, imperialism, and ethnicity.

In many ways the shift from definitive descriptions to judgemental responses marked by *Diana: Her True Story* has made visible the processes by which the meaning of *Diana* has historically been constructed. From her first appearance in public as the intended bride of the Prince of Wales, media constructions of Lady Diana Spencer conformed to the dominant mode of royal representations.[5] Access to 'what Diana is really like' was conducted in terms whereby character, personality and biography were merged and subsumed into a discourse of iconicity. In this, constructions of Diana conformed to the customary ways of representating and discussing royalty identified by Michael Billig and others. More recently though the *Diana* question has rarely been posed in terms of an identity assumed to be present. Instead it takes the form of issues such as that of Diana's official status and future life, the upbringing of Princes Harry and William, and questions such as 'Do you think Diana is right to go on Panorama?' and 'Should Charles be allowed to marry Camilla?'[6] At the same time as this shift has taken place, a battery of apparatuses has been developed for gathering and articulating popular responses to such questions. 'Popular opinion' has been solicited and publicised by opinion polls, by phonelines sponsored by the tabloid press and on teletext. In its recent history then, the *Diana* sign appears to be associated both with the undermining of certain hegemonic codes, and with a certain democratisation of the production of cultural meaning. In this paper I will be investigating the implications of these developments for dominant codes of gender, national identity, sexuality and class. In order to do so, I will attempt to historicize the sign of *Diana*, considering it both in terms of semiotics, and also in terms of its material production, dissemination, and consumption. The historical development of the *Diana* sign, it will be argued, is best seen as a process of *popular deconstruction*.

The history of Charles' and Diana's break-up could be seen both as foregrounding the codes by which the meanings of 'royalty' are constructed, and at the same time as unmasking a series of attendant, dominant constructions of gender, national identity, family, sexuality, and social class. This might seem particularly interesting to cultural critics on the lookout for signs, and accustomed, under the influence of poststructuralism, to look for the deconstruction of signifying practices. In the case of *Diana*, it appears, the prising away of signifier from signified, and the foregrounding of the relation between signifiers, has happened, and is happening, within the realm of popular culture, without the interpretative pressure of the academic critic. The development of the iconicity of *Diana* could be seen therefore as undoing the reciprocal relations which had served to bind together a series of prestigious codes of gender, sexuality, social hierarchy, and national history. Put simply, the popular deconstruction of *Diana* can be read as unmasking some of the ways in which images of domesticated femininity, of heterosexual romantic love, of social and cultural authority, have secured dominant status.

Cultural critics have stressed the ideological role of the royal family in reproducing particular models of identity. For example, in her 1983 book *Female Desire: Women's Sexuality Today,* Rosalind Coward makes a brilliant analysis of what she calls 'the longest-running soap opera in Britain'. She concludes:

> 'The Royals' eternalizes traditional values, glorifies women's route
> to power through individual sexual attraction, and defines women as
> exclusively bound up with these values.[7]

Coward demonstrates how the power with which representations of the royals cohere this knot of meanings is dependent on the construction of the *royal family* as a timeless, unchanging embodiment of national identity. She quotes from the address given by the Archbishop of Canterbury at the wedding of Charles and Diana, as follows:

> We are fortunate in having at the heart of our national life ... the
> presence of a family, providing a sense of continuity and pointing to
> the most profound themes of human life which do not change from
> century to century.[8]

Coward points out that the resolution of these themes by reference to the family unit automatically excludes any consideration of the entry of women into the world of work, while noble rank defines these resolutions outside the realm of economics altogether. Obviously what she cannot consider is the impact of a Royal divorce on these meanings. In what follows, I will examine the implications of what I termed earlier the popular deconstruction of the *Diana* sign for these ideologies and the power relations they underpin.

I want to begin by developing further analysis of an element of this process touched on by Coward; the importance of the binary opposition of ordinary/extraordinary for the royals in general and for Diana in particular. Roland Barthes, Judith Williamson, Tom Nairn, and Michael Billig have all discussed the importance of combinations of the ordinary and the extraordinary in representations of the royal family.[9] Robert Runcie's description of the timeless royals quoted above provides a good starting point to consider the historical fortunes of this royal synthesis. A crucial element of the House of Windsor's post-war self-construction has been the playing down of a claim for authority based on its connection with a specific historical past, and an emphasis instead on drawing its legitimacy from its relationship with what coheres the nation in the present. The key to the popularity of the British royal family from the 1960s on was that, rather than legitimating itself through a nostalgic evocation of a specific history, it defined itself in relation to the supposedly time*less*. In the early 1980s the chief function of the *Diana* sign was to play a crucial role in securing this conception of the Windsors.

Diana as 'both...and'

Early descriptions of Lady Diana Spencer took up the notion of her bringing a naturalness and informality to the royal family. Unsurprisingly, representations of the 1981 Royal Wedding frequently adopted a discourse of doubling, of 'both...and'. This is a familiar form for wedding discourses, but is especially productive on Royal occasions, since it allows all kinds of syntheses to be keyed into the heterosexual union of two individuals. In the hardback souvenir book *Invitation to a Royal Wedding* (1981), author Kathryn Spink describes the wedding as effecting a synthesis of 'historical and contemporary, commercial and spiritual, public and personal'.[10] She was outdone however in the foreword to her own book by the Dean of St Paul's, the Very Reverend Alan Webster. In the space of a few hundred words, Webster staged four complementary sets of oppositions: St Paul's was royal and yet also 'the Peoples' Cathedral; it was also both holy and challenging. The words of the wedding service were ancient and modern.

(It was actually an amalgam of the Church of England Series I marriage service and prayers from the new Alternative Service Book; most remarked upon was the dropping of the wife's promise to 'obey' from the 1662 Prayer Book, a break from the tradition which had been upheld by the Queen, Princess Margaret and Princess Anne.)[11] Webster went on to stress the ecumenicalism of the service itself; with representatives from Anglican, Free Church and Roman Catholicism, it was historic yet also enacted a 'new unity'. Finally the 'place, service and music' of the wedding are 'special', while its purpose 'is the same as that in every wedding, religious or civil, in every culture and country'.[12] In typical Windsor fashion then, the heterosexual romance narrative of Charles and Diana is made to support a vast range of official, religious and public syntheses.

These syntheses did not necessarily produce a totally – if speculatively – united nation. But the binary structuring did define non-royalists outside communal norms both explicitly and implicitly. Even celebratory texts such as Spink do not present the whole of Britain as swept away with royalist fervour in July 1981. She records the following as dissenting from the royalist community, without overt judgement. The ruling Labour group on North East Derbyshire District Council decided to fly the red flag from the Council's flagpole on July 29 'as a matter of principle'; the Labour administration on the GLC declined an invitation to the wedding with '[n]o one elected us to go to weddings. They elected us to try to get the buses running on time.' Also in Derbyshire, Clay Cross councillors organised anti-monarchist plays, and one councillor declared that when Diana rides into St Pauls in a glass coach she will also be 'riding on the backs of the working class and not realising what a mess the country is in'.[13] An anti-anti-royalist position was made more explicit in a children's book of the wedding published under the name of TV presenter John Craven. Here, the existence was admitted of anti-royalists who 'had their televisions and radios switched off all day', some of whom escaped to republican France, though the joke was on them because President Mitterand had gone to the wedding.[14]

While their coupling was produced in this way, both Charles and Diana were frequently represented as themselves split doubles, though in significantly different ways. For Charles, the issue was in synthesising 'heart and head', in choosing a love match who would not only provide a long-term companion but also heirs to the throne.[15] By contrast, Diana was figured as simply embodying binary oppositions. Initially this was often represented in terms of what she would have to learn as part of the royal family – Spink describes her as a 'fresh, unblemished "English rose" who will be given the distinctive Royal grooming'. The naturalness of this rose, exemplified by Lady Diana's 'refreshing giggle' is in need of 'royal restraint'. Given this royal training, Diana began to appear as a perfect synthesis.[16] *Diana* was constructed as effortlessly embodying binary oppositions clustered around that of the ordinary/extraordinary. She was the ordinary girl specially chosen to play a part in a fairy tale romance. In return she would bring a down-to-earth quality to the royal firm. As the Ladybird book *HRH The Princess of Wales* put it in 1982:

> ...Diana turned out to be an uncommon mixture of old-fashioned virtues and modern vivacity. She was homeloving, dutiful, and wanted 'lots and lots' of children; she was discreet and unpretentious, despite her aristocratic background. Yet she possessed the good looks, charm, and outgoing manner the public role of royalty requires.... She was, in fact, the girl next door to the Royal Family.[17]

Similar meanings were constructed in the apparently accidental exposure of Diana en route from her flat to work as a kindergarten teacher, endlessly repeated on news bulletins and subsequently on commemorative videos. Here television cameras caught not only a blushing, giggling young woman, soon nicknamed 'Shy Di', but also her car, a red Mini Metro. Car – whose name was developed of course from the original British motor to emblematise a classless society – and job cemented her image as 'good with children', and produced readings of Diana as modest in terms of gender, ambition and of class.

The both/and construction of Diana as ordinary and extraordinary was further cemented by subsequent publications such as the previously quoted *Royal Wedding* by Gordon Honeycombe, packaged as if it were one's own photograph album; and the 1983 hardback available from British Home Stores *Diana Princess of Wales: The Book of Fashion*. The latter in particular both represented Diana as unique and set her up, minus 'HRH', for emulation.[18]

In retrospect at least, it is clear that these magical syntheses were predicated on constructing Diana primarily in terms of gender, and of obscuring or fictionalising notions of social and economic class. These combinations of real-life and fairy-tale; of everywoman and Princess, were facilitated by emphasising a particular model of femininity conceived of as transcending not only class but also time and even culture: a domestic femininity as caring, deferential, defined by reference to a more powerful male. Diana's own history provided plenty of material for this construction, especially for example the coupling of her academic weakness with her 'goodness with children'. According to the above-mentioned 1982 paperback *Charles and Diana*, subtitled 'Their Story Told By John Craven, including children's memories of the wedding', both of these qualities were apparent in Diana from an early age. A certain Miss Ridsdale, headmistress of the boarding school to which Diana was packed off at the age of eight, told John:

> I was very pleased that she won a very special cup, the Helpfulness Cup. This was given by the teachers to any child who had been helpful in many ways without seeking reward.The staff discussed spontaneous acts of kindness that they had spotted, and Diana was awarded the cup.[19]

In these constructions of Diana and the Windsors, gender and social class are articulated in significant and mutually reinforcing ways. Diana's femininity naturalises not just her own deferential position but also underwrites the authority of Charles. Her identity, conceived through her femininity, is a matter of embodiment; while Charles' royalty is constructed as a set of responsibilities to be assumed, partly by reference to his 'natural' bride. In the kind of reciprocal reinforcement that gives such strength to these constructions, not only is patriarchal power naturalised by assumptions of Charles' royal prerogative, but the social hierarchy of which royalty is a part is in turn naturalised by patriarchal assumptions. The *Diana* sign played a crucial part in securing these connections, which is why of course it was so strongly welcomed as a means of strengthening and modernising the monarchy. But it was immediately and by definition always a sign of weakness. In Derridean terms, *Diana* stood for and was the *supplement* that guaranteed the royal authority of the Windsors.

In sum then *Diana* was initially constructed for the British public in terms of both/and, and she was presented as embodying universal feminine qualities. These served to tighten the knot of class, gender, and authority; the dominant constructions of class, gender, race and national identity.

Diana as 'either...or'

The story of the *Diana* sign, ever since rumours of marital problems gained wide credibility, has been the story of the fracturing of its synthesis of those binary oppositions. The process of the popular deconstruction of the *Diana* sign has been accompanied by its inability to sustain these contradictory meanings simultaneously. Confidence in the content, or the signified of Diana has waned, at the same time that Diana has come to be represented not as 'both...and', but as 'either....or'. It is no coincidence that, also over this period, the power of royalty both to sustain its own prestige, and as part of the reciprocally reinforcing signification of patriarchal and economic authority, has declined. At the same time, arguably, Diana's femininity has been understood less as something natural and essential, and more in terms of cultural and historical determinants (less as embodying qualities to be viewed, more in terms of the production of children, construed in a variety of terms, from the use of Diana's body for breeding stock, to debates over the upbringing of the heir to the throne). But while Diana has become a problem for the royal family, *Diana* (the sign) has become a problem at the level of signification. As a free-floating signifier, *Diana* can point in multiple political directions, constructing a variety of meanings and operating in the service of different politics. The semiotic deconstruction of *Diana*, of itself, is politically polyvalent. Space makes it impossible here to exemplify this from the various mainstream and subcultural representations of Diana; I hope elsewhere to examine these and the various strategies evolved in the mass media and in popular culture to handle this problem of Diana. I will close here with a brief description of the Diana problem as it presented itself to mainstream media, before going on to examine one of the principal strategies invoked to deal with it, which I have called 'structured contradiction'.

Rumours of marital breakdown, followed by the announcements of separation and divorce, presented pro-royalist conservative discourses with a major strategic problem. How to represent internal hostility within the paradigmatic heterosexual couple in the nation? How to ease out of the picture not only the woman who was the most popular member of the royal family, but also the sign which had effectively grounded the claims of the royals to represent the nation at large? This problematic was and is by no means confined to conservatism and pro-royalism, but extended across the range of discourses connected with the British royal family, and across the variety of people whose own sense of national, global, gendered, social, or cultural identity was to any extent invested in the 1981 wedding. In the tabloid press, the resulting confusion was such that no coherent opinion or response was produced. Instead, a series of strategies were developed in order to handle diametrically opposed affiliations, structured along the lines of the 'either...or' construction of *Diana*. One of the principal paradigms used was that of 'structured contradiction'.

Eventually widely disseminated among the British popular press, this strategy first featured strongly in the cover story of the December 1993 edition of *Tatler*. This ten-page feature, headlined, 'Diana: monster or martyr?' contained two columns, one hostile to Diana and one supportive, and shorter comments by fifty celebrities, with the results of a survey of '1,000 hand-picked, well-informed people who quite probably have danced with the Princess of Wales or at least with a man who has'.[20] The principles of selection for the fifty 'opinion leaders' are possibly still more obscure. The list is a mad, or possibly inspired mixture of journalists, pop performers, nightclub owners and interior designers, minor aristocracy and hangers-on. It includes such luminaries as Ruby Wax, Madonna, Peter York, Julie Burchill, Sir Peregrine Worsthorne, Trevor Nunn, Joan Bakewell, Imogen Stubbs, Count Nikolai Tolstoy, David Sullivan (pornographer and now owner of Birmingham City F.C., somewhat euphemistically described here as newspaper proprietor), the Hon. Mrs Rocco Forte, Sue Townsend, Dennis Skinner MP, nightclub-owner Johnny Gold, the UK's Eurovision song contest hope Lisa B, Fiona Pitt-Kethley, Dr Freddie Nicolle (whose specialism lies in plastic surgery), Frank Muir, and Michael Winner.

In the main articles, *Daily Express* diarist Ross Benson argues the case for Diana's monstrousness, while Anthony Holden defends her. Tellingly, both arguments hang on the multiplicity of identities readable into Diana's image. Benson articulates a familiarly misogynistic account of femininity as surface: beneath the 'panstick of illusion', he writes, lies a manipulative and capricious nature. 'What we have been witnessing', he continues, 'is the victory of image over evidence and the institution of the monarchy has been sorely damaged as a result'.[21]

By contrast, in the column quoted from at the head of this chapter, Holden contextualises the ambiguity of *Diana* with respect to its production and consumption in discourse. Diana is not just 'many things to many people,' but the 'people's princess is pawn to K-4 in any conversational gambit'.[22] Holden comes very close here to suggesting that the key to *Diana* lies in its production from codes of meaning, far from any definable or 'authentic' content. As his article goes on though, Holden draws back from the deconstructive implications of this position by going on to claim real personal knowledge of Diana after all. Nevertheless, its place in the multi-voiced discussion of Diana-ness presented in this issue of *Tatler* automatically limits the credibility of Holden's pretensions to insider knowledge. Moreover, not only the tonal ambiguity of his remarks about the monarchy, but also his sense of Diana-ness as being up for grabs set the pattern for much later coverage of Diana and the divorce issue. It should also be said that the terms in which *Tatler* put the Diana question – 'monster or martyr' – appear unusually misogynistic compared with later representations, which are both more sympathetic to Diana personally and offer a more imaginative sense of her life possibilities.

The tabloid press used the model of structured contradiction in a number of ways. Their initial response to the announcement of Charles' and Diana's separation and later divorce was to present the issue in terms of a debate. They carried pro- and anti-Diana columns, and set up phonelines for readers to articulate support for either party, or for specific courses of action. While it should not be underestimated how these functioned to manage and to structure popular responses, nevertheless they allowed unprecedented power over signification to the readership. At the same time, the framing of discussion by reference to popular interest in the social issues of gender roles, authority and others, carried on the process of denaturalising the codes.

Coverage in these sections of the press not only played a part in deconstructing the codes that had produced popular understandings of Diana, but also granted readerships some control over signification. The 'popular' is still being managed, not least through the setting of the question itself, but nevertheless there were signs of confusion in the expert posture of the tabloids. Instead of portraying themselves as purveyors of inside information, the popular press adopted a series of commentary discourses from a range of positions. While again these operated in some ways to manage popular meaning, the proliferation of such discourses tended to undermine authoritative statements of identity and position. Thus for example on 20 November 1995, the *Sun* published the column by Ann Robinson previously discussed, which championed Diana as having 'evened up the score for every cheated wife and mother'.[23] Two days later the same newspaper ran a pro-Charles editorial which sought to protect the Windsor succession from Diana's alleged suggestion that the crown should skip a generation to her eldest son.[24] Similar cracks showed nearly a year later in the *Sun*'s attempt to argue that its reprinting of frames from a video purportedly showing intimacies between Diana and James Hewitt was justified, on the grounds that it proved her fears (of royal spies) correct.[25]

Of course, consistency is not necessarily demanded of the popular press, and to a large extent the pluralisation of readings of Diana may be contained by strategies such as this. However, the proliferation of mutually exclusive meanings of the *Diana* sign continues to problematise the ideological authority of dominant constructions of royalty, gender, and nationhood. At time of writing, it does not appear that this disruptive effect will be much contained should Charles succeed in installing Camilla Parker-Bowles officially as a replacement for Diana. Such a move, it is already clear, could even proliferate the controversies produced by the fallout from the failure of the 1981 marriage, adding fox-hunting and the role and status of the Church of England to the issues already broached. It seems that whereas formerly the imbrication of royalty with multiple codes of identity and authority was the secret weapon in sustaining British conservatism, the unravelling of these connections has increased its vulnerability.

Postscript

This paper was conceived and written some time before the shocking accident which occurred in the early hours of 31 August 1997 in a Paris underpass, when Diana, Princess of Wales was killed in a car crash, together with her close friend Dodi Al Fayed and their driver. Rather than attempting to revise the paper to take account of this tragedy and the widespread grief it elicited throughout the world, it has been decided to let this piece stand as a partial and specific account of certain aspects of the importance of this remarkable woman.

The Author

Dr Jude Davies is a Senior Lecturer in the School of Cultural Studies at King Alfred's College of Higher Education, Winchester. He has published articles in the *Journal of Popular Culture* and *Screen*, and is co-author of a forthcoming book on contemporary American film.

References

1   Andrew Morton, *Diana: Her New Life,* Michael O'Mara Books, London, 1994, p. 9.
2   Anthony Holden, 'Diana: Monster or Martyr?', *Tatler,* vol. 288 no.12, December 1993, p. 151.
3   This is not to overemphasise the role of Morton's book in definitively fixing *Diana*, but to stress its historically pivotal role.
4   Anne Robinson, 'Anne Robinson joins the *Sun*', *The Sun*, 20 November 1995, p. 3.
5   For two complementary analyses of 1980s discourses of royalty, see Coward 1983 and Billig 1992, cited and discussed below.
6   See *The Sun,* 20 November 1995, p. 3, and 22 November 1995, p. 8; and also ITV Teletext poll, September 1996.
7   Rosalind Coward, 'The Royals', in *Female Desire: Women's Sexuality Today*, Paladin, London,1983, pp. 161-71, p. 171.

8   Coward, 'The Royals', p. 165.

9   Roland Barthes, *Mythologies*, trans. Annette Lavers, Paladin, London, 1973; Judith Williamson, *Consuming Passions*, Boyer, London,1987; Tom Nairn, *The Enchanted Glass: Britain and Its Monarchy*, Vintage, London, 1994; Michael Billig, *Talking of the Royal Family*, Routledge, London, 1992, Chapters 3 and 4.

10 Kathryn Spink, *Invitation to a Royal Wedding*, Colour Library Books, New Malden,1981, p. 91.

11 See for example Gordon Honeycombe, *Royal Wedding,* Book Club Associates, London, 1981, p. 177.

12 Spink, *Invitation*, p. 11.

13 Spink, *Invitation*, p. 67.

14 John Craven, *Charles and Diana*, Arrow Books, London, 1982, p. 76.

15 See for example Spink, *Invitation*, p. 15.

16 Spink, *Invitation*, p. 75.

17 Brenda Ralph Lewis, *HRH The Princess of Wales*, Ladybird Books, Loughborough, 1982, p. 4. Directly below this passage there is a photograph of the engagement ring on Diana Spencer's hand. Also of interest is Audrey Daly, *Royal Wedding: A Ladybird Souvenir of the Royal Day,* Ladybird Books, Loughborough, 1981, which appeared a mere five days after the event.

18 (Text by) Jane Owen, *Diana Princess of Wales: The Book of Fashion*, Colour Library Books, Guildford, 1983.

19 Craven, *Charles and Diana*, p. 40.

20 Various, 'Diana: Monster or Martyr?', *Tatler,* vol. 288, no. 12 December 1993, pp.148-155, 218-219; p.150.

21 Various, 'Monster or Martyr?', p. 150.

22 Various, 'Monster or Martyr?', p. 151.

23 Robinson, 'Joins the *Sun*', p. 3.

24 Uncredited editorial, 'Your Country Needs You', *Sun,* 22 November 1995, p. 16.

25 'Di Spy Video Scandal', *Sun,* 8 October 1996, pp. 1-5. The video was almost immediately exposed as a hoax.

THE PERSONAL PAST

6

Your Granny Had One of Those!

How Visitors use Museum Collections

Christine Johnstone

Many museum curators spend much of their time analysing material culture. This is not surprising, given that a museum is defined as an institution that collects, documents, preserves, exhibits and interprets material evidence and associated information for the public benefit. For curators, product definition and product differentiation are crucial elements in marking out their professional territory, and defining their own expertise. It has never been sufficient to describe something by its raw material and gone are the days when general museums had staff curating just silver, just wood, or just textiles. Even if there are sufficient resources to specialise in this way, many museum objects are made of two or more materials. Form and function must therefore be looked at instead. What was it used for? Who made it? How was it made? And then there's the date too – extremely important in museums where history is cut in half somewhere around the time of the English Civil War.

In my own museum service at Wakefield, we have curatorial expertise in archaeology, art and social history. All these experts can legitimately lay claim to specialist knowledge in an area like ceramics, so a not untypical fudge has been developed to specify curatorial responsibilities. All ceramics made before 1700 are the responsibility of the Keeper of Archaeology, and all contemporary craft ceramics are cared for by the Keeper of Art. All those specifically relating to Pontefract are looked after by the Curator of Pontefract Museum and any made in Castleford also fall to the Keeper of Archaeology, because of her personal expertise in this area. Anything else is allocated to either the Keeper of Art or the Keeper of Social History, depending on its position on a complex matrix of old/new, ornamental/useful, craft/mass-produced and cheap/expensive. We then rely on computerised documentation to help identify and eliminate areas of confusion or duplication.

Such detailed and documented analysis is something that museums are very good at, and which curators, by and large, enjoy. Indeed, social history curators boast that they can classify all human life with SHIC, the Social History and Industrial Classification system. Under this comprehensive system if the object is classified as, for example, 1.4122 it comes from a dental clinic, if 1.4123 a physiotherapy clinic. If it's 2.8161, it's a dolls house; if it's 2.8162 it's a model farm. The classification 3.3211 is for a man's main garment covering the body above and below the waist and 3.3212 for a man's main garment covering the body above the waist and to knee level.[1]

Classification systems undoubtedly have their uses, and curators do need to know what the objects that they look after were made for. But the whole emphasis of this approach is on production; whether it is the manufacture of individual items, the construction of a whole collection as an acquired artefact, or the creation of displays as a temporary assemblage.

In this paper, I want to look down the other end of the telescope, and examine not how well curators can produce a product, but how visitors consume it. All objects are made to be consumed, particularly, in the context of my own work, those with a historical significance. Consumption of a product as complex as a group of old and varied objects raises many interesting issues. In my work, and in this paper, I am concerned with those questions which relate to the different expectations and analytical tools of the producer and consumer. When the consumer has the same world-outlook as the producer – a Mondrian connoisseur looking at a Mondrian exhibition curated by a Keeper of twentieth-century fine art, for instance, or a teacher of Key Stage 2 history looking at an exhibition of Roman life in Britain – then they share the same emotional closeness to or distance from the object, and probably have a similar level of practical or intellectual knowledge about it. In other areas – children at a dinosaur exhibition, or indeed, tourists in almost any museum – the curators are guaranteed to know more than the visitors, and inevitably stand in a closer relationship to the objects on display. In one particular area however, that of twentieth-century social history, many visitors seem to have a much more immediate, personal and emotional engagement than that experienced by most curators. Often they have specific knowledge of the use and perhaps manufacture of specific objects; knowledge that the curator lacks. Visitors engaging emotionally with twentieth-century social history displays can always be recognised by their cries of 'Your Granny had one of those!'

Recent history directly touches most people's lives. Almost everyone knows something of their parent's individual histories. Not a few know something about their grandparents or great–grandparents. Karl Curry, for example, relates how: "My grandfather used to tell me stories, you know when you're small, and you sit and your grandfather tells you tales about the pit.... He worked at Whitwood did my grandfather."[2] If one assumes generational gaps of 25 years, this means the average 30 year old can relate to material from the Second World War, the First World War and even the 1890s. A 70 year old, similarly, has direct memories from the 1930s and may even know family tales back to the 1850s. Though Karl only began work as a miner in 1967, through the memories of his grandfather he gains knowledge of the conditions in a pit that he has never worked in, at a time before he was born.

In addition to personal memories, most people are surrounded by, and familiar with, material evidence of the last 200 or 250 years. Even the landscape of Milton Keynes includes the occasional old building, railway line or canal! Housing, industries, public buildings, field boundaries and transport networks are all dominated by the changes made to the British landscape since 1750.

Most people live out historical narratives in their everyday lives, perhaps without even realising it. In Wakefield, a typical resident might leave their Homes fit for Heroes 1920s council house, and catch a bus past the 1910s terraced houses, through the common land enclosed in the 1790s, past the 1860s spinning mill and the 1840s prison, under the 1860s railway viaduct, past the 1760s chapel and the 1890s theatre, through the 1909 road-widening scheme, and into the 1950s bus station. From there she or he will walk through the 1990s pedestrian scheme to a 1980s shopping centre named after a local authority which was abolished in 1974![3] People are thus sensitised to the past: via their own memories, those of their friends and family, and also by their immediate surroundings.

Curators usually attempt to choose objects for display rationally and carefully, trying to recognise the many levels of meaning the objects might carry. In the context of each different display, the meanings attached to, and intended for the object will inevitably vary. Curators distinguish between objects along the classificatory lines of, for instance, how it was produced, its primary or secondary uses, its date, purpose, or visual appeal. But objects are usually included in displays for more complex reasons, which demonstrate the curators' engagement as museum professionals with historical material. A tin bath might be part of a display because it illustrates the lack of plumbing in mining villages; a sports badge because 'we need something about leisure'; some 1984-5 strike ephemera because of the devastating economic effects of the subsequent pit closures, and a painting because it is by this year's favoured artist.

Most visitors, however, will interpret these objects through a different set of meanings. The display has, for them, a largely emotional and commemorative value since they appropriate and adapt the objects within the context of their own experiences. Here are some individual responses to the objects I listed above, which may have little or nothing to do with the intentions of the curator who included them in the display.

On the tin bath:

> On a cold night, with your night clothes airing on the polished steel fender, feeling the heat from the deep fire of the kitchen range, your towel warming on the oven door and the Light Programme on the wireless, having a bath was delicious.... The bath itself stood on an old towel on the hand-pricked rug and the mellow gas light added to the fireglow, giving the whole activity a natural, pleasurable enjoyment.[4]

And:

> Having a bath when I was young was quite something.... I don't think I would like to go back to having a bath in front of the coal fire, but I have fond memories of sitting in a warm bath with a glowing fire in front of me. Somehow it gave me a sense of security.[5]

On the sports badges :

> Hull City and Hull FC made me proud and Clive Sullivan left a lump in my throat.[6]

On the strike ephemera :

> A lot of hardship in that one. It was an experience. There won't be many who've been out on strike for twelve months. I mean, I can remember dad proudly talking about the six months strike and what they'd done, and I remember taking him down to Allerton Bywater to see all the police and dogs and horses, and I said, "Look what we're bloody tackling!"[7]

And on the painting:

> I've been fishing in places like this. I like fishing, its my sport.[8]

Visitors cherry-pick for emotional engagement as they wander through displays of twentieth-century history. Curators can put together timelines and sequential displays, in every showcase and all exhibitions, but visitors are not interested in chronological strait jackets. At most they will follow a tightly focused exhibition in the order it was designed to be 'read' – left to right, top to bottom – but they will not do this in a large generic display. Instead, they are interested in the personal and emotional resonance of the ordinary, the commonplace. Something unique or uncommon – the biggest, the oldest, the only, the most expensive – is not as popular as the everyday, because it is the everyday object that they are more likely to recognise from their own lives.

In addition, the resonance often occurs in unexpected places. Curators have learnt to expect that most adults have clear and detailed memories of a coal-fired range, or the old trams. But a photograph of the Rugby League cup being paraded round the city will only have resonance for one visitor because he is the little boy snapped waving out of the window; or the whole exhibition on life in Roman Britain is meaningful for two other visitors only because it is located in the room where they met each other, at a 1940s dance.

Research by Nick Merriman shows that most people have a strong sense of the past, but that many do not approach the past through guided, edited formats like chronological exhibitions, guided tours or reference books. Their approach is often intangible, being based on their family, their home, and the area they live in or come from. Material culture, such as treasured possessions, sometimes has an important role to play in making this sense of the past tangible, but many rely purely on memory, imagination and conversation, in which history is passed on verbally.[9]

The same research highlighted the way in which old objects are important to many different kinds of museum visitors, mainly because of the links the objects had with the visitor's family. Over 78% of frequent museum visitors own objects which are over 50 years old, 62% of regular visitors, 50% of occasional visitors and 48% of rare visitors. For regular, occasional and rare visitors the most important reason why an old object is attractive is because of its family links (46–52%). Only the frequent visitor puts beauty above family links, for other groups it comes a poor second, or even third.[10]

Unpublished research among museum visitors at Wakefield also throws light on what people want to see in museums, and who they expect to see it with. When consulted in 1996, as part of the project to redevelop Wakefield Museum, children under twelve overwhelmingly expressed a desire to see exhibitions and displays on toys and on sport (82% and 64%). Teenagers wanted famous people (70%), and music, health and toys (65– 61%). Young adults (age 19–30) had the most diverse interests, but more than

66% of them wanted to see (in descending order) religion and beliefs, women's history, hidden history, pubs, the Romans, textile history, sport, music, wars and battles, the Victorians, belonging to Wakefield, industry, poverty and historical evidence.

It is this diverse reaction to the museum's representation of history that is reflected in the following views of a Castleford resident:

> I sometimes wonder what the Romans ever saw in this place. I mean, look at it! That is if you can see anything through that yellow haze. They say they settled here for strategic reasons. It's at the confluence of two rivers. Now it stands for the effluence of two rivers. I mean, what did they do for entertainment? Do you think they mixed with the locals? I doubt it. If a legionnaire picked up a Cas [Castleford] lass where would he take her? Maybe they had Chariot Races up at Ponte [Pontefract]. Or perhaps he took her to see the Christians thrown to the lions at Wheldon Lane [Castleford RLFC ground]. Nah! Where would they get the lions? Or the Christians for that matter? I wonder if they used local coal to heat their baths? I wonder if they used local lads to dig it up? Nah! They'd be wood burners. No use for coal then, or now come to think of it. So what did they see in Cas? Maybe they heard the birds singing on Fairburn Ings [local RSPB reserve], or maybe it was the ale. They liked a drink, you know. Perhaps it was just what I said earlier, strategic reasons.[11]

Older adults, like children and teenagers, seem to have narrower preferences. Visitors aged 31–60 wanted to see old buildings and hidden history (64%, 55%), those aged 61 and above preferred hidden history and transport (61%, 56%).

From these choices, it seems clear that younger people want to see things that relate to their present experience (toys for children, music for teenagers); or to their wider interests outside the museum (famous people for teenagers, religion and beliefs, and pubs, for young adults). Older people are more interested in subjects that they remember from earlier in their own lifetimes (old buildings, hidden history, transport).[12]

At the same time, the same visitors were asked who they visited with. Excluding organised groups (almost exclusively schools, the district college and adult training centres), all but the young adults were likely to visit with their families (children 43%, teenagers 41%, young adults 33%, older adults 49%, oldest adults 40%). The percentage of visits made alone was, as might be expected, proportional to age (children 2%, teenagers 5%, young adults 33%, older adults 35% and oldest adults 44%). The percentage visiting with friends was almost as clearly inversely proportional (children 33%, teenagers 31%, young adults 33%, older adults 12%, oldest adults 8%).

Young people, then, come in groups, not alone. The group is almost as likely to be a peer group of the same age, as a family group of different ages. Older people do not visit with their peer group. They are most likely to be with a family group of different ages, or else visit on their own. Combining these trends, it appears that adults, especially older adults, want to connect lives together in a chain of experience, and pass on that experience through memory, triggered by objects and images.

Nick Merriman's research shows that many people gain access to the past in a closely personal way, through their relatives and the family heirlooms that they share. Typically these might include a dolls house, a silver locket, medals, the grandmother's wedding ring, family photographs, a silver fob watch, a tea service, a child's rocking chair, antique furniture, or a painting.[13] Social history collections in museums can often provide substitutes for these important emotional triggers, when the visitor cannot access the original remembered object. It may not be Granny's, but Granny had one just like that.

If we consider the list above, the family jewellery may have long since disappeared one or two generations ago, and belong to another branch of the family. Before the mid 1960s, many families had no camera on which to record family events. Tea services got broken, and furniture was at some point considered too big or too old-fashioned for the new home. Other well-remembered objects were just too big to move. A kitchen range, for instance, might have been left behind and the family's first black and white television relegated to the dustbin as obsolete. Other objects found a subsequent, secondary use. 'Baths were not a once-in-a-lifetime purchase and when they showed signs of wear they were relegated to the allotment to help force the rhubarb.'[14]

The role museum collections can play as substitute 'heirlooms' is even more pronounced for adults who have experienced profound geographical disruption. Older adults born in Africa, South Asia, the Caribbean and Europe, but now living in Britain, have found museums invaluable for teaching both their children and grandchildren, and the wider community, about their own experience as children and young adults in other countries. Many came to Britain with, at best, just a few suitcases of possessions, often from a background of relative poverty or desperate persecution. They are unlikely to own the family photographs, jewellery, tea sets and antique furniture that Nick Merriman has identified as being such an important part of people's understanding of history. Exhibitions on the Caribbean contribution to the Second World War, on the Jewish communities in

Poland, on textiles from Gujerat, or on the political founders of Pakistan, can all help to flesh out the stories told by these parents and grandparents.

Museum objects can also provoke strong emotional responses, even when there is no direct personal or family link with the visitor. World conflicts, or deeply-held political beliefs, can often be important emotional stimuli, even if the visitor's family was never at the centre of the event. The 40-year-old, born in Kent, may experience profound emotions when visiting the Cabinet War Rooms, simply because the Battle of Britain has become an intangible factor in his or her own self-identity. Similarly, many African Caribbean adults have very positive emotional reactions to material from Africa – material which they have never owned either in Britain or the Caribbean, which they can only see (in Britain) in museums, but which they most certainly regard as part of their personal family history. In the words of one African Caribbean adult visiting an exhibition of traditional West African carvings at Hackney Museum – 'if its going to leave Africa at all, its good that it's here where we can see it'. In this particular case, the museum's role was vital, as the objects on display were borrowed from an anonymous local collector, and would not be shown publicly anywhere else.

So, given this thirst for objects with emotional resonance, how does the curator of a twentieth-century social history collection respond? First, curators must learn to accept that there is no single view of history. Everyone has their own experiences, their own narrative trajectories through which they consume history, and everyone does it in a different way. The curator may use history to gain personal satisfaction ('ephemera is so much more interesting than silver'), or even power ('that is all social history, and I need more resources to deal with it professionally'). The academic may seek glory ('no one's ever discovered that link before') or recognition ('I know more about that than anyone else'). The community leader may want recognition for his/her community ('look at the role we played in the Second World War'), or for his/her authority as leader ('there is no diversity of views in this community, everyone shares my beliefs'). The amateur local historian may want proof ('what did that building look like?'), or acknowledgement ('here's some more information about the history of that family'). The visitor wants family entertainment ('a good place to bring the kids'), excitement ('I never knew that'), or verification of past experience ('your Granny had one of those').

None of these ways of interpreting material culture, or consuming the past, can be dismissed out of hand. None are invalid, and none can be ignored. A curator who tells individual visitors that their reactions to an exhibition are misinformed or incorrect is imposing his or her own singular

74

interpretation on a display whose meanings are, for the visitors, multiform, various and bound up in the authority of their memories and emotions.

From this it follows that displays need both depth and breadth. Curators of social history collections should provide object-rich contexts to match the visually rich memories of the visitors, plus information about the objects for those who are interested. Curators and designers must create the freedom, implicitly even give permission, for visitors to make personal connections with the collections, and to share those links as they chose. The possibilities are open ended and diverse, and must be so, for each object has as many meanings as there are people with personal visual memories to fit it.

On a practical level, at Wakefield Museum, this means that our bid to the Heritage Lottery Fund to regenerate Wakefield Museum includes many measures to facilitate visitors' interactions with the collections. More objects will be displayed, as an added mezzanine floor creates more space and pull-out 'discovery drawers' increase the density of objects in exhibitions. All 10,000 historic photographs will be put on computer, with their contexts, so that visitors can browse through them and print any copies that they want.

At the same time, we will learn from the public consultation in 1996. Toys particularly appeal to children, so they will be displayed at child-height, with text of the appropriate reading age. Music only appeals to teenagers, so will be available only on headphones. All the displays will be arranged so that the visitors can walk through them in any direction they choose, be it chronological, or by subject, or by concentrating solely on the things they are familiar with.

In this way, we hope to produce an open-ended, multi-stranded history of Wakefield, which maximises the public benefit of the collections. If we are successful, we will be deafened by cries of 'Your Granny had one of those!'.

The Author

Christine Johnstone completed her doctoral thesis on nineteenth-century living standards at the University of York in 1979. Since then she has worked as a Social History curator in publicly funded museums. She is currently Senior Keeper and Keeper of Social History at Wakefield Museum and Arts in West Yorkshire.

References

1   SHIC working party, *Social History and Industrial Classification (SHIC)*, 2[nd]edition, Museum Documentation Association, Cambridge, 1993.

2   Karl Curry's comments in G. William, *Remembering How it Was: Mining in the Leeds Area,* Leeds City Council, Leeds, 1993, p. 23.

3   Darnley Estate, Plumpton Terrace, Westgate End, M.P. Stonehouse Ltd, Wakefield Prison, the Leeds-London railway line, the Unitarian Chapel, the Theatre Royal, Marygate and Cross Square, Wakefield bus station, Northgate and Kirkgate, the Ridings, West Riding County Council.

4   Winifred Eaton, 'Baths at Home 1930', *Bathtime*, Yorkshire Arts Circus, Castleford, 1988, p. 2.

5   Pauline Wigglesworth, 'Baths at Home 1950' , *Bathtime*, p. 11.

6   Jayne Taylor, 'Sporting Life', *Social History in Museums* , vol. 22, 1995–6, p. 37.

7   Keith Parker's comments in William, *Remembering*, p. 41.

8   John Millard, 'Art History and Half–baked Gimmicks', *Social History in Museums,* Vol. 22, 1995–6, p. 20.

9   Nick Merriman, *Beyond the Glass Case,* Leicester University Press, Leicester, 1991, p. 121.

10 Merriman, *Beyond the Glass Case*, p. 125.

11 R. Schule, ed., *The Heart of a Town: Castleford Tales,* Yorkshire Arts Circus, Castleford, 1994, pp. 65– 66.

12 The choices offered in the consultation, and the visual prompts associated with them, were as follows: The armed forces – photograph of Boer War recruiting sergeant; belonging to Wakefield – 1991 Census leaflet; childcare – 1950s photograph of man with pram; civic pride – photograph of 1890s fire brigade; clothes – 1970s dress catalogue; county town – photograph of the opening ceremony at County Hall; death and burial – 1920s undertaker's invoice; entertainment – photograph of 1930s fairground; the environment – photograph of sewage works; exploration – map of Charles Waterton's route across Guyana [the Charles Waterton natural history collection occupies about 15% of the museum's displays]; families – 1930s advertisement showing a three generation family; famous people – the young Princess Diana; favourite objects – Arthur Atkinson's record-breaking rugby ball; food – photograph of a shop window cheese display; furniture – painting of a late Victorian sitting room; the future – Wakefield 2000 logo; generations – 1950s photograph of three women; health – photograph of hospital ward; hidden history – contemporary leaflet about disabled people's rights; historical evidence – drawing of Wakefield in the 1880s; home life – 1930s advertisement for electricity in the home; incomers – contemporary Chinese restaurant menu; industry – photograph of miners and pit ponies; love and courtship – 1970s Valentine's card; markets – photograph of cattle market; modern life – photograph of children at school; music – Gilbert & Sullivan programme; the 1930s – catalogue for tin baths; the 1950s – photograph of

Woolworths in Kirkgate; old buildings – drawing of Market Cross before demolition in 1866; playing games – 1930s booklet about card games; politics – 1970s election leaflet for the Conservative party; poverty – photograph of a woman making matchboxes at home with her children; pubs – advertisement for Trinity bitter; religion and beliefs – contemporary Roman Catholic Easter service leaflet; the Romans – postcard of gold aureus coin; Sandal Castle – aerial view of ruins; schools and college – photograph of 1916 classroom; sport – photograph of cricket team; shops – photograph of Kirkgate in 1910; textile history – drawing of woman with spinning wheel, about 1800; toys – photograph of toddler with pull along horse; transport – photograph of steam train; the Victorians – photograph of shops and pedestrians in 1885; wars and battles – photograph of air raid damage; Charles Waterton and his animals – drawing of Charles Waterton capturing cayman; wealth – photograph of Walton Hall; women's history – 1984-5 Miners' Support Group certificate; work – catalogue for 1930s washing machines.

13   Merriman, *Beyond the Glass Case,* p. 127.
14   Eaton, in *Bathtime,* p. 2.

7

Monuments and Memory

The Great War in Wales

Angela Gaffney

Memorials to those killed in the Great War are probably the most numerous and widespread of all public monuments in Britain. Wales is no exception with a prominent 'national' monument at Cardiff and many local memorials throughout the country. Almost eighty years after the end of hostilities, public and academic interest in the war and its aftermath has shown no sign of waning. In recent years studies on Great War memorials have become as widespread and diverse as the memorials themselves. Memorials have been studied as works of art, as public sculpture and as repositories of political ideas and national aspirations.[1] There can be no doubt that different approaches have contributed to our knowledge and understanding of memorials, but there is a need for studies on local responses and reactions to the war as embodied in the commemoration process; studies that will emphasise the importance of memorials to the generations who lived through the conflict and struggled to come to terms with the emotional impact of the war.

By the time the guns finally fell silent in November 1918, an estimated nine million men had lost their lives in the Great War; over seven hundred thousand of these were British servicemen.[2] Adrian Gregory suggests that an estimated three million Britons lost a close relative in the Great War although, as he points out: 'This figure represents only the "primary bereaved", (parents, siblings, widows and orphans). In addition, the "secondary bereaved" ought to be considered, those who lost a cousin, uncle, son-in-law, a colleague, a friend or a neighbour'.[3] The loss of life on this scale ensured that bereavement became a shared experience throughout Britain and the years after the Armistice witnessed a determination to provide a lasting tribute to those who had died.[4] Early attempts to influence public choice over memorials were made with exhibitions on war memorial designs held at the Victoria and Albert Museum and the Royal Academy in 1919, and in August of that year a pamphlet was published in an attempt to ensure appropriate wording for war memorials.[5] Yet there was no official central direction or funding; war memorials were a spontaneous act. The resulting monuments yield unique insights into the attitudes of the Welsh population towards the war and towards post-war society.

Casualty lists published in British newspapers throughout the Great War gave daily notice of the catastrophic impact on society. The decision taken in 1915 to ban repatriation of bodies would have far reaching consequences in the memorialisation process. The formalities of burial had been taken over by officialdom in the form of the Imperial War Graves Commission; a bureaucratic and remote process into which the bereaved had little input. Catherine Moriarty has written:

> Burial and cemeteries abroad had then become the exclusive concern of the IWGC. Relinquishing their role as citizens, thousands of men had become components in the military machine and in death they were to be buried and officially commemorated as such. To many at home this arrangement caused widespread distress...The vast majority, unable to visit the battlefield cemeteries in the immediate post-war period needed, in the absence of a body, some readily available focus for their grief. They too, needed to stage a symbolic honouring, in the absence of a corpse.[6]

It was this need for a permanent, tangible reminder of the dead; a re-inscription of them at the centre of the community that motivated so many communities to erect war memorials. It also provides an explanation for the desire to erect memorials in communities who have already suffered tragedy, often on a far greater scale, than that inflicted by the Great War. Many Welsh communities were centred around extractive or heavy industry and were well used to facing tragedy or death as the price to be paid for industrial progress. The Glamorgan and Monmouthshire valleys in South Wales had witnessed rapid social and industrial change as the high quality steam coal fuelled the ships of the Imperial Navy. By the outbreak of the Great War, the coal output from South Wales was in the region of 56.8 million tons per year with a work force of over a quarter of a million. The pits were notoriously difficult to mine and the accident statistics are a grim testament to the dangers faced on a daily basis by the workers. In October 1913 the coal mining community of Senghenydd in South Wales endured the worst accident in British mining history. An explosion underground at the Universal Colliery killed four hundred and thirty-nine men and boys.[7] This occurred just twelve years after a similar explosion claimed seventy nine lives at the same pit. In the centre of the square in Senghenydd is an impressive clock tower in a prominent position at a road junction. The monument records, however, not the mining accident of 1913 but the sixty-three men from the village who were killed in the Great War. In July 1919 a public meeting, under the auspices of the local Reception and Memorial Committee, was held to decide on the form of war memorial. The original scheme had been to build a monument in the main square in Senghenydd. At the meeting, various alternative suggestions were put forward including a Memorial Hall, Swimming Baths, Monument, Gymnasium Rooms and the offering of Scholarships. After much discussion and an open vote it was decided to continue with the original resolution and to erect a monument on the local square.[8] It was financed entirely by public subscription and unveiled in March 1921 by Percy Ward, General Manager of the Lewis Merthyr Collieries who owned the Universal Colliery. Local newspapers reported that several thousand people watched the procession and unveiling ceremony.[9] The memorial was unveiled only eight years after the pit tragedy which had claimed so many more local lives than the war yet until recently there was no official memorial to the 1913 disaster.[10] It is evident that local communities were willing to subscribe to and finance the erection of a war memorial during times of severe economic hardship and emotional trauma and it may be that such communities were so hardened to the reality of death in the workplace that they were able to separate such tragedies from local involvement in a wider conflict. Death underground was undoubtedly viewed as a harsh but unavoidable fact of life in the valleys of South Wales.

Accounts of rescue operations which followed major pit explosions include stories of great courage of, and immense danger for those involved in the struggle for survivors. A sense of urgency is apparent, even when all hope of life has faded, as it became equally important to retrieve bodies from the mine whenever possible. Michael Lieven articulates this in his account of the 1913 explosion in Senghenydd:

> Many of the rescuers were the relations, often brothers, of the dead
> and this added to the sense of irrational urgency. In part the sense of
> desperation was due to strongly held feelings about the significance
> of a proper burial and of a horror, common in all coal fields, of
> leaving bodies in a mine.[11]

Death and burial on the battlefield also denied those left behind the opportunity to participate in the funeral ritual. Bernd Huppauf points out: 'Those mourning at home had lost a human being. But there was no visual object for their mourning, no corpse to which they could say a last farewell in the burial ritual.'[12] Erecting a war memorial; the ritual involved in the unveiling ceremonies and the position of the memorial invariably at the centre of a community, acted as an emotional catharsis enabling the bereaved to begin to accept the death of a loved one and to contemplate moving forward once more. In this context, commemoration of the individual was an extremely important element in the process of mourning as the local war memorial became a surrogate grave providing an essential focus for individual and collective grief.

Little interest was shown in more comprehensive commemorative projects and a potent example of this occurred in 1919 when Cardiff City Council attempted to organise a conference aimed at the establishment of a Welsh National War Memorial. A letter was sent out from Cardiff in May 1919 to two hundred public bodies throughout Wales with the optimistic view that 'the proposal is one which it is confidently anticipated will appeal to all Welshmen and receive the unanimous support of the whole Principality.'[13] The letter was largely ignored by local authorities throughout Wales and it is clear that the invitation was treated with a mixture of indifference, suspicion and hostility. It was only the intervention of the 'national' newspaper, the *Western Mail*, that ensured the building of the memorial in Cardiff unveiled in 1928 by the Prince of Wales. Five years earlier he had unveiled the North Wales Heroes' Memorial in Bangor and subsequently North Walians displayed little interest in either subscribing to or becoming involved with the movement in Cardiff. This apathy was shared by the majority of local authorities in the Principality as by mid 1919 many public and private commemorative projects were under way which took precedence over the proposed national memorial in Cardiff. Studies of the movements to establish county and borough memorials for Carmarthenshire and Merthyr Tydfil also suggest that a desire for local commemoration provided a stronger link in the commemoration of the Great War throughout Wales than a desire to display national or regional unity. In Carmarthenshire the scheme for the proposed County War Memorial was to extend the local Infirmary and to erect a monument outside the Infirmary buildings. Yet even this decision evoked critical comments from representatives of towns within the county. The *Carmarthen Journal* reported that:

> Mr. Dan Williams, Llanelly...saw a difficulty with regard to the venue of the proposed county memorial...They did not see why they, in debt in Llanelly in connection with their own Hospital, should contribute towards a wing at the Carmarthen Hospital. If Carmarthen people wanted an extension for their own Hospital they should pay for it.[14]

Similarly, the borough of Merthyr Tydfil experienced great difficulties in its prolonged endeavours to fund and build a substantial war memorial. A public meeting in December 1922 initiated the movement for a memorial but it was assumed without doubt that it would be a memorial for the complete borough of Merthyr Tydfil. Disapproval was apparent straightaway. At a ward meeting held in Dowlais strong views were expressed in favour of a local memorial. A representative of local ex-servicemen voiced the opinion that:

> the feeling of the Dowlais people was dead against a Borough Memorial but in favour of a local one...Captain Musgrove said Dowlais ex-servicemen wanted a cenotaph erected in Dowlais where relatives of the fallen could place wreaths on the anniversary of their sacrifice, and what was more, they were determined to get it.[15]

The proliferation of local schemes and the resulting memorials throughout Wales are testament to the strength of local affiliations, loyalties and identity. Local newspapers frequently sought to compare communities still without a memorial to those who had 'done the right thing' or were in the process of doing so. An appeal to civic pride was often combined with the implicit accusation that the absence of a memorial, or a movement to build one, displayed a lack of honour and respect for the dead. Newspaper comments were acerbic in their condemnation of local indifference to sacrifices made in the Great War. An editorial comment in the *Aberdare Leader* made this clear after much local debate had taken place over the lack of a memorial:

> At one time there was much talk of Aberdare going to do a lot for the survivors of the Great War and also for the memory of those who fell. We were going to erect a cenotaph and a new memorial hall and ever so many other monuments of gratitude and appreciation. But all those elaborate schemes have gone the way of the best laid schemes of mice and men and the abstract homes fit for heroes to live in. "Lest we forget" indeed! We have forgotten already. Buying poppies is far cheaper than building halls and houses.[16]

Aberdare eventually gained its memorial which was unveiled in March 1923. Unveiling ceremonies were often described as the highlight of the local year and were comprehensively reported in the press. There appears to have been an unveiling hierarchy headed by the Lord-Lieutenant of the County or his deputy followed by high ranking military personnel, local landowners, industrialists, the local Member of Parliament or local councillors. The leading officers of the local War Memorial Committee, which normally reflected the structure and hierarchy of local society, would be much in evidence. The appearance of royalty, or, even better in Wales, David Lloyd George, was a rare but treasured occurrence.

Throughout the 1920s the construction of war memorials made an unprecedented visual impact on the urban and rural landscape and it is clear that the movement to commemorate the Great War offered a unique opportunity to make a very public statement of civic pride and honour. Whilst the desire to pay tribute to the sacrifices made by local men and women was fundamental to memorial movements, the protagonists behind larger civic memorials may well have had specific ideas regarding how their own areas of social jurisdiction could and should be perceived by the larger community.

A note of caution needs to be sounded, however, in any attempt to connect the widespread movement to erect war memorials and the construction of civic identity in the post-war years. Civic pride did have a role to play, but in the many hundreds of smaller memorials it can only be credited as a minor actor. In town and country, local commemoration provided those left behind with an immediate, daily reminder of the sacrifice made by husbands, fathers, lovers, sons or brothers. This is especially relevant in rural communities where national, county and borough memorials could be perceived as impersonal and remote both psychologically and physically. Hence the great difficulties that many regional movements encountered when trying to raise funds for commemorative projects. The stories behind the building of such memorials peel away the facade of national unity, certainly within Wales, and reveal a society determined to place commemoration of the individual within local communities above the creation and consolidation of broader civic and national images.

Commemoration of the dead became a flourishing business in the decade after the war and as such provided useful commercial opportunities for some whilst others sought to put forward individual or collective statements on how the war should be remembered. For example, inscriptions on war memorials often invoked notions of honour, sacrifice and loyalty and memorials in Wales were no exception whether the sentiments were expressed in Welsh or English. A common dispute took place over the form of memorial: should war memorials serve the living or honour those who had died? Halls and hospitals were popular forms of utilitarian memorial but often faced opposition from those who felt such memorials were not a fitting tribute to the fallen. There was also the fear that war memorial projects might be used as a convenient guise to gain facilities which should have been provided by local government. In November 1918 the people of Barry in Glamorgan, along with virtually every other community in Wales, sought to commemorate the fallen. Yet it was twelve years before the cenotaph was unveiled and a further two years before the War Memorial Hall was finally opened in November 1932. Barry Urban District Council felt that a new public hall would enhance the prestige of the town but the idea was opposed by local ex-servicemen and members of the public who felt that the spirit of the tribute was inappropriate.[17] The two memorials remain in Barry; the cenotaph just a few feet from the entrance to the Memorial Hall, as if in defiant opposition to those who espoused such a practical memorial and a permanent reminder of the very different needs that existed within communities after the Great War.

The frequent disputes over forms of memorial highlight the difficulties in achieving a consensus over the most appropriate way to commemorate the dead. The potential loss of meaning attached to a utilitarian form of memorial was one of the major reasons cited for opposing this form of commemoration. Those in Barry who argued against a public hall saw their fears realised when in January 1933, just two months after the hall had been opened, it was decided that the word 'War' should be dropped and that Barry's commemoration of those who died in the Great War should be known simply as the Barry Memorial Hall.[18] A memorial in the form of a monument, however, occupied an almost 'sacred' space within the community; a space that was rarely challenged by inappropriate use or subsequent neglect. A local memorial was a very public affirmation of community with the memorial itself acting as a 'marker' by signifying its exclusivity and uniqueness. It proclaimed a local contribution to the war not only by mourning its young men, but by making a clear statement that these were our young men echoing; thus Edna Longley's comment that 'Commemorations are as selective as sympathies. They honour *our* dead, not your dead.'[19]

The study of war memorials in Wales reveals the human price of participation in the Great War and provides invaluable evidence as to how communities chose to remember the war and commemorate individual and collective loss. Questions of site, size, cost and form of war memorials stimulated discussion and, on occasion, controversy in Wales, but it appears that the need to commemorate the fallen was not a matter for public debate.

The use of the Welsh language on memorials remains the most notable difference between Welsh and other British memorials within the United Kingdom, yet language was the least contested issue of commemoration in Wales. By far the most common memorial inscriptions are bilingual and largely reflect those that can be found on war memorials throughout Britain. This duality extends to the place of the Welsh language within the ceremonies to unveil war memorials where Welsh prayers were recited, Welsh hymns were sung, and the ceremony normally concluded with the Welsh national anthem. Yet this did not amount to a visible and enduring statement carved in stone of a sense of an independent Welsh identity. Rather it co-existed with imperial iconography in the form of anthems, occasionally by the sculpture of the memorial itself and by the predominant use of the Union flag. The memorial itself was the focal point of the unveiling ceremony and draping the structure in the Welsh flag would convey a powerful message of identity to the onlookers; yet at every ceremony studied to date, it was the Union flag that appears. On the rare occasions when the Welsh dragon did make an appearance it was always used in conjunction with the Union flag. Even the memorial in Lloyd George's own constituency of Caernarfon was draped with both the Welsh and Union flags and both national anthems were sung at the ceremony.[20] The Welsh contribution to the imperial cause was evident in the commemoration process and provides tangible evidence of a nation at ease with its own position within the British state and the Empire. The position of Wales within the wider British polity was confirmed and that position was neither contested nor challenged by the experience of war.

The major cause for controversy in the commemoration process in Wales was the location of a memorial. Pierre Nora has suggested that: 'Statues or monuments to the dead...owe their meaning to their intrinsic existence; even though their location is far from arbitrary, one could justify relocating them without altering their meaning.'[21] Analysis of the commemoration process in Wales, however, suggests that location was crucial to the meaning of a memorial. The location invested a memorial with meaning for those who had fought and survived and demanded adequate tribute to their fallen comrades; for those who sought to make a public statement on civic pride and dignity in the community's sacrifice; for the representatives of church and clergy seeking to reaffirm the consolatory and healing power of a God whose credibility had for some been severely tested and found wanting by the experience of war. Above all, the location was crucial for the bereaved as a site of individual and collective mourning.

Alan Borg has commented on later memorials to subsequent conflicts and suggests that they are 'little more than obligatory gestures to the memorial tradition' and that they do not 'spring from a genuine response to the tragedy of war. It is this that distinguishes the First World War memorials, for they were designed and built out of authentic feelings of pride and sorrow.'[22] There is no doubt that it is the memory of the Great

War that remains etched on the urban and rural landscape in the tangible form of war memorials. Detailed study of the means by which communities argued, co-operated and compromised over their building reveals how the experience and memory of the Great War pervaded society in the inter-war years and continues to do so today.

The Author

Angela Gaffney is a Research Fellow with the Centre for Advanced Welsh and Celtic Studies, University of Wales. She is based in the Art Department at the National Museums & Galleries of Wales, Cardiff and is working on the *Visual Culture of Wales* research project.

References

The ideas and examples contained in this paper are drawn from my Ph.D thesis: '*Poppies on the up-platform': Commemoration of the Great War in Wales*, University of Wales, Cardiff, 1996.

1   Examples include: J.M. Mayo, *War Memorials as Political Landscape: The American Experience and Beyond*, Praeger, New York, 1988; G.L. Mosse, *Fallen Soldiers, Reshaping the Memory of the World Wars*, Oxford University Press, New York, 1990; A. Borg, *War Memorials from Antiquity to the Present*, Leo Cooper, London, 1991.
2   J.M. Winter, *The Great War and the British People*, Macmillan, London, 1986, p.71. An estimated 280,000 men from Wales served in the Great War and the Welsh National Book of Remembrance lists the names of thirty-five thousand who did not return.
3   A. Gregory, *The Silence of Memory*, Berg, Oxford, 1994, p. 19.
4   For a concise account of commemoration of those killed on active service before the Great War, see C. Moriarty, '*Narrative and the Absent Body. Mechanisms of Meaning in First World War Memorials*' Unpublished Ph.D Thesis, University of Sussex, 1995, pp.16-34. For a guide to Boer War memorials in Britain, see J. Gildea, *For Remembrance and in Honour of Those Who Lost Their Lives in the South African War 1899-1902*, Eyre and Spottiswode, London, 1911.
5   See C. Harcourt Smith, *Inscriptions Suggested for War Memorials*, Victoria and Albert Museum, London, 1919.
6   C. Moriarty, 'The Absent Dead and Figurative First World War Memorials', *Transactions of the Ancient Monuments Society*, vol. 39, 1995, pp. 7-40.

7 For details of the Senghenydd explosion, see J.H. Brown, *The Valley of the Shadow*, Alun Books, Port Talbot, 1981; R. Williams and D. Jones, *The Cruel Inheritance*, Village Publishing, Pontypool, 1990, pp. 74-82; M. Lieven, *Senghennydd, The Universal Pit Village 1890-1930*, Gomer Press, Llandysul, 1994, especially pp. 215-68.

8 *Caerphilly Journal*, 19 July 1919. See also *South Wales Daily News*, 17 July 1919.

9 For full details of the unveiling ceremony see *Western Mail*, 2 March 1921 and *Caerphilly Journal*, 5 March 1921.

10 A memorial to the victims of the 1901 and 1913 pit disasters was unveiled in October 1981 in Senghenydd.

11 Lieven, *Senghennydd, The Universal Pit Village 1890-1930*, p. 236.

12 B. Huppauf, 'War and Death: The Experience of the First World War' in M. Crouch and B. Huppauf, eds., *Essays on Mortality*, University of New South Wales, Sydney, 1985, pp. 65-87.

13 Letter from J.H. Wheatley, Clerk to Cardiff City Council to The Clerk, Mynyddislwyn Urban District Council, 30 May 1919.

14 *Carmarthen Journal*, 6 October 1922.

15 *Merthyr Express*, 13 January 1923. The impressive memorial at Merthyr Tydfil was finally unveiled in November 1931. Other areas within the Merthyr borough went ahead with their own memorials including Merthyr Vale and Aberfan, Pant and Treharris. Although no central memorial was built, the inhabitants of Dowlais still insisted on smaller memorials within local church and chapels.

16 *Aberdare Leader*, 19 November 1921.

17 Dire consequences arising from the potential misuse of memorial halls were raised by the Reverend Jubilee Young in an address to the Caernarvonshire Baptist Festival held at Pwllheli in 1928. During his speech he noted that 'Wales erected hundreds of memorial halls to her gallant sons, but the use made of those halls was an insult to the memory of those heroes. On their polished floors young husbands and young wives danced themselves to divorce courts.' *Western Mail*, 16 June 1928. I am grateful to Mari Williams for this reference.

18 *Barry Urban District Council*, meeting of Memorial Hall Management Committee, 23 January 1933. See also *Barry and District News*, 27 January 1933 and *Barry Herald*, 27 January 1933.

19 E. Longley, 'The Rising, the Somme and Irish Memory' in M. Ni Dhonnchadha and T. Dorgan, eds., *Revising the Rising*, Field Day, Londonderry, 1991, p. 29. Italics in text.

20 No example has yet been found of a memorial draped in the Welsh flag alone. At the unveiling of the Welsh National War Memorial in Cardiff in June 1928, the three entrances to the 'shrine' were draped with the Union Jack, the White Ensign and the flag of the Royal Air Force. *Western Mail*, 13 June 1928.

21 P. Nora, 'Between Memory and History: Les Lieux de Memoire',

Representations, vol. 26, 1989, pp. 7-25.

Borg, *War Memorials from Antiquity to the Present* , p. 84.

8

Psychoanalysis and Marxism in the Making of the Self

Memory Versus History

Allegra Madgwick

Everything about this title refers to the recent past and in a way that conjures melancholy, obsolescence and anachronism. After all, who is any longer concerned with finding a rapprochement between psychoanalysis and Marxism? As Eugene Wolfenstein states baldly apropos his 1993 attempt to do precisely that: 'There are those, after all, who think that psychoanalysis and Marxism are out of date'.[1] Indeed there are, and this is particularly true of Marxism which now figures as no more than a memory overlaid by regret, embarrassment and forgetfulness.[2] (I leave out those who are crowing over the corpse, as this amounts to an over-represented tendency in public political debate at least.) As for the self, who would want to wheel out this poor, beleaguered, victim of murder – a murder not committed once but repeatedly – this self which is undoubtedly dead of overkill? It seems there is nothing more dated than the recent past, this being as true for intellectual fashion as it is for any other sort of fashion. For the recent past raises the question of how to treat the past: as memory, with its sense of the contingent, the unreliable and the subjective; or as history, with its connections to the public record and collective meaning.

Ironically the problem of the recent past is one addressed by both Marxism, as a theory of what is to be done with history, and by psychoanalysis, as a pragmatics of memory. It is in this sense that this essay will invoke psychoanalysis and Marxism as ways which, perhaps obsolescently, seek transformation from the past through the medium of interpreting it. Even the idea that meaning might be found in the past is precarious given an intellectual climate that has confidently announced 'history's end' (Fukuyama) but at the same time is thoroughly entrenched in the West through the relentless psychologising of experience that Philip Rieff identified as early as 1966, in *The Triumph of the Therapeutic*.[3] An obvious conclusion to be drawn from the contradictory fate of attempts to attribute meaning to the past is that 'metanarratives' are in bad shape while psychoanalytic insights have become ubiquitous. What I intend to argue is that the different fates of explanatory theories on a macro level versus explanatory theories that are applicable to smaller units of society ('class' versus 'psyche' if you like), obscure affinities between both theory's construction of the past. In particular what Marxism and psychoanalysis share is a sense of the past as the malign influence that defeats change, and as a liberating potential if consciously appropriated. This argument endorses and expands upon Stephen Marcus's reading of the similarity between Marx and Freud which he grounded in their respective conceptions of history, but with the added dimension of the self seen as indeterminably carrier of memory and subject of history.[4]

Marx's and Freud's differences have been foregrounded in the readings offered by radical post Marxist and post Freudian theorists. The idea that the two might work together according to the dubious principle of sexual complementarity, to make good what each lacked, was quite a late development in the complex encounter between them. Robert Young accurately sums up the hopes of this particular turn to Freud via Lacan, and Marx through Althusser, when he writes: 'To everyone's convenience, suddenly it seemed as if Marxism and feminism could acquire a theory of the subject, and psychoanalysis a theory of the social'.[5] This was certainly a development from earlier socialist positions on the relationship between psychoanalysis and Marxism as demonstrated by Lucien Seve's summation of the debate, published in 1964, and which Elizabeth Roudinesco suggests came to have the force of the 'official doctrine' for Socialist countries. Seve is quite unequivocal about both the superiority and incompatibility of Marxist, as opposed to psychoanalytic explanatory models for the human subject, which can only be interpellated through history and not psychology. As he says:

> The fundamental error of Freud and most psychoanalysts after him, in the general conception of human reality they presuppose is … to believe that one can explain history by psychology and not psychology by history…. That is why it seems extremely debatable to establish a parallel between Marx and Freud as having both equally dissipated the illusion of the human subject, the former through his ex-centred conception of history, the latter through his ex-centred conception of the psyche.[6]

That Seve did not get the last word in the matter is demonstrated by the resurfacing of the attempt to reconcile Marx and Freud on the question of the human subject. In its turn this reading came under pressure through the realisation that psychoanalysis already had a theory of the social and that Marxism was premised on a negation of subjectivity.[7] But analysing the 'incorrectness' of the argument is not my purpose. Instead I want to trace the effect of the wish to reconcile a Freudian version of the subject with a Marxist reading of history on British Marxist autobiographical writing, that arose at a point where this reading/misreading was dominant.The perception existed of an intellectual division of labour between Marx and Freud where history and materialism belonged to Marx and Freud's domain was memory and subjectivity. This offers a partial explanation for the fact that Marxism has had a far profounder influence on the discipline of history than psychoanalysis. Given that Marxism addressed itself directly to history and contained some exemplary examples of historical writing, its effect on methodology and content was and is profound. The growth in social history, history from below and, particularly pertinent to this paper, oral history were all part of the Marxist inspired shift in the way history was studied, written and taught. It should also be said, as T.G. Ashplant recognises in his article on *Psychoanalysis in Historical Writing,* that history, at least in a British context, was one of the few disciplines in the humanities that remained relatively untouched by psychoanalysis.[8] One of the areas where Marxist historical writing and psychoanalytic theory did seem pertinent to each other was, however, in the production of oral history.

Throughout the late seventies and eighties the British journal *History Workshop,* the main organ for disseminating socialist and feminist historiography, published articles interrogating the effect of psychoanalysis on history writing and in particular how it might be relevant to oral history. The parallels drawn by both Karl Figlio and Luisa Passerini, who contributed to this debate, make use of the function of speech within an analytic framework and how this reflects on what goes on in an oral history interview. The two techniques are not at all the same in their aims but may well involve similar issues when it comes to interpreting the speech of the other. What needed to be taken into account when conducting an oral history interview was seen to be comparable to the issues an analyst would be alert to when listening to a patient; that is, that as much attention had to be paid to what was not said as to what was, and that the analyst/interviewer was not an objective observer but would inevitably participate in the process through the phenomenon of transference and countertransference. As Passerini says of the work she did interviewing workers who had lived through Italian fascism:

Oral sources refused to answer certain kinds of questions; seemingly loquacious, they finally prove to be reticent or enigmatic....I received what to my ears were either irrelevant or inconsistent answers. 'Irrelevant' answers were mainly of two types: silences and jokes.... Lifestories were told without any reference to fascism...A second type of silence...was present in striking chronological gaps between 1922-23.[9]

The connections between the analytic process and Passerini's experience are clear if we read this quote alongside one of Freud's famous essays on technique, where he describes the shifts in the analytic task in this way: 'Remembering and abreacting, with the help of the hypnotic state, were what was at that time aimed at. Next, when hypnosis was given up, the task became one of discovering from the patient's free associations what he failed to remember'.[10] What is also at stake in the task of reconstructing the past is the nature of what is forgotten – not, as Passerini notes, trivial material of no historical interest but what was most traumatic historically and emotionally. For Passerini the repressed would be connected to a traumatic political history whereas for Freud the material will be connected to childhood sexuality. That the two sources of trauma testified to by laughter and forgetting are harder to separate than at first appears, is acknowledged but not elaborated upon by Karl Figlio, when he writes that both oral historians and psychoanalysts have begun to wonder 'what constitutes a real event'.[11] The real event that Figlio refers to is, of course, the controversy over the traumatic effect of sexual seduction/abuse that occurs in fantasy or in fact, and forms the substance of what has been forgotten. That this issue has been struggled over on the terrain of memory inflects the point being made here.[12] The reading of the past as repressed trauma that has to be faced echoes Fredric Jameson's gloss on Marx, which Carolyn Steedman uses to preface *Landscape For A Good Woman*, when he says: 'History is what hurts, it is what refuses desire and sets inexorable limits to individual as well as collective praxis'.[13] So the connections being drawn between oral history and psychoanalysis concern both the process of production and the nature of the material produced.

At this point we will return to the neglected element in this account which concerns 'the making of the self.' Ronald Fraser, who had established a reputation as a Marxist historian through his oral history of the Spanish Civil War, *Blood of Spain*, published *In Search of a Past* in 1984.[14] The latter was an autobiography based on oral history interviews conducted with the servants of the manor house where Fraser grew up and on the sessions Fraser had during a three-year-long analysis that he undertook as an adult suffering from depression. Two years later the social historian Carolyn Steedman, whose work has focused particularly on childhood, published an autobiographical account of her mother's life and her own working class childhood, *Landscape for A Good Woman*.[15] In the book Steedman interrogates both psychoanalysis and Marxism as interpretative frameworks for the lives she is writing about, only to reject them both for their inability to address the experience of working class women like her mother. In the same year that Steedman's book appeared, the art critic Peter Fuller, who had been strongly influenced by Marxist critic John Berger, produced *Marches Past*, a journal that documented Fuller's four year analysis undertaken in the seventies because of what Fuller describes as problems of a 'psychiatric nature'.[16] For the critic Laura Marcus, '[a]ll three texts share a concern with the tensions between social and psychoanalytic accounts of subjectivity'.[17] Through looking at these texts I want to re-evaluate the positioning of psychoanalysis as the investigation of memory as subjectivity produced in time, and Marxism as a theory of a psyche evacuated by or reducible to historical conditions. It is obvious that the books will be different even though they can be legitimately said to share a common project, and I hope to avoid homogenising these accounts. In a sense, they can be seen as exemplary in their difference – representing as they do contradictory responses to a political agenda that had wider resonance then these particular voices.

To reiterate Marcus, the autobiographical works of Fraser, Steedman and Fuller emerge out of a historical conjuncture, which Marcus connects to the influence of modern feminism and it's politicisation of sexed subjectivity. Whilst endorsing that reading in the case of Steedman and at a pinch Fraser, it is more obvious to me that these works are in dialogue with an older radicalism. In some senses they are a defence of Marxist categories for defining subjectivity: for Steedman, and more ambivalently for Fraser, that means using class as a defining category for recounting their history; for Fuller 'history,' in a somewhat idiosyncratic appropriation of Marx's conception, becomes what works against a sense of personal disintegration. In support of Marcus it should be noted that these books occupy what previously had not been seen as obvious territory for left wing writers – autobiography and first person testimony became central to feminist politics whilst being quite peripheral to left wing political writing. The choice of genre could be seen as an implicit reaction to the changing nature of what was considered political writing, which resulted directly from the validation via feminism of what Maria Lauret has called, 'feminist fictions of subjectivity'.[18] What is interesting about this moment is that it is precisely at the point where the personal becomes the vanguard of an impetus towards political change, that theories of a unified identity or self are being deconstructed by post structuralist theory. These books are hybrid in the sense that they emerge out of a dialogue with past influences which are coming under increasing pressure from a changing political and theoretical agenda. Marcus critiques both Fuller and Fraser for their use of an account of an analytic cure which, she suggests, for Fraser means the reproduction of a conventional and uncritical division between self and society and, in Fuller's case, invokes psychoanalysis as merely a way of refiguring 'self awareness as a phenomenon'.[19] In contrast, she suggests that Steedman's use of the case study (of Dora) as a device in her narrative undercuts the construction of an inner life which is separable from social determinants – to show that such a conception of the self is a bourgeois possession rather then a universal structure. It is certainly true that Steedman reads as the more 'radical' of the texts in its move towards the negation of any closure that could rehabilitate her mother's life into an already available cultural story, but I want to undercut Marcus's reading by questioning her reproduction of the conventional placing of psychoanalysis as a theory orientated towards the 'self' and Marxism towards the 'social'. These texts offer grounds for rethinking that binary through a reversal of its logic – it is my contention that Marxism actually figures in these texts as the site of a transformative ideology of the self to which psychoanalysis stands as a corrective in its materialising of the subject.

These books share a genealogical inheritance. Fuller knew Fraser through both of their work on *New Left Review*, and Steedman's book is seen by Marcus as '...an implied critique of Fraser, [which] points to the fact that the gates surrounding the "big house" form the limits of psychoanalysis and bourgeois understanding; the lives that exist outside the gates remain outside these limits'.[20] Each book, however, has different – though related – motivations. Steedman is quite clear that she was conducting a battle on two fronts. She wanted to argue against the versions of working class life produced by British male socialist historians, and to argue with the contemporary feminist versions of identity that pointed to gender as a more fundamentally determining category for identity then class. In a substantial later gloss on *Landscape for A Good Woman*, she writes:

> What I had to engage with in working class autobiography were: notions of cheerful decency, poor-but-honest happiness.... I think that it is a book designed to hurt, to tell them (who are them?) that they have not experienced – have not had, can't ever have – that which places you on the outside, and makes you bitter and envious enough to want to hurt.... [The book] is ungrateful...towards

feminism as well ... in that one of my organising principles ... is the pitching of class against gender, and class is allowed to win, as the more interesting, important and revelatory interpretative device.[21]

This combative spirit is not shared by either Fuller or Fraser. Both are struggling for a sense of integration. For Fraser this means confronting fundamental splits in his psyche which are inseparable from the fundamental divide between classes he grew up with. Fuller marks his own sense of lifelessness or lack of reality by a longing for participation in self obliterating 'history.' But whilst Fraser is moving towards a dream of wholeness Fuller seems to be concerned with a sort of self annihilation. Both desires are interpellated through and in relation to Marxism far more than psychoanalysis. The moment when Ronald Fraser discovers both a rationale for his methodology and the motivation for writing his book occurs during this dialogue with his analyst:

> I outline the newly discovered aim of combining two different modes of enquiry – oral history and psychoanalysis – to uncover the past in as many of its layers as possible. "At first, I thought I wanted your help to overcome the difficulty of writing about the past: now I see that the difficulty is part and parcel of the past. This 'voyage of inner discovery' ... has to be combined with the account of the other voyage into the social past".[22]

Fuller's motivation is screened through retrospective disavowal – an obliteration of the attachments of past selves, with which he no longer identifies. Although this can be, and was read as, a reactionary reading of a radical past, it also comes closest to a sense of psychoanalytic practice as being as much about murdering the self as it is about 'finding it'. And in a sense, Fuller's moving away from Marxism is a more representative if undertheorised example of the intellectual shifts of the past decades, than those who have openly or (more credibly) covertly, held on to their old loyalties. In his introduction Fuller makes it clear that he finds much of his journal hard to stomach:

> What really grates, throughout the text, is my much reiterated belief that, as Victor Serge...once put it, "The only meaning of life is conscious participation in the making of history".... Evidently, all this talk about "history" was at once, a denial of what was really wrong and....a perverse attempt to right that wrong, to break through to 'real relations' somehow.... Marxism can, and in my case probably did, provide a dangerous patina of projections and

rationalisations for what are often psychological conflicts masquerading as social and historical insights.[23]

Each narrative offers a different way to interrogate memory and the making of a self through the medium of a shared political culture. Steedman can be said to obliterate the self. The book is the story of her own girlhood but told through the prism of what she knows – the familial myths – of the lives of her parents. Steedman does not seem to be directly concerned with reproducing a representation of herself – this is anti-Bildungsroman. In no way are we offered the portrait of a feminist, artist or socialist as a young girl. In fact Steedman quite deliberately places herself outside of her own family romance, as both observer and victim of its somewhat impersonal dynamics. But for Fraser too the self, despite embodying a dream of integration, is as chimerical. As Fraser says in a later interview concerning his book, 'The book's search is for an 'I', a subject who would be capable of writing it'.[24] The interesting point is that for both Fuller and Fraser it is Marxism, not psychoanalysis, which seems to offer the possibility of an unalienated, whole and integrated self as part of its project. And it is the process of psychoanalysis that detaches both men from the sense that it would be possible to either heal a divided self, or to lose it in a larger project.

The self is not a taken-for-granted structure in any of these narratives. Steedman ignores the self to the point almost of what Ernest Jones called *aphansis* or the death of desire. Her dissection of the poverty of interpretation ends her book when she asks for a politics that having seen 'what can be made out on the margins,' would 'refuse to celebrate it' and instead 'say "so what?"; and consign it to the dark.'[25] Fraser never achieves a moment of revelation that can move him beyond the constructions and myths of his childhood – one of which has been a fantasised split between his 'bad' real rich parents and his 'good' but not real surrogate parents amongst the servants who looked after him. Fraser's narrative is a good example of what Steedman calls 'the creation of a psychic structure in historical circumstances'.[26] When Fraser goes out to destroy the 'myth' that he has constructed of his past through conducting interviews with surviving servants he finds instead that, '[w]hat happened was the opposite: their testimonies seemed to confirm the myth'.[27] For Fraser, the historical attempt to uncover and transcend the mythical foundations of his personal history does not result in the discovery of a more authentic version of the past, but in an entrenchment of what he had already imagined it to be. Fuller also has a sense of wanting to escape from a confining reality – almost from the boundaries of sentient selfhood. He expects to be liberated into history, into the wide stream of suffering humanity which would necessitate escaping from his own past. As he says, 'I can only ever see the world from a point somewhere behind *these* eyes; I can only ever know it filtered and mediated and distorted through the gills of this my claustrophobic, indestructible history'.[28] History for Fuller works as prison and potential for self-forgetting – this double movement is what he discerns in the prison writings of his hero Victor Serge, who connects himself to historical processes in a way that counteracts the inertia and the meaninglessness of time spent in jail.

In conclusion, I have tried to use these books to make a case for seeing the British Marxism of the eighties as a repository of hopes and disillusions concerning the self in a way that psychoanalysis was not. Even if Steedman rejects British socialism, what remains for her is a commitment to class as the determining factor in delineating the unrepresentable past she writes about; and for Fraser and Fuller, Marxism is what holds out the promise of either the location of a more realistic version of the past or an obliteration of a despised self in the collapse of private meaning amidst political action. In other words Marxism, far more than psychoanalysis, is connected to the development of subjectivity for these authors at least as potential – an imagined moment of disalienation can be read in these narratives in a way that undercuts psychoanalysis as a discourse about developing a more integrated self. After all, psychoanalysis offers anything but transcendence – its dream of the good life looks suspiciously like the death of the dream of anything better. Fredric Jameson makes it clear that Marxism posited something beyond the dissolution of the bourgeois subject 'mapped by psychoanalysis'. As he says:

> For Marxism ... only the emergence of a post-individualistic social world, only the reinvention of the collective and the associative ... can overcome the isolation and monadic autonomy of the older bourgeois subjects in such a way that individual consciousness can be lived ... as an "effect of structure".[29]

My contention is that it is this element of Marxism which has been most effectively forgotten in the forms of thought that have seen psychoanalysis as about the self and Marxism as about history – the hopes for the emergence of a different sort of self cannot be attributed to psychoanalysis. At one point, and to some people, Marxism offered what Louis MacNeice described in his poem *Autumn Journal* as 'a life beyond self but self-completing'.[30] Perhaps, as is the rule in all forgetting, that which it is the most painful to remember is what becomes distorted and lost. To read

Marxism/psychoanalysis as either/or explanatory models ignores the way that at one point in their history, at least, they depended on each other as the means of deconstructing the past through psychoanalysis and reconstructing the self through Marxism.

What I am writing about is, of course, the recent past and in a sense this paper emerges out of a contradictory state of urgency and melancholia. The recent past is still contemporary. Any attempt to evaluate its impact can seem both premature – it lacks the distancing patina provided by historical research into more distant epochs – and suspect – in that any reconstruction of this past is also at the same a self-interested invention of it. The plot lines that justify such endeavours seem fatally well-worn as well. You can claim to be discovering or reassessing something mysteriously overlooked or misinterpreted with the implication that you are in a posistion to 'tell it like it is' – or 'was.' Or less grandiosely you might be attempting to rescue something – from oblivion and forgetfulness and for the record – because that something seems precious and necessary. The disavowal of an awkward past in the name of modernity is the dominant model in current political discourse. What is certainly true is that the question of how to think about or use the past has not been resolved and that these books, insofar as they are working in the territory, offer an antidote to the glib or magical assumption that the past somehow no longer signifies.

The Author

Allegra Madgwick is completing a doctorate on 'Psychoanalytic Theory and its Relation to Autobiographical Narrative' at Queen Mary and Westfield College, London. She has co-edited a book on oral history, *Inventing Ourselves* (Routledge, 1989) and will be publishing an article 'Perversion and Literature' in the near future.

References

1   E.V. Wolfenstein, *Psychoanalytic Marxism: Groundwork,* Free Association Books, New York and London, 1993, p. 1.
2   For a rather belated attempt to resuscitate or at least pay tribute to the corpse see Jacques Derrida's address to the 1993 international conference 'Whither Marxism?', now published as *Spectres of Marx,* Routledge, New York and London, 1992.
3   P. Rieff, *The Triumph of the Therapeutic; Uses of Faith after Freud,*

University of Chicago Press, Chicago and London, 1966.

4   'Just as Marx regards the history makers of the past as sleepwalkers, "who required recollections of past world history in order to drug themselves concerning their own content," so Freud similarly regards the condition of dream-formation, of neurosis itself, and even of the cure of neurosis, namely the analytic experience of transference. They are all of them species of living past history in the present. If the last of these works out satisfactorily, then a case history is at the end transfigured. It becomes an inseparable part of an integral life history. Freud is, of course, the master historian of those transfigurations'. S. Marcus, 'Freud and Dora', in C. Bernheimer & C. Kahane, eds., *In Dora's Case: Freud, Hysteria and Feminism,* Virago, London, 1985, pp. 56–91, p. 75.

5   R. Young, 'Psychoanalysis and Political Literary Theories', in J. McDonald, ed., *Thresholds: Psychoanalysis and Cultural Theory*, Macmillan, London, ICA, 1991, pp. 139–157, p. 140.

6   Quoted in E. Roudinesco, *Jacques Lacan: A History of Psychoanalysis in France 1925–1985,* Free Association Books, London, 1990, p. 536.

7   E. Laclau, 'Psychoanalysis and Marxism', *Critical Inquiry*, vol.13, 1987, pp. 330–33, p. 330.

8   T.G. Ashplant, 'Psychoanalysis in Historical Writing', *History Workshop: A Journal of Socialist and Feminist Historians,* vol. 26, 1988, pp. 102–119.

9   L. Passerini, 'Work Ideology and Consensus Under Italian Fascism', *History Workshop,* vol. 8, 1979, pp. 82–108.

10   S. Freud, 'Remembering, Repeating and Working Through (Further Recommendations on the Technique)', in *The Standard Edition of the Complete Psychological Works of Sigmund Freud*, trans. J. Strachey, vol. 12, Hogarth Press, London, 1991, p. 147.

11   K. Figlio, 'Oral History and the Unconscious', *History Workshop,* vol. 26, 1988, pp. 120–132, p. 130.

12   The interpretation of sexual abuse in our time deserves a careful history. What is interesting to note is how what was at first a political critique that fought against the psychologising away of abuse has been reappropriated by an individualistic 'therapeutic' culture. The argument today significantly does not talk about patriarchy and men's power in the family but instead about 'false memory syndrome' and the power for manipulation abrogated to the therapist.

13   F. Jameson, *The Political Unconscious: Narrative as a Socially Symbolic Act,* Methuen, London, 1987, p. 102.

14   R. Fraser, *In Search of a Past; the Manor House, Amnersfield, 1933–1945,* Verso, London, 1984.

15   C. Steedman, *Landscape for a Good Woman; a Story of Two Lives*, Virago Press, London, 1986.

16   P. Fuller, *Marches Past,* Chatto & Windus, London, 1986, p. 6.

17   L. Marcus, 'Enough About You, Let's Talk About Me', *New Formations,* vol. 1, 1987, pp. 77–95, p. 78.

18   M. Lauret, *Liberating Literature; Feminist Fiction in America,* Routledge, London and New York, 1994, p. 97.
19   Marcus, 'Enough about You, Let's Talk About Me', p. 93.
20   Ibid. p. 88.
21   C. Steedman, *Past Tenses; Essays on Writing, Autobiography and History,* River's Oram Press, London, 1992, p. 43.
22   Fraser, *In Search of a Past,* p. 118.
23   Fuller, *Marches Past,* pp. 10–11.
24   R. Fraser, interviewed in *History Workshop*, vol. 20, 1985, p.185.
25   Steedman, *Landscape for A Good Woman,* p. 144.
26   Steedman, *Past Tenses,* p. 3.
27   Fraser, interviewed by *History Workshop*, p. 180.
28   Fuller, *Marches Past,* p. 42.
29   F. Jameson, *The Political Unconscious,* Methuen, London, 1987, p. 125.
30   Louis MacNeice, *Collected Poems,* Faber & Faber, London and Boston, 1979, p. 144.

9

'We Wish He Had Been a Better Poet and a Manlier Fellow . . .'

Frederick Furnivall's Thomas Hoccleve

Antonia Ward

Frederick James Furnivall, whose judgement of Thomas Hoccleve forms the title of this paper, ends the introduction to his 1897 Early English Text Society edition of *Hoccleve's Works: The Regement of Princes* with this apology: 'I am sorry these Forewords are so slight and scrappy...Let them serve until the old poet's next editor treats him thoroughly'.[1] For all their supposed slightness and scrappiness, Furnivall's remarks provide a useful case study for an analysis of the historicising of masculinity. Furnivall, as well as scrutinising Hoccleve's poems, metre and language, measures Hoccleve for masculinity, and finds him wanting. In doing so, Furnivall reveals more about the variables of nineteenth-century masculinity than he does about Thomas Hoccleve.

In this paper I show how such criticism interprets the literature of the past using the gender criteria of the present. Specifically I look at the discourses of masculinity employed by Furnivall in his introduction to Hoccleve's poems. I propose that when a critic interprets an author's masculinity, he or she does so from within – and with reference to – the dominant discourses of masculinity of their own time. As Andrew Tolson has suggested:

> masculinity is a culturally specific and socially functional 'gender identity', with peculiar (often negative) consequences for men themselves. [...] If gender is cultural and social, then it is also *historical* - sexuality is not the same for different generations. There is no 'universal' masculinity, but rather a varying masculine experience of each succeeding social epoch.[2]

I suggest that the ways in which a number of critical studies of Hoccleve draw attention to issues of masculinity may be in part symptomatic of just such an historically contingent masculine experience. I use Furnivall and the end of the nineteenth century as a case study; I then go on to show how – despite changes in ideas about what constitutes masculinity – at the end of the twentieth century Hoccleve's masculinity is still being called into question.

I

Thomas Hoccleve was born in or around 1367. Records show that he worked as a civil servant – a clerk in the Privy Seal – until his death in 1426. He also wrote poetry; some 13,000 lines of it. In this poetry he refers to himself, both as an author and as a clerk, and he describes himself as having suffered a period of mental illness, when his friends avoided him and his memory 'went to pley'.[3] Today, Hoccleve is read, if he is read at all, in three main contexts: as Chaucerian disciple, as a contentious example of early autobiography, and for one of the first literary descriptions of a nervous breakdown.[4]

Frederick Furnivall was born in 1825 and died in 1910. He was the founder of the Early English Text Society, the Chaucer Society, the New Shakspere Society, and the Browning Society. A trained barrister whose extracurricular interests in philology, English Literature and the education of working men soon took up all of his time, Furnivall has been described as 'one of the great rock-blasting entrepreneurs of Victorian scholarship, the kind of man who if his energies had taken another turn might have covered a continent with railways'.[5] Fairly catholic in his tastes and cavalier in his editing, Furnivall wrote lengthy 'Forewords' to many of his editions, and he was not averse to including within them long digressions on practically any of his personal passions; from rowing – which he advocated ardently, to religion – which he didn't advocate at all. He apparently prided himself on writing exactly as he spoke, and he spoke exactly as he thought; or as Sidney Lee put it in the *Dictionary of National Biography*, 'Devoid of tact or discretion in almost every relation of his life.'[6]

In 1892 and 1897, when Frederick Furnivall printed the works of Thomas Hoccleve for the Early English Text Society, they became available to a reading public in a (relatively) accessible text for the first time since their composition. The 'old poet's next editor' has still not materialised; Furnivall's two volumes remain the only complete works of Hoccleve available and are still in use today. Consequently, almost all twentieth-century readers of Hoccleve reach the text through the idiosyncratic editorship of Frederick Furnivall. This idiosyncrasy is significant because Furnivall's own life and times are legible in his readings of Hoccleve's life and work, and because these in turn have influenced all subsequent scholarship on Hoccleve. Furnivall's 1890s editions can be located in a paradigmatic moment for issues of masculine identity. In addition to - and perhaps because of - this historical context, at the same as time as Hoccleve is reclaimed as worthy of publication, Furnivall initiates a practice of questioning the poet's masculinity. Specifically, this can be seen in his 1892 introduction to the *Minor Poems*, where he characterises the poet as a:

> weak, sensitive, look-on-the-worst side kind of man [...]. But he has the merit of recognizing his weakness, his folly, and his cowardice. He makes up for these by his sentimental love of the Virgin Mary, his genuine admiration for Chaucer, his denunciation of the extravagant fashions in dress, the neglect of old soldiers, &c. We wish he had been a better poet and a manlier fellow; but all of those who've made fools of themselves, more or less, in their youth, will feel for the poor old versifier. [...] There's a good deal of human nature in man. So we'll not throw stones at old Hoccleve.[7]

Furnivall's description of Hoccleve as a 'weak, sensitive, look-on-the-worst-side kind of man' reveals less about Hoccleve's writing than it does about Furnivall's own era. His first adjective, 'weak', for example, reflects a number of Victorian discourses of masculinity which can be located on the male body. As Bruce Haley has shown, the topos of health was important to Victorian constructions of masculinity.[8] In the following extract from 'The Science of Health', Furnivall's friend Charles Kingsley illustrates contemporary fears about 'whether the British Race is improving or degenerating'.[9] His rhetorical conversation warns of dire consequences if people were to ignore 'that they have bodies as well as minds and souls':

> There may be those who would answer [...] - "You say, we are likely to grow weaklier, unhealthier. And if it were so, what matter? Mind makes the man, not body. We do not want our children to be stupid giants and bravos; but clever, able, highly educated, however weakly Providence or the laws of nature may have chosen to make them. Let them overstrain their brains a little; let them contract their chests, and injure their digestion and eyesight, by sitting at desks, poring over books. Intellect is what we want. Intellect makes money. Intellect makes the world. We would rather see our son a genius than an athlete.[10]

Kingsley answers:

> Well: and so would I. But what if intellect alone does not even make money...unless it is backed by an able, enduring, healthy physique, such as I have seen, almost without exception in those successful men of business whom I have had the honour and pleasure of knowing? [...] What if, for want of obeying the laws of nature, parents bred up neither a genius nor an athlete, but only an incapable unhappy personage, with a huge upright forehead, like that of a Byzantine Greek, filled with some sort of pap instead of brains, and tempted alternately to fanaticism and strong drink?[11]

The list of physical ailments which Kingsley identifies matches Hoccleve's own laments on the side effects of a career as a writer:

> Wrytyng also doth grete annoyes thre,
> Of which ful fewe folkes taken heede
> Sauf we oure self; and thise, lo, thei be:
> Stomak is on, whom stowpyng out of dreede
> Annoyeth soore; and to our bakkes, neede
> Mot it be greuous; and the thrid, our yen,
> Vp-on the whyte mochel sorwe dryen.
>
> What man that thre & twenti yeere and more
> In wryting hath continued, as haue I
> I dar wel seyn it smerteth hym ful sore
> In euere veyne and place of his body;
> And yen moost it greeueth trewely
> Of any crafte that man can ymagyne:
> ffadir, in feth, it spilt hath wel ny myne.[12]

This combination of dyspepsia, backache and eyestrain would perhaps have been a familiar list of complaints to Hoccleve's Victorian editor. For example, failing eyesight is just one ailment which carried cultural connotations for nationality and sexuality in Victorian discourses of the male body. Worries about racial and national degeneration at the end of the century were focused as worries about the strength and stamina of the male body. In an article unambiguously entitled 'The Deterioration in the National Physique' printed in *The Nineteenth Century* in 1903, George F. Shee wrote that 'For some time past the physical condition of the nation has been a matter attracting the grave attention of thoughtful men.'[13] Eyestrain was considered by some to be no small part of this degeneration. In the same year that Shee was fearing for the health of the nation, George M.

Gould was tracing 'The Origin of the Ill-Health' of writers such as De Quincey, Carlyle, Huxley and Browning.[14] This 'Ill-health' included what Gould calls 'the eye-strain factor':

> every tenth person of the slaves of civilisation, all those who are compelled to work with their eyes at the reading, writing and handwork distance, are today having havoc played with their minds, dispositions, and workaday lives, by this unrecognised disease factor. I am told that an abnormally large percentage of criminals and the youth consigned to reformatories have high degrees of optical and other defects of the eyes.[15]

Fears about degeneration in the male body were accompanied by fears about the degeneration of mankind itself. One source for such degeneration was found in the 'degenerate stock' which was producing such miserable specimens of masculinity, and one cause for degenerate stock was found in masturbation. Hoccleve's physical complaints correspond with Victorian medical discourses on masturbation. Dr. David Skae, in this 1873 description of 'the unhappy victim' of masturbation, takes his examples of the connection between masturbation and mental and bodily illness from the popular press. Symptoms include:

> nervous debility, mental and physical depression, palpitation of the heart, noises in the head and ears, indecision, impaired sight and memory, indigestion, loss of energy and appetite, pains in the back, timidity, self distrust, groundless fears, and muscular relaxation.[16]

The list of symptoms corresponds frighteningly well with Hoccleve's own complaints. Even leaving aside Hoccleve's putative madness, which could be connected to ideas of 'masturbatory insanity', the physical symptoms of Hoccleve's occupational hazards come precariously close to locating him within an emergent discourse of masturbatory identity.[17]

It was partly in an attempt to redress these worrying trends of weakness and degeneration that discourses of 'muscular manliness', especially the ideas of 'muscular Christianity' and the cult of athleticism, became prevalent at the end of the nineteenth century. Participation in organised sports was promoted in schools, and sporting prowess was increasingly applied to the image of the ideal man. Furnivall himself helped to promote these values. George Bernard Shaw described Furnivall as someone 'who, being what was called a muscular Christian (slang for a sporting parson), could not forgive Jesus for not putting up a fight at Gethsemane.'[18] Furnivall promptly lost his faith but retained his fanaticism for physical recreation, rowing fourteen miles on the Thames every Sunday until his eighty-fifth year. After his death a friend wrote of Furnivall 'He was so keen on all bodily exercise', adding in brackets 'I have seen him interested in ping-pong even!'[19]

An explicit connection of athleticism and manliness can be seen in Furnivall's comments about Hoccleve's bravery, or lack of it, in the masculine pursuits of sport: 'I see no evidence that he had ever crost a horse: and he was too much of a coward to play football or any rough game.'[20] By the 1890s, football was becoming increasingly popular, and was described by one headmaster as 'a means of testing the manly prowess of representative teams of schools, colleges, clubs, villages, or other communities...'.[21] What is significant here, however, is that Furnivall is not actually isolating an incidence in the text of Hoccleve describing an unwillingness to play football, or in fact any sport; the lines which Furnivall cites to back up his description, from stanza 22 of the 'Male Regle', are in fact about physical violence towards other men: Hoccleve says 'I was so ferd with any man to fighte'.[22] Furnivall is reading what Hoccleve calls his 'manly cowardyse' as something which makes him 'the sort of man who doesn't like football', a judgement that even today would provide an instant characterisation of a masculine identity. Perhaps Furnivall would have forgiven Hoccleve many more things if he had played football with his colleagues Prentys and Arundel for the Privy Seal Five-a-Side team.

Hoccleve's job as a clerk in the Privy Seal, however, was another area which could have influenced Furnivall's characterisation. What information about his author's masculinity could Furnivall have read into Hoccleve's occupation? As John Tosh has identified, the social status of the clerk at the end of the nineteenth century was far from certain: 'The hapless office clerk fell between two stools; in middle class terms his occupation was servile, while the labourer despised his soft hands and poor physique.'[23] Peter Stearns in his review of masculinity, *Be A Man!*, identifies that for white-collar workers at the end of the nineteenth century 'technology, while not nearly so ominous as for the working male, threatened possible displacement from the 1880s onward; a combination of typewriters and female secretaries, for example, virtually did away with the male clerk in many offices.'[24] Hoccleve, being such a 'hapless office clerk' and having such a 'poor physique', provides little that is unequivocally 'manly' to his middle-class Victorian editor.

Hoccleve emerges in his poetry as preoccupied with – and frank about – his lack of money, at a time when 'many white collar workers fell back on their own version of instrumentalism, wrapping their manhood in their

108

earning level'.[25] With his texts embodying the machinations of patronage from the viewpoint of the patronised, Hoccleve's work violates an intrinsic part of Victorian masculine reputation. John Tosh describes how the Victorian male needed:

> an income from work [...]. But not just *any* work. It wasn't enough that the work be dependable or even lucrative - it had to be dignified. For middle-class work to be dignified, it had to be absolutely free from any suggestion of servility or dependence on patronage.[26]

This is the same preoccupation which is the subtext to Kingsley's polemic in 'The Science of Health'. As Ed Cohen points out, both Kingsley and his devil's advocate agree that the goal of a man's life, be he genius or athlete or neither, is to make money.[27] What might Furnivall, coming from such a culture, have made of Hoccleve's petitionary poems, which have been described as the finest collection of begging letters in the history of English Literature?

Furnivall, then, found Hoccleve's masculinity problematic because his physical weaknesses and occupational status were at odds with the dominant masculinities of the 1890s. But if by the end of the nineteenth century attitudes to work were beginning to promote 'the idea that what a man did in his working life was an authentic expression of his individuality', this was to be an even more important influence for twentieth-century masculinities.[28] This correlation of occupation and identity can be seen in some twentieth-century criticism of Hoccleve, which reflects contingent discourses of masculinity just as explicitly, and just as unwittingly, as its Victorian predecessors. While the reference point for dominant masculinities may change with 'each succeeding social epoch', literary critical readings of Thomas Hoccleve's masculinity, it seems, remain the same. When in 1989 John Burrow found 'the directness of Furnivall's response' to Hoccleve 'delightful' but 'very old-fashioned indeed', he was distancing himself from a methodology superseded by 'historical,.. New, and formalist or structuralist criticism', rather than from Furnivall's gendered response.[29] In what follows I show the persistence of gendered readings of Hoccleve's masculinity since Furnivall.

II

That Hoccleve's career was no meteoric rise to the higher levels of the civil service, and that he was never granted the ecclesiastical benefice 'without cure of souls' which he hoped for, can be verified by documentary evidence.[30] Malcolm Richardson discusses this in his 1986 article 'Hoccleve in his Social Context'.[31] It could well be re-titled 'Hoccleve and his Professional Failure'. Richardson introduces 'the unfortunate poet Thomas Hoccleve', and lists Hoccleve's failures to achieve promotion in the Privy Seal, describing him as 'a conspicuous under-achiever'.[32] He even adds Hoccleve's marriage to his bad career moves: 'There was little Hoccleve could do to worsen his position. He found something, however: he got married'.[33] Presenting this as another in a line of habitual self-destructive acts, Richardson waxes vitriolic in his contemporary comparisons: 'Hoccleve had done nothing to prepare himself for marriage. Consequently, his laments resemble those of modern students who complain bitterly that they cannot have at the same time a university education, two children, and a new automobile.'[34] When Richardson sums up his theory that 'the poet was not the victim of a malignant fate, but of himself', he reflects the late twentieth-century meritocratic principle that a man is master of his own fate.[35]

Richardson's account of 'Hoccleve in his Social Context' in fact shows Hoccleve's masculinity in Malcolm Richardson's social context. By emphasising Hoccleve's failure to achieve a degree of occupational success sufficient to satisfy his twentieth-century career-minded critic, Richardson predicates his assessment of Hoccleve on 'economic manhood' as it was legible in 1986. In the same way that Furnivall's criticism reflects variables of masculinity in the 1890s, Richardson's article reflects the 1980s. In the decade of the young upwardly mobile professional, Hoccleve, perhaps, fails to conform to a dominant masculinity because he was not a yuppie.

It is the direct identification between the work a man does and the man a man is that has led to the direct identification of Hoccleve the author as Thomas the protagonist. Consequently, it is in part Hoccleve's 'unsuccessful' career that makes his literary critics read him as unsuccessful as a man. Critics who are convinced by the autobiographical persona in Hoccleve's poems consistently read Hoccleve as a real man but not as a 'real man'. How similar to Furnivall's characterisation 'a weak, sensitive, look-on-the-worst-side kind of man' is Jerome Mitchell's statement that 'the personality that emerges from the Prologue to the *Regement of Princes* is that of a weak, timorous, self-centred, but very human individual.'[36]

Why, then, do some critics find Hoccleve's personality problematic? Perhaps there is a clue in Mitchell's phrase 'self-centred'. I suggest that it is the very fact that Hoccleve writes about himself that is seen as so disturbing. An unease can be detected in Albrecht Classen's reading of the

'Male Regle', which he talks about as revealing 'too much of Hoccleve's inner self in autobiographical terms... Hoccleve repeatedly provides us with unmediated information about his private life, his intimate feelings, his idiosyncrasies and other aspects of his personality.'[37] This is perhaps why A. C. Spearing, comparing Hoccleve with Chaucer, describes Hoccleve's use of the first person as 'vulnerable', or why Derek Brewer describes Hoccleve as 'amusing but undignified'.[38]

Hoccleve not only talks about himself – he is guilty of the traditionally feminine trait of talking too much. H. S. Bennett in 1947 described 'Hoccleve's constant gossiping about himself', while A. L. Brown says of Hoccleve 'He was garrulous.(...) He wrote, and presumably talked too much...'.[39] A. C. Spearing gives an explicit reading of Hoccleve's speech as female: 'At times, in his self-absorbed chattiness, Hoccleve sounds like the Wife of Bath, forgetting where she has got to in her exhaustive account of her marital history.'[40] Jerome Mitchell also correlates autobiography with emasculation: 'Hoccleve has painted a miniature self-portrait by means of specific, descriptive details and through intimate, unabashed remarks about his own rather effeminate personality.'[41] John Burrow openly acknowledges that Hoccleve's self-referential details might not be socially acceptable. In fact, Burrow applies attitudes of masculine social identity to contemporary critical reaction to Hoccleve. Discussing the discrepancy in the poems between Hoccleve's moral counsel and his confessions of inadequacy, Burrow states that:

> Readers who credit Hoccleve with no awareness of this contradiction commonly react to his orthodoxies with something of that mixture of embarrassment and derision which society reserves for those of its members who try too hard to be one of the boys.[42]

He ends with the summary that 'it is readers least embarrassed by these details who are most likely, I think, to appreciate the character of this remarkable, though uneven, writer'.[43] Frederick Furnivall's legible affection for 'the poor sensitive old poet' comes perhaps because he was 'least embarrassed' by the intimacies of Hoccleve's writing: in fact, he himself addressed his readership in a similar way, believing that the societal nature of his methods of publication (that is, both that he published for the good of society as a whole, and more specifically, that he printed texts from within the framework of the Early English Text Society), meant that he was 'entitled to write Prefaces as to a circle of my friends'.[44]

In questioning Hoccleve's masculinity – whatever masculinity might mean at any particular historical moment – the Hoccleve critics discussed above are reinforcing the masculinity of their own 'circle of friends'; other readers, scholars and students. By pointing to Hoccleve's failure of masculinity, scholars since Furnivall assume that their readers can view Hoccleve from the same position of untroubled masculinity as they can themselves. In order to know what constitutes trying too hard, one has to know already what it takes to be 'one of the boys'.

Thus the study of masculinities in and through criticism on Hoccleve has ramifications for the academic study of masculinity – and for the study of academic masculinity. When Malcolm Richardson makes his character assassination of Hoccleve 'Hoccleve, as we know, was the type of man who sees his own glass half empty and his companion's glass half full.' perhaps we should concentrate not on the pop-psychology of his reference, but on the inferences of nescience and intimacy between critics and readers which are implicit in the phrase 'as we know'.[45]

To return, then, to the quotation from Furnivall's 'Foreword' with which we began, when Furnivall says 'we wish he had been a better poet and a manlier fellow', he not only describes his reaction to Hoccleve, but also prescribes 'ours'. When John Burrow calls this the 'frank man-to-man response of Furnivall to his author', his comment reveals the significance of Furnivall's characterisation for the study of masculinity.[46] To see criticism as a 'man-to-man response' denotes an interaction between two men – and therefore between two distinct discourses of masculinity. It is not only Hoccleve's masculinity which is at issue here, but also Furnivall's. When the Victorian scholar pledges that he'll 'not throw stones at old Hoccleve', he draws attention to his own position, perhaps, in a glasshouse where his own masculinity can be seen.

The Author

Antonia Ward is a member of the Department of English and Related Literature and the Centre for Women's Studies at the University of York. She is currently researching constructions of masculinity in Middle English literature and Victorian medievalist scholarship.

References

I would like to thank Trev Broughton, Felicity Riddy, Alastair Minnis and Hugh Stevens for their comments on earlier drafts of this paper.

1   F. J. Furnivall, ed., *Hoccleve's Works: The Regement of Princes and fourteen minor poems*, EETS ES 72, London, 1897, p. xix.

2   A. Tolson, *The Limits of Masculinity*, Tavistock Publications, London, 1977, p. 13.

3   Hoccleve, 'Thomas Hoccleve's Complaint', l. 51.

4   See, for example, S. Lerer, *Chaucer and his Readers*, Princeton University Press, Princeton, 1993; J. A. Burrow, 'Autobiographical Poetry in the Middle Ages: The Case of Thomas Hoccleve', in J. A. Burrow, ed., *Middle English Literature: British Academy Gollancz Lectures*, Oxford University Press, Oxford, 1989, pp. 223-246; J. Simpson, 'Madness and Texts: Hoccleve's *Series*' in J. Boffey and J. Cowen, eds., *Chaucer and Fifteenth Century Poetry*, KCLMS, London, 1991, pp. 15-29.

5   J. Gross, *The Rise and Fall of the Man of Letters*, Weidenfield and Nicholson, London, 1969, p. 169.

6   S. Lee, 'Frederick James Furnivall', in *Dictionary of National Biography Second Supplement*, Smith, Elder and Co., London, 1912, pp. 60-66, p. 65.

7   F. J. Furnivall, ed., *Hoccleve's Works: The Minor Poems*, EETS ES 61, London, 1892, p. xxxviii.

8   B. Haley, *The Healthy Body and Victorian Culture*, Harvard University Press, Cambridge, Mass., 1977.

9   C. Kingsley, 'The Science of Health', *Health and Education*, Daldy, Isbister & Co., London, 1875, pp. 1-25, p.1.

10 Kingsley, 'The Science of Health', pp. 16-17.

11 Kingsley, 'The Science of Health', p. 17.

12 Hoccleve, 'The Regement of Princes', ll. 1016-1029.

13 G. F. Shee , 'The Deterioration in the National Physique', *The Nineteenth Century*, May 1903, 797-805, p. 797.

14 G. M. Gould, *Biographic Clinics: The Origin of the Ill-Health of De Quincey, Carlyle, Darwin, Huxley and Browning*, Redman Ltd., London, 1903.

15 Gould, *Biographic Clinics*, p. 13.

16 E. Cohen, *Talk on the Wilde Side*, Routledge, New York and London, 1993, p. 57.

17 See Cohen, 'Taking Sex in Hand: Inscribing Masturbation and the Construction of Normative Masculinity', *Talk on the Wilde Side*, pp. 35-68.

18 G. B. Shaw, *Sixteen Self Sketches*, Constable, New York, 1949, p. 95.

19 J. Munro, ed., *Frederick James Furnivall: A Volume of Personal Record*, Henry Frowde, London, 1911, p. 1.

20 Furnivall, *Hoccleve's Minor Poems*, p. xxxv.

21 H. H. Almond, 'Football as a Moral Agent', *The Nineteenth Century*, December 1893, pp. 899-911, p. 901, quoted in A. Mason, *Association Football and English Society 1863-1915*, Harvester Press, Brighton, 1980, p. 224.

22 Hoccleve, 'La Male Regle de T. Hoccleve', l. 170.

23 J. Tosh, 'What Should Historians do with Masculinity? Reflections on Nineteenth-Century Britain', *History Workshop Journal*, vol. 38, 1994, pp. 180-202, p.186.

24 P. N. Stearns, *Be A Man! Males in Modern Society*, Holmes and Meier, New

York and London, 1990, p. 150.

25   Stearns, *Be A Man!*, p. 150.

26   Tosh, 'What Should Historians do...?', p. 185-186.

27   Cohen, *Talk on the Wilde Side*, p. 40.

28   Tosh, 'What Should Historians do...?', p. 186.

29   Burrow, 'Autobiographical Poetry', p. 224.

30   J. A. Burrow, *Thomas Hoccleve: Authors of the Middle Ages: English Writers of the Late Middle Ages; No. 4*, Variorum, Aldershot, 1994, p.11, p. 34.

31   M. Richardson, 'Hoccleve in his Social Context', *The Chaucer Review*, vol. 20, 1986, pp. 313-22.

32   Richardson, 'Social Context', p. 313.

33   Richardson, 'Social Context', p. 319.

34   Richardson, 'Social Context', p. 320.

35   Richardson, 'Social Context', p. 320.

36   J. Mitchell, *Thomas Hoccleve: A Study in Early Fifteenth Century English Poetic*, University of Illinois Press, Chicago and London, 1968, p. 15.

37   A. Classen, 'The Autobiographical Voice of Thomas Hoccleve', *Archiv für das Studium der Neuen Sprachen und Literaturen*, vol. 228, 1991, pp. 299-310, p. 303.

38   A. C. Spearing, *Medieval to Renaissance in English Poetry*, Cambridge University Press, Cambridge, 1985, p. 114; D. S. Brewer, ed., *Chaucer and Chaucerians: Critical Studies in Middle English Literature*, Nelson, London, 1966, p. 28.

39   H. S. Bennett, *Chaucer and the Fifteenth Century*, Clarendon Press, Oxford, 1947, p. 147; A. L. Brown, 'The Privy Seal Clerks in the Early Fifteenth Century', in D. A. Bullough and R. L. Storey, eds., *The Study of Medieval Records*, Clarendon Press, Oxford, 1971, pp. 260-81, p. 271.

40   Spearing, *Medieval to Renaissance*, p. 115.

41   Mitchell, *Thomas Hoccleve*, p. 11.

42   Burrow, 'Autobiographical Poetry', p. 238.

43   Burrow, 'Autobiographical Poetry', p. 246.

44   F. J. Furnivall, ed., *The Stacions of Rome, The Pilgrims Sea-Voyage* etc., EETS OS 25, London, 1867, p. viii.

45   Richardson, 'Social Context', p. 315.

46   Burrow, 'Autobiographical Poetry', p. 225.

THE POLITICAL
PAST

10

Medievalism and the Ideology of Industrialism

Representations of the Middle Ages in French Illustrated Magazines of the July Monarchy

Michael Glencross

The appropriation of the past to serve ideological interests in the present has been a hallmark of French cultural discourse in the modern period.[1] Such types of consumption of the past have been marked by perceptions of both continuities and discontinuities in the nation's history. At no point in time was historical appropriation more critical and conflictual than during the Restoration (1814–1830) and the July Monarchy (1830–1848), and no period was more central to this debate than the Middle Ages, which became the object of competing claims to legitimate the post-revolutionary settlement.[2] The royalist, Catholic appropriation of the Middle Ages, dominant in the early Restoration and evident in the writings of authors like Chateaubriand and Bonald, had given way by the late 1820s to a new liberal consensus which read medieval French history as a narrative of the destruction of feudalism and the decline of the aristocracy, accompanied by the rise of the bourgeoisie in alliance with the monarchy. In this article I shall examine some of the representations of the Middle Ages in the society created by this consensus, the July Monarchy, and in a medium which was invented during the period, the cheap illustrated magazine. My analysis of the material will explore the tensions between the contemporary ideological interest – in both senses of the word – in the pre-industrial society and culture of the Middle Ages and the simultaneous defence of the supposed and perceived benefits of industrialisation. In my conclusion I will consider briefly to what extent medievalism in French culture of the period was gender-based.

Before studying the way in which the Middle Ages were consumed by the readership of this new type of periodical it is useful to outline the material and cultural conditions in which the magazines were produced and to describe some of the features of their internal structure and organisation.[3]

The appearance of the first cheap illustrated magazines in France in 1833 marks an important new stage in the development of the French press and shows the impact of industrial technology on cultural forms. The production of these magazines was made possible firstly by the invention of the steam-powered printing press which enabled much longer print runs than previously possible, thereby decreasing the unit cost of production and creating new opportunities for mass cultural consumption. Secondly, wood-engraving techniques were adapted to the demands of mass production by the use of teams of engravers working on separate end-grain wood-blocks which were then assembled to make up the complete illustration. As a result wood-engraving which at the beginning of the century had been the hallmark of luxury printed books became in the course of the 1830s the stock-in-trade of a cheap, mass-produced popular form.[4] Not surprisingly both the technical conception and the commercial exploitation of this new medium occurred first in the most advanced industrialised country of the period, England. All the magazines founded in France in 1833 acknowledged, readily or grudgingly, the model of Charles Knight's *Penny Magazine*, which began in 1832 and continued publication until 1845 under the auspices of the Society for the Promotion of Useful Knowledge.[5]

The success of the *Penny Magazine*, which led the Society for Promoting Christian Knowledge to produce the rival *Saturday Magazine* (1832–1844), was due primarily to the quality and quantity of its illustrations. Its French epigones were eager to ensure their success by similar means, often using the services of English engravers and reproducing by agreement the same images. Illustration was certainly not an innovation in magazine publishing in France in the early 1830s but until then it had been confined to expensive serials, especially fashion magazines. Apart from its cheapness, due to the mass production techniques already mentioned, this new type of publication was characterised by the use of wood-engraving rather than lithography. The main advantage of the former medium was that text and image could be combined on the same page since both could be cut from wood. The integration of printed word and image is therefore central to exploiting the capacities of this medium. Full-page illustrations without accompanying text are consequently unusual. The normal spatial organisation is one in which text precedes image, the latter serving to summarise and express in a clearer, simpler form the written message. The need for suitable illustration is obviously one of the most important constraints operating on the choice of subject matter. Hence the frequency of articles devoted to topography, natural sciences, biography and architecture. The essential purpose of discourse in this combined medium is, then, didactic. It is interesting to note here that contemporary lithography on the other hand is the mode of realisation of what Richard Terdiman has termed the counter-discourse of July Monarchy journalism, an essentially critical visual code, realised in satirical publications such as *Le Charivari* and *La Caricature*.[6]

Apart from the industrialisation of production methods the birth and growth of illustrated magazines show the early development of consumption in nineteenth century France, the creation of what William R. Reddy has called a market culture if not a market society.[7] This process of the commodification of culture is visible in the metaphors embedded in the periodical titles. The magazine is a store-house, a museum or a mosaic, an accumulation of collectable items regularly provided for public consumption. The picturesque itself, as foregrounded in the title of the most successful of all these publications, the *Magasin Pittoresque*, becomes less an attribute of the natural than a reproducible adjunct of the industrial. The reader of each weekly issue is thus presented with a collection of discrete items on a range of subjects varying from science to literature. This unpredictability and heterogeneity of content provided the reader with variety but was not a recipe for encouraging his or her fidelity to the title. To help achieve this the competing publications had, from the beginning, recourse to the use of themed series of articles especially on historical topics and, from the late 1830s, incorporated serialised fiction following the immense success of the first *romans feuilletons* which appeared in the daily press in 1836.[8]

In the rapidly evolving and fiercely competitive world of journalism during the July Monarchy only two cheap illustrated magazines survived the 1830s, the *Magasin Pittoresque* and the *Musée des Familles* but these two publications continued to evolve and to coexist for the whole of the remainder of the nineteenth century, until 1938 and 1900 respectively, thereby far outliving their English counterparts. Their interest for the cultural history of the July Monarchy is, however, due not only to their enduring commercial success, a feature they had in common, but to the way in which each reflected a contrasting but related aspect of contemporary French culture: the impact of the economic, political and social ideas of Saint-Simon and his followers in the case of the *Magasin Pittoresque* and, for the *Musée des Familles*, the effect of industrial capitalism on the world of printing and publishing. This divergence is attributable to the dominant roles played within each publication by, on the one hand, Edouard Charton, a disciple of Saint-Simon and founder in 1843 of the first French illustrated news magazine, *L'Illustration,* modelled on the *London Illustrated News*; and, on the other, Emile de Girardin, the most successful and innovative entrepreneur in the French press during the July Monarchy. Other illustrated magazines which had also been launched in 1833 such as the *Magasin Universel* and the *Mosaïque* were unable to withstand the competition and had ceased publication by the end of the decade, but they too contain useful material for a study of medievalism in the 1830s.

The most common element of medieval culture represented in these magazines is that of architecture, especially the Gothic cathedrals of Northern France. This emphasis is typical of French medievalism of the period, especially after the publication of Hugo's novel *Notre-Dame de Paris* in 1831. The first medieval cathedral described in the *Magasin Pittoresque* is in fact that of Rouen,[9] not Paris, but Hugo's influence is clear in a later article on the cathedral of Notre-Dame which uses his terminology of the sublime and the grotesque to explain the aesthetics of medieval art.[10] The magazine sees itself as part of that nineteenth-century consensus which rejected the Enlightenment's disdain and neglect for an essential part of the nation's cultural heritage and sense of continuity.

The most interesting article on medieval art published in the early issues of the *Magasin Pittoresque* is not, however, devoted to one of the major Gothic monuments but to the misericords of a church in Corbeil near Paris which depict aspects of everyday life in the Middle Ages.[11] The text is accompanied by illustrations of the misericords, the originals of which had been destroyed but were known from earlier drawings. The article emphasizes the gap between the wealth of medieval sources available for the study of kings and nobles and the lack of documentation about the customs and conditions of the people. The author of the article values the medieval sculptures as a direct expression of medieval life, superior to the fictional recreations found in nineteenth-century novels. Medieval art is here valued as document not monument.

A similar approach is found in the *Magasin Pittoresque*'s treatment of medieval literature. The magazine differs from its main rival the *Musée des Familles* in the prominence it gives to Old French literature, probably the result of the collaboration of important medievalists of the period such as Hippolyte Fortoul and Achille Jubinal, who are both listed as contributors though their articles are unsigned. As is usual in the study of medieval French literature in the 1830s pride of place is given to the Carolingian not the Arthurian cycle, to epics celebrating a collective national identity rather than to romances recounting the amorous exploits of individual knights of the Round Table. Above all, medieval literature is seen as valuable in its very naivety and as historically useful even in its use of anachronism since it discloses in its purest form the social customs and moral values of the Middle Ages. Historical truth is necessarily revealed in the most apparently fantastical fictions.

More than literature, it was history which constituted the main focus of contemporary interest in the Middle Ages, whether in works of scholarship or in popularising publications such as illustrated magazines. In the case of the *Magasin Pittoresque* the coverage of medieval French history falls into two categories: firstly anecdotal accounts of incidents or episodes in French history, usually centred on the actions of an individual; secondly general presentations of aspects of medieval social history such as chivalry, feudalism and rise of the communes. It is articles in this second category which best reveal the ideological values informing this magazine.

As I have already mentioned, the founder and long-time director of the *Magasin Pittoresque*, Edouard Charton, was a follower of the social and political doctrines of Saint-Simon.[12] Though Charton formally broke with the movement in 1831 when it turned itself into a fully fledged religious sect, he remained convinced of the validity of its founder's social, political and economic theories. In Saint-Simon's thought the Middle Ages and the nineteenth century are in both a contradictory and a complementary relationship. They are based on two opposing principles of conquest and work, military or industrial activity. However, both belong to what Saint-Simon calls organic, rather than critical ages of history, that is they are structured to form a hierarchical but consensual system. Industrialism supersedes feudalism and a new industrial class replaces the old feudal aristocracy but the Middle Ages are seen not as a nostalgic refuge against the ravages of industrial capitalism but as a sort of perfectible prefiguration of modernity. Saint-Simon's central theses on medieval French history, the importance of the principle of conflict and the emancipation of the communes, were taken up in liberal French historiography of the 1820s, notably by Thierry who worked for a time as Saint-Simon's secretary. These ideas had become common currency by the time of the founding of the *Magasin Pittoresque* and they find an expression, albeit in a simplified and reduced form, in various articles on medieval subjects.

Whilst it is legitimate, even necessary, to make explicit the political and social philosophy underlying the magazine it is important not to give a falsely intellectual impression of the actual content of the publication. Its main aim, as formulated in its first issue, was to present to its readership in words or pictures anything which constituted 'an interesting subject for day-dreaming (rêverie), conversation or study'.[13] In terms of the representation of the Middle Ages this translates into articles on the picturesque side of medieval life, notably chivalry. Hence a series of articles, some with full-page engravings, entitled 'Scenes of the Middle Ages'.[14] These articles describe chivalric ceremonies such as the arming of the knight, tournaments, the loss of knightly status as a punishment for crime and trial by combat. The sources used and quoted in these articles belong to the antiquarian movement of the eighteenth century and earlier represented by scholars such as La Curne de Sainte-Palaye whose famous study on chivalry, first published in 1751, had been edited and republished by Charles Nodier in 1826. The continuing interest in the customs of chivalry shows how the same social practices can be reinterpreted according to the dominant ideology. The aristocratic revival of interest in chivalry, which had been a strong feature of French culture of the early Restoration, was an expression of the taste for medievalist trappings cultivated by the newly restored monarchy. After 1830, on the other hand, chivalry tended to be seen less as a celebration of military values and social exclusiveness and more as a moral model adaptable to industrial society in the form of charity towards the deserving poor.

This socially moralising exploitation of medievalism is also apparent in what is the most extended treatment of a medieval theme in the *Magasin Pittoresque*, a serialised historical fiction set in the fifteenth century and entitled 'Le Serf' (1841). This narrative is a companion piece to two other moral tales published earlier and set respectively in the nineteenth century ('L'Apprenti', 1837) and in ancient Rome ('L'Esclave', 1840). The purpose of the trilogy is to demonstrate to the reader via a fictional narrative the value of self-help and moral improvement through effort and work. Despite the different social and historical settings each narrative reveals a dialectic between work and idleness, another typically Saint-Simonian theme. The choice of the fifteenth century as period setting for the medieval tale is in no way accidental. Like Hugo in *Notre-Dame de Paris*, the author chooses a period of transition and tension in which four social groups, nobles, clerics, bourgeois and serfs are in conflict. After a series of hostile encounters with authority figures representing feudalism, the Church and the bourgeoisie, the main protagonist, the poor, rebellious, but intelligent young hero Jehan, discovers in the end a gospel of social harmony and progress which fulfils the Christian ideal of equality. Social conflict is thus transcended and the link between the Middle Ages and the nineteenth century asserted through a synergising evangelism.

In comparison with the *Magasin Pittoresque*, both the *Magasin Universel* and the *Mosaïque* were ephemeral publications which now rarely rate even a passing mention in historical surveys of the French press. Each of them, however, contains a considerable number of articles on medieval topics which confirm the general direction of popular interest of the time in the Middle Ages. The two most prominent features of this medievalism are the rehabilitation of Gothic architecture in France but also in neighbouring European countries, and the study of medieval French history. The first article of the first issue of the *Magasin Universel* is representative here: it is devoted to the chapel of Henry VII in Westminster Abbey and reproduces an engraving printed in the English publication *The Saturday Magazine*. The account of the evolution of medieval architecture given by the *Magasin Universel* shows the tension within the bourgeois culture of the July Monarchy between, on the one hand, the need to discriminate between the vulgar and the tasteful and, on the other hand, the attempt to distinguish between the decently practical and the decadently luxurious. The Gothic style of the late Middle Ages is interpreted as an art of decadence in which 'good traditions are lost, elegance and simplicity give way to affectation and to the search for exaggerated effect, and the desire to innovate leads artists into inevitable excesses'.[15] The relations between the medieval and the industrial must, then, be placed within the framework of the conflict between the desire for cheaper mass produced goods made available to a wider public and the need to maintain social distinction. Such tensions are clearly revealed in, for example, accounts of industrial exhibitions.

The re-evaluation of Gothic architecture in the 1830s should not, however, be confused with a glorification of medieval culture in general. Publications like the *Magasin Universel* and the *Mosaïque* firmly assert their belief in the reality of social progress. The social self-confidence of the bourgeoisie is in no way threatened by the aesthetic superiority accorded to medieval over modern architecture. Not surprisingly, there is no place in this ideology for a celebration of popular, rural culture. Hence the lack of articles on medieval vernacular literature. Medieval history is, on the other hand, considered a perfectly suitable subject for treatment since the historian's mission is to assert truth not to provide comforting or distracting fictions.

In this spirit the *Mosaïque* offers its readers a long series of articles on the kings of France going right back to the Merovingians. The history of France is firmly returned to the traditional account of kings and dynasties, a version of the national past which liberal Romantic historians such as Sismondi and Thierry had already argued against and attempted to rewrite in the 1820s. Nevertheless, despite the traditionalist nature of this announced programme the actual articles, particularly the later ones in the series, present an account much closer than might be expected to those of liberal historiography, in that they too emphasize the central importance of the freedom of the communes and the emergence of a new social class. This process is described in the following terms in an article on the reign of Philip I:

The progress of civilisation, the growth of luxury, the development of sumptuous tastes and needs, by making new demands on labour, new creations in the arts and industry, favoured the class which worked, which produced... They lost the conviction of their weakness and of their individual powerlessness, and acquired an instinctive awareness of their collective force.[16]

Once more the medieval and the industrial are not mutually exclusive but inclusive, and the echoes of the Saint-Simonian cult of the industrial quite clear.

To complete this brief survey of medievalism in illustrated French magazines I need to turn to the second most successful example of the genre, the *Musée des Familles*, and to compare its ways of consuming and reproducing the medieval past to those already studied. From its very beginnings this magazine defined itself in relation to and in distinction from the *Magasin Pittoresque*. In its ability to differentiate itself from its rival lay the formula for its success. This process can be clearly seen at work over the period between 1833 and 1835 when the magazine was seeking its identity and originality. Whereas the opening article of the periodical's first issue took English magazines as models to be imitated, by 1835 editorial policy had changed and, in a clear disparaging reference to the *Magasin Pittoresque*, the subscribers are told that the era of the illustrated magazine with its contents copying English material is now past. Readers, it is claimed, now want articles which have an authentically French flavour and 'no longer give off the smell of the sea and the smoke of coal'.[17] By 1837 the *Musée des Familles* repudiates the term magazine and lays claim instead to that of a literary review, ironically another category originally imported from across the Channel but already by this time naturalised and nationalised as French. To complete this move up-market the publication included in each monthly issue a journal of the literary and scientific events of the month. It now defined itself as a museum and meeting-place for the leisured, middle-class *habitués* of literary salons, a far cry from the labouring classes patronisingly invoked in Jules Janin's opening article of 1833, in which he set out the aims of the new magazine. The cultural space occupied by the *Musée des Familles* belongs firmly to the world of leisure not that of work, even though it sees the function of literature as being one of moral improvement more than entertainment.

Given this market positioning it is hardly surprising to find that the articles on the Middle Ages are less barely factual and historical than those in the other illustrated magazines so far examined. The articles on medieval topics are much longer than in rival publications and include contributions by successful writers such as Alexandre Dumas *père* and Pitre-Chevalier in addition to those of well-known medievalists such as Raynouard, Paulin Paris and Paul Lacroix (better known as 'le bibliophile Jacob'). The range of medieval topics is, though, predictable: the orders of chivalry, episodes from French history and accounts of the origins of Paris monuments like the hôtel de Cluny and the Sainte-Chapelle. Apart from articles on the mystery plays, medieval French literature is again conspicuous by its absence. In general the texts project a Middle Ages in which artistic beauty contrasts with social squalor, a period in which art created 'such striking marvels, almost without thinking, and founded upon every narrow, dark and filthy street a fairy palace as finely wrought as an ivory jewel'.[18] Hugo's aesthetic vision of the grotesque and the sublime underlies the decorative, picturesque medievalism of the *Musée des Familles* as much as its more functional, moralistic variant in the *Magasin Pittoresque*.

Early nineteenth-century medievalism, particularly in England, has typically been interpreted as a rejection of the disruptive, fracturing effects of both economic and political revolution, as a nostalgic return to a stable, hierarchical and organic form of social organisation.[19] In this article I have argued the link between medievalism and industrialism, in a cultural form which was itself the product of industrialisation, the illustrated magazine. I wish to conclude with some brief remarks on the gendering of conceptions of the Middle Ages evident in this material. Despite pious declarations of intention to appeal to a wide and undifferentiated readership, the success and very survival of the illustrated magazines I have surveyed depended on their ability to identify and satisfy the interests of specific social groups. If we accept the validity of a distinction in contemporary bourgeois society between a male-dominated public sphere of production and the female-orientated domestic world of consumption, it is useful to consider to what extent medievalism reinforced or undermined the gendering of culture in the July Monarchy. I would argue that the dominant mode of medievalism in French culture at the beginning of the nineteenth century was female-orientated. Its focus was the lady and its locus was Provence. This is the so-called *genre troubadour*, a survival in fact of *ancien régime* culture. During the Restoration and especially after 1830 a new dynamic, conflictual vision of the Middle Ages becomes the norm, whose focus is the people and whose locus is the North of France. In genre terms a lyrical mode gives way to an epic or dramatic one. In the industrialising society of the July Monarchy a gap is created between male or female medievalism. Most of the manifestations of medievalism I have examined in this paper belong to the male model, functionalist and productive. The decorative model is, though, more evident in the medievalism of the *Musée des Familles* which is less strident in its embracing of industrialism than the *Magasin Pittoresque*.

Further evidence for the gendering of the French Middle Ages can be found in a short-lived regionalist illustrated magazine, the *Mosaïque du Midi* published in Toulouse between 1837 and 1842, an interesting source because it contrasts sharply with the Paris-based magazines examined so far. As could be expected from a publication appealing to a Southern French audience it projects a view of French culture and society still fixed within the outdated conventions of the *genre troubadour*. It preserves therefore an archaic, rural, pre-industrial and feminised medievalism far removed from the industrialised variant of its Parisian originals and rivals.

My final example of the gendering of contemporary French medievalism comes from a better known sources, Michelet's essay *Le Peuple* of 1846. The gradual rejection of the Middle Ages is one of the most notable features in the evolution of Michelet's ideas, as is his increasing celebration of what he considered to be the feminine principle in creation. It is no coincidence that in *Le Peuple* he denounces simultaneously the Middle Ages and nineteenth-century industrial society. The spectacle of the squalor of the great industrial cities immediately evokes for Michelet a vision of the Middle Ages, an image of suffering and oppression. It is also worth noting that in Michelet's writings the critique of nineteenth-century industrial society forms the basis of his negative view of England. Michelet is at least consistent in his critique of industrial capitalism and the inequalities and injustices of contemporary English society, whereas the contributors to many of the illustrated magazines discussed earlier proclaim the economic benefits of industrialism in France but denounce its socially corrosive effects in England.

The success of the cheap illustrated magazine in France from 1833 onwards, as measured in terms both of its circulation and its longevity, is proof of the emergence of a readership which identified with the ideological values and interests promoted by these publications. Industrial and social change were, then, the two sources of this new cultural form. In some ways these magazines were to an emerging industrial society what the works of the *bibliothèque bleue* – the French equivalent to the English chapbooks – had been to rural communities, a means of entertainment, of instruction and of social control. As I have shown, the illustrated magazine is an important but neglected source for the culture and ideology of the July Monarchy dominated by the interests of an emerging industrial bourgeoisie. Within this framework textual and graphical representations of the Middle Ages are particularly significant: they reveal many of the tensions and contradictions of the July Monarchy, notably those between popular and élite culture, between urban and rural society, between consumption and production, between public and private spheres and between male and female roles. Medievalism functions as a useful discloser of most of these trends and shows how the medieval past could serve as a convenient displacement for the problems of the present.

The Author

Michael Glencross is a Senior Lecturer in French at the University College of Ripon & York St John. His main research interests are in early nineteenth-century French literature and cultural history. He is the author of *Reconstructing Camelot: French Romantic Medievalism and the Arthurian Tradition* (Brewer, 1995), and is at present working on a book on the French illustrated magazine in the culture of the July Monarchy.

References

1   On the presence of the past in French history see R. Gildea, *The Past in French History*, Yale University Press, New Haven/London, 1994.
2   There are a number of important recent studies of the place of historiography in French culture of this period: S. Bann, *Romanticism and the Rise of History*, Twayne, New York, 1995; C. Crossley, *French Historians and Romanticism*, Routledge, London, 1993; L. Gossman, *Between History and Literature*, Harvard University Press, Cambridge, Mass., 1990.
3   Useful studies of cultural and social conditions in this period in France include the following: L. Auslander, *Taste and Power: Furnishing Modern France*, University of California Press, Berkeley, 1996 (especially pp. 186–224); W.R. Reddy, *The Invisible Code: Honor and Sentiment in Postrevolutionary France 1814–1848*, University of California Press, Berkeley, 1996 (especially pp. 184–227); R. Terdiman, *Discourse/Counter-Discourse: The Theory and Practice of Symbolic Resistance in Nineteenth-Century France*, Cornell University Press, Ithaca, 1985; W. Whitney, *France at the Crystal Palace: Bourgeois Taste and Artisan Manufacture in the Nineteenth Century*, University of California Press, Berkeley, 1992 and R. H. Williams, *Dream Worlds: Mass Consumption in Late Nineteenth-Century France*, University of California Press, Berkeley, 1982.
4   See Ségolène Le Men's essay on book illustration in France in the 1830s in P. Collier & R. Lethbridge, eds., *Artistic Relations: Literature and the Visual Arts in Nineteenth-Century France*, Yale University Press, New Haven/London, 1994, pp. 94–110.
5   On the *Penny Magazine* see P. Anderson, *The Printed Image and the*

Transformation of Popular Culture 1790–1860, Clarendon Press, Oxford, 1991, pp. 50–83. Of related interest are: C. Fox, *Graphic Journalism in England in the 1830s and 1840s*, Garland, New York/London, 1988 and M. Shiach, *Discourse on Popular Culture: Class, Gender and History in Cultural Analysis, 1730 to the Present*, Polity Press, Oxford, 1989, especially pp. 71–100. For a recent feminist reading of contemporary English women's magazines see M. Beetham, *A Magazine of Her Own? Domesticity and Desire in the Woman's Magazine, 1800–1914*, Routledge, London, 1996.

6   See Terdiman, *Discourse/Counter-Discourse*, p. 152.

7   W. Reddy, *The Rise of Market Culture: The Textile Trade and French Society, 1750–1900*, Cambridge University Press, Cambridge, 1984.

8   Of these magazines only *L'Illustration* has been the subject of a detailed study and even this is a disappointing and largely anecdotal work, J.-N. Marchandiau's *L'Illustration 1843/1944, vie et mort d'un journal*, Privat, Toulouse, 1987. Surprisingly, there are only passing references to illustrated magazines in P. ten-Doesschate Chu & G. Weisberg, *The Popularization of Images: Visual Culture under the July Monarchy*, Princeton University Press, Princeton, 1994.

9   *Le Magasin Pittoresque*, vol. 1, 1833, pp. 12–14.

10   *Le Magasin Pittoresque*, vol. 1, 1833, pp. 83–5.

11   *Le Magasin Pittoresque*, vol. 2, 1834, pp. 148–50.

12   For a (critical) overview of Saint-Simon's thought, including his conception of industrialism, see J. Hayward, *After the Revolution: Six Critics of Democracy and Nationalism*, Harvester Wheatsheaf, New York/London, 1991, pp. 65–100. Also Crossley, *French Historians and Romanticism*, pp. 105–138 and N. McWilliam, *Dreams of Happiness: Social Art and the French Left, 1830–1848*, Princeton University Press, Princeton, 1993 (especially pp. 31–53).

13   *Le Magasin Pittoresque*, vol. 1, 1833, p.1. All translations from the French text are my own.

14   *Le Magasin Pittoresque*, vol. 2, 1834, p. 33, p. 58, p. 89, p. 129.

15   *Le Magasin Universel*, vol. 1, 1833, p. 206.

16   *La Mosaïque*, vol. 3, 1837, p. 229.

17   *Le Musée des Familles*, vol. 2, 1835, p. 409

18   *Le Musée des Familles*, vol. 5, 1838, p. 125.

19   This view is best set out in A. Chandler, *A Dream of Order: The Medieval Ideal in Nineteenth-Century Literature*, Routledge & Kegan Paul, London, 1971.

11

Braveheart

More than just Pulp Fiction?

Fiona Watson

History, quite rightly, is public property. Though we all do not share the same history, and certainly do not have the same views about it, interpretations of past events are debated, contested and revised in all forums of life, from the family gathering to the academic tome. But perhaps nowhere is history more public than in the movies, a medium which not only presents a particular viewpoint, but lets its audience – for a brief moment at least – virtually live through the events depicted.

The hype that followed Mel Gibson's portrayal of the thirteenth-century Scottish 'freedom-fighter', William Wallace, in the Hollywood epic *Braveheart* seemed to come out of nowhere. Indeed, it had to be released twice in America before it took off with sufficient momentum to dominate the 1996 Oscars. Scotland, the ostensible setting for the movie,[1] was certainly taken by surprise, though the Braveheart-fever which followed its European première in Stirling in September 1995 gave expression to already existing beliefs about the nation's past. These in turn reflected contemporary concerns over Scotland's future.

The following extract from *Cencrastus*, a Scottish arts magazine, highlights rather well some of the difficulties involved in trying to use history for what is essentially entertainment. The piece takes the form of an imagined conversation between Wallace (the narrator) and another prickly Scot, the poet Hugh MacDiarmid, in a sort of Scottish Valhalla. MacDiarmid, as usual, was laying forth (if you have problems with the Scots, just read it out loud):

> 'Furst of aw', says he [MacDiarmid], 'The filum is jist no' accurate!'
> Ah had tae agree wi' him ... For yin thing, Ah did not shag the
> Princess o' Wales or ony ither suddroun dame. ... But that's no' whit

129

riled him. Naw. He went oan aboot the embarrassin' accents, the contemptuous ignorance o' Sco'ish history and the proper place for the auld Scots tung in what should hae been a multi-linguistic production reflectin' the contemporary yase, by the way o' P and Q Celtic, Auld Norse, courtly Norman French an' Church Latin.

'But Shuggie',[2] Ah said tae him, 'It wid ne'er sell, man!'. 'Ye canna cater for the masses bi talkin' doun tae thaim', says he. 'Ye need gie thaim the haill jingbang for it tae maitter. Hauf a history is nae history at aw!'.[3]

The business of half a history is a crucial one, to which I will return. But an equally important and related question is, 'whose history?'. Blind Harry, on whose poem, *The Wallace*, the film script was predominantly based, claimed to have made use of a 'Latin Buk' supposedly written by Wallace's chaplain as the basis of his story; this was a common literary device, used even by the likes of Chaucer, to give more weight to the growing vernacular literary tradition. The poem was actually derived from earlier chronicles, some of which have not survived, but also, and more importantly, popular oral folktales which had sprung up in the 170 years since the hero's death.

By the 1470s, when *The Wallace* was written, Sir William was already a popular hero in the literal sense, the focus of non-élite, and hence generally unrecorded, history. This was despite the obvious anomaly that the man himself came from a different social background, as the younger son of a minor landowner. On the other hand, Robert Bruce, the hero-king and subject of the first epic poem about the period one hundred years earlier – John Barbour's *The Bruce* – was the focus of élite adulation.

Despite elaborating on what was a long-standing popular tradition, Harry's primary intention was to provide a moral tale for his own times, which is another way of saying that it was a piece of political propaganda. Though the passage of time has obscured this crucial element, Harry's contemporaries would have recognised that *The Wallace* was a direct attack on the policy of rapprochement with England espoused by the unpopular Scottish king, James III. In particular, it had disgusted a number of Harry's patrons, such as Sir William Wallace of Craigie. The latter's namesake, as a popular hero who only ever dealt with the English at the end of a sword, was thus the ideal candidate to represent the pure undiluted patriotism which Harry and his sponsors claimed to champion.[4] Part of this process was the creation of not only the definitive 'spirit of Wallace', but also fictional scenarios of thinly-disguised contemporary political events (contemporary to Harry, not Wallace). Unfortunately for those interested in the thirteenth-century man, Harry's version has formed the basis of almost all subsequent versions of Wallace's life.

Braveheart, despite obviously hanging its hat on an historical peg, has little or no basis in historical reality. By that, I mean reflecting the evidence available from the period when Wallace lived, rather than one hundred and fifty years later. Just because Harry's *Wallace* is old does not mean that it is old enough. However, the film did not claim to portray such a thing, and it is not Gibson's or anyone else's fault that some – many – viewers chose to believe that it did. According to the *Daily Telegraph*, commenting on the 1996 Oscars: 'As for the script's widely criticised historical howlers, Gibson was defensive. "This movie falls somewhere between fact and legend", he told me. "But there's some basis of truth in it"'.[5]

Braveheart was certainly about 'the truth', but, like Blind Harry, its creators were not worried about mere historical fact getting in its way. However, in considering the general reaction to the film, primarily in America, but also in Britain, it is clear that the presumption of a strong element of 'historical truth' played an important role in giving its underlying message greater credibility. So while Mel Gibson can be excused for doing his job – creating a cinematographic success against the odds – any analysis of the film, in terms of the public's reaction to it, must consider what the viewer thought of the history he or she believed was being offered.

As with Blind Harry's *Wallace*, *Braveheart* did not actually come out of nowhere but operates within a contemporary context. It does so both in the message which is most successfully conveyed, and in the cinematographic methods employed to disseminate it. As well as lifting his 'history' almost straight from Harry,[6] Randall Wallace, *Braveheart*'s script-writer, together with the film's director, Mel Gibson, also recognised the essential element of the poem and created their own moral tale for our times. Though they are not necessarily advocating a specific political policy, they are certainly attempting to present a particular politically-charged ideology.

As the superabundance of comments on *Braveheart* on the Internet makes clear, the key elements of that ideology were not lost on many of the film's viewers. There is certainly an essential methodological flaw in using Internet sites as the main source of opinion about the film, since they are predominantly constructed by those who are obsessed by it and naturally appeal to others who feel the same way. However, the loudest voices in the media on both sides of the Atlantic, and especially in Scotland, did reflect similar attitudes at the time of the film's release.

The Interneters' remarks generally identified three key elements in the film's ideology. The first, and arguably the most important, is the role of the individual. As Hollywood is keenly aware, there is an ongoing human

131

need for heroes. Cinematographically such men (and they usually are men) have come in all shapes and sizes, but, by definition, they are products of their time. Mel Gibson's William Wallace is a very traditional hero, in the Ben Hur/ Spartacus mould. He appealed to many Interneters both because he changed the course of history and because he was 'ordinary', not born to greatness: 'The most compelling aspect of the film is its true portrayal of how ONE man galvanized a small nation against brutal tyranny' or 'Braveheart shows the power one man can have in a country that he strongly believes in'.[7]

Such comments, which are fairly typical, reflect the sense of political disenfranchisement which is an increasingly common phenomenon in the developed world, certainly in America and increasingly in Britain. Such feelings of insignificance and powerlessness, which very much inform our postmodernist world, are undoubtedly important in individual lives. However, the desire for a saviour for our own times, personified in the heartfelt statement, 'If only there was someone alive now who truly believed in freedom, justice and the average person', could, ironically, presage a turning away from the collective liberties fought for in this century.

Wallace, both historically and even mythologically, achieved his prominent position precisely because he had tunnel vision, an inability to see any other point of view than his own. On the other hand, the vacillation prompted by the dilemma faced by Angus McFadyen's Robert Bruce was ultimately seen, as was no doubt intended, as weak and unattractive. It is too close to our own experiences in a liberal society where right and wrong are not as clear-cut as it (supposedly) used to be. The post-modern world has, ironically, provoked a renewed belief in the need for the Truth in this increasingly confusing world, accompanied by a desire to believe that, like Wallace, we would be heroic enough to fight to the death for it. Historians have often used the past to counterbalance such a view of the inherent morality of belief to the death (not necessarily your own, of course), but society is remarkably indifferent to the idea that we have been through all this before, except in certain specific instances, (such as the war in the former Yugoslavia). Any number of comments from the Internet make this historical short-sightedness remarkably clear.

The cynicism which came out of the sixties and seventies had already given way to a desire for a greater security in conformity and regulation long before *Braveheart* came to tell us where we should stand. Uncomfortable films are certainly still being made: the recent examples of *Seven*, *Twelve Monkeys* and even, up to a point, *The Rock*, attest to the popularity of movies about the cancer within American government and society even in Hollywood. However, mainstream cinema audiences are primarily paying for old-fashioned escapism, as the huge profile of actors like Arnold Schwarzenegger and Sylvester Stallone exemplifies. Indeed, as U.S. film critic, Gene Siskel, noted in the run-up to the 1996 Oscar ceremony which brought *Braveheart* five awards, 'The biggest surprise is the exclusion of serious movies in the best picture category ... I believe Academy voters simply did not see *Dead Man Walking* and *Leaving Las Vegas*'.[8]

The search for meaning and 'truth' in terms of spirituality was another key theme identified by Internet commenters on the film. Interestingly, *Braveheart* was often seen as a 'Catholic' film:

> When I saw *Braveheart* I realized instantly that if Mel Gibson wasn't an orthodox Catholic then he must have been my kind of pagan with a good-humoured appreciation for Catholicism. I have never seen such a forceful depiction of courageous Catholic convictions as were written into the *Braveheart* script.

This aspect of the film was strongly emphasised in a review under the title 'Best Movie of 1995' written by William Fahey, a graduate student of the Catholic University of America, in the California State University campus magazine. For example, once again Robert Bruce's difficulties in choosing between idealism and safety is described as being that of a '... crisis of belief which ... symbolizes the struggle each of us must face before experiencing freedom', in this case, presumably, the freedom of religious belief.

More explicitly, Fahey highlights the attractive nature of the religion pursued by Wallace and his compatriots:

> There is neither a simpering nor a conniving Christianity in *Braveheart*. Here priests manfully intone Latin; soldiers say their *pater nosters* and receive the Holy Eucharist before battle. The hero steals scarcely a kiss before proposing marriage and – *mirabile dictu* – does not consummate his marriage until there is a marriage to consummate'.[9]

The theme of martyrdom is also stressed, Wallace's execution being perhaps inevitable in this context in order to reinforce the message that, in both life and death, his purpose was to affirm 'a moral order'. Mel Gibson is known for his espousal of what is called 'family values' on both sides of the Atlantic; *Braveheart* gave him the opportunity to promote those beliefs to a worldwide audience.

That basic morality was all the more powerful for being so simplistic: 'Better to die free than to go on living in chains'. However, only one internet correspondent compared the portrayal of thirteenth-century Scotland under English rule to a modern example of similar proportions, in this case, the enforced assimilation of East Timor to Indonesia. Most others lamented the perceived lack of freedom in Western society, a sentiment that should be deeply worrying to our political leaders and is grossly disrespectful to those who really are suffering under oppression:

> In our culture there is no room for freedom. What passes for freedom
> is marginal at best. There is no way for a man to defend his honour.
> Today, if a man tried to live free and defend his honor he would be
> placed in a loony bin.

Passion – both for the cause and for the woman – is deemed to be missing in our own times and was to be found then, a belief which doubtless ties in well with contemporary views about the rootlessness and disorientation prevalent particularly among men in a post-feminist world.

Braveheart is certainly about a period in history when men were men and women were women and the goodies and baddies were clearly distinguishable:

> Finally something for those of us who believe there was a time when
> wrongs were righted, bravery was encouraged, God was respected
> and men carried swords.

The old-fashioned qualities – family values again – promoted by the film doubtless appealed particularly to conservative viewers, but let us not underestimate how essentially – and attractively – chauvinist *Braveheart* is and how often in history the fight for 'freedom' is actually only engaged upon for one section of society, whether the excluded or included group relates to gender, race or class.

It is not difficult to understand why *Braveheart* is such a product of its time. So-called Western societies are at a bit of a loose end: the Cold War is over, the Middle East is too divided as yet to form an Islamic superbloc and China is too important economically to demonise. It's no wonder that we don't know who the enemy is, though there seems to be a concensus that there must be one. Even the recent glut of sci-fi films such as *Independence Day* and the spoof, *Mars Attacks*, though successful in box-office terms, failed to grip the imagination to the same degree as their predecessors because there were no analogies to be made with threats closer to home. We know deep down that fearing little green men is ridiculous, but not if they are a cloak for red, yellow or black ones.

Which perhaps leaves us with no choice but to go back in history to pick on the ex-bully, the imperial power par excellence – England. Many Interneters, but – as you might expect – the Scottish ones particularly, directly challenged any liberal attempts to castigate the movie for its blatantly anti-English stance – they only got what they deserved, was the basic view. One Interneter even made the remarkable claim that:

> One of my friends is a 26 year-old Englishman named Simon ... After seeing the movie Simon said with tears rolling down his cheek "will you ever forgive me, can you ever forgive me for being English and killing William Wallace?"!

One lone voice did try to redress the balance, stating that:

> I felt I had to send you a letter after some of your entries regarding English people apologizing for being English and being ashamed of their countrymen. My country fought two world wars and lost millions of lives to protect the freedom and democracy we know of today. When Hitler conquered Europe and France surrendered Britain stood alone, against the evil of the Nazis. ... Bankrupt, we were victorious because we stood for a cause we believed in. Freedom. Good against Evil.

This is another form of the same myth, though it is unlikely that it was recognised as such by those who now so passionately espouse the cause of poor old Scotland.

And, in terms of a contemporary agenda, poor old Scotland is the crux of the matter. Scottish historians, of which I am one, are perhaps less comfortably esconced in their ivory towers than their colleagues south of the border simply because there is a full-blown political debate taking place around them in which the nation's past is very much used as an offensive weapon. There is no academic nationalist school of Scottish history, which is perhaps a good thing, encouraging a wide range of interpretations of the past. However, this very acceptance of ambiguity and complexity among professional historians can lead those with a nationalist agenda (whether political or cultural) to be attracted to particular sorts of history from a less academic background, repeated over and over again, to hammer home the salient political points.

But this is an old story and I doubt if any nation can claim immunity from it. Each people's history is surely, in essence, that which the nation collectively feels its past to have been. Equally, the sources from which this collective perception derives are many and varied and certainly not constructed only from academic output. Of course, on closer inspection there will be both local and personal deviations of greater or lesser significance. However, this does not seem to affect the overarching *sense* of the nation's past – that almost religiously-held and usually unquestioned assessment of what it all boils down to – which unites the disparate elements of its population and their diverse histories into a common identity. The fact that important sections of that population – most obviously, women and, more recently, ethnic minorities – are not represented in the detailed history supposedly creating that overriding perception does not seem to make much difference, though they might promote change over time.

There is a great similarity between the relationship between 'the facts' and a nation's sense of history, and 'the facts' and their distilled essence portrayed in the movies. Film-makers make no apology for their loose interpretation of what is known about particular events in order to portray a wider 'truth'; historians might whinge about details, but, the movie-makers claim, *they* are interested in the spirit, not the letter, of the past. This is underlined by a response to a query from an Interneter to the MacBraveheart web site[10] relating to some of the more glaring historical inaccuracies in the film, such as the portrayal of Wallace as a highlander and the fling he had with the Princess of Wales. The (Scottish) owners of the web site stated that:

> We feel that on balance the inaccuracies which have been introduced are justified on the basis that they contribute to the overall objective which was to produce a movie which was a work of art and of entertainment, which at the same time was inspiring and emotionally gripping. Very few of the changes are 100% invention. Most have been brought in (relocated in time perhaps) from some other recorded events in Wallace's life or at the time of the Wars of Independence.

These are sentiments which Mel Gibson, as the film's director, would doubtless have shared, though as a historian, I would have to say that there is indeed quite a lot of 100% invention, whether by Harry or the film-makers themselves. In an interview between the historian, Eric Foner, and the film-maker, John Sayles, the latter is asked if he and his colleagues care at all what historians think about their films. The answer – and this is surely true for *Braveheart* – is that they do not. Sayles goes on to say that history is 'a story bin to be plundered, and depending on who you are and what your agenda is, it's either useful or not'. The historical details must not get in the way of the story-telling.

However, their conversation does indicate that the historian and the film-maker, or at least an independent film-maker like Sayles, may have a lot more in common than first meets the eye. Foner points out, in a passage describing the relationship between the historian and alternative views of the past, that 'the hardest thing for people who don't think much about history to realize is that there may be more than one accurate version of history'. However, he goes on to justify academic history by saying: 'On the other hand, there are limits. If my point of view was completely divorced from the evidence, other historians would know that my views were implausible, and they would point that out because the evidence is there and there are standards'. As Sayles then acknowledges, the logic of the position that anything goes is, for example, Holocaust denial.

The idea that history is not a series of pre-determined events told by a single narrator is one that struck a chord with Sayles, who admitted that: 'I've often had the experience of seeing a historical movie and then reading some history and – and thinking that the history is a better story, a more interesting story, and certainly a more complex story'.[11] Complexity, particularly in terms of portraying events from a number of perspectives, is even more difficult to do in the movies than it is in a book – there is a real danger of failing to engage the audience's emotions with the main characters if there are too many competing points of view. In *Braveheart*, which intended to make money and manipulate its audience, there was no doubt about who merited our sympathy, just as we knew when to laugh, when to cry and when to cheer.

But reality is rarely that simple, even in the thirteenth century. The more distant past is regarded as fair game by both film-makers and the public because, so it is believed, we don't really know what happened anyway. It is true that we know very little about the real William Wallace; but we certainly know a lot about the war he was fighting, the society he lived in, and the other protagonists on the Scottish side, members of the elites and thus better documented. In the film, the latter were, with one exception, quite unrecognisable as historical figures, so concerned were the film's makers to ensure that Gibson/Wallace shared the goodies' centre stage with no-one apart from his love interests and the ambiguous, but ultimately Wallace-redeemed, Robert Bruce.

The final question to be answered, which relates to the business of half a history, is, to put it bluntly, so what? If the people of Scotland wish to believe that their forebears were all terribly good-looking, brave and put-upon by the evil English, and if the rest of the world wants to admire them accordingly, well, why not? On a number of levels, it doesn't matter at all, especially since *Braveheart* has done wonders for Scotland's tourist industry and my own student numbers. It is now up to us how we present alternative versions of Wallace and Scotland's past generally, once we have these new devotees through the door.

But at other levels – particularly that of Scotland's political identity – there is perhaps room for concern and the historian should not shrink from joining in the debate, though as an equal, not a more-qualified, participant. This has become a matter of urgency given that the Scots are expected to vote 'yes' to a separate parliament on the very date of Wallace's great victory seven hundred years ago. That referendum, together with a similar one in Wales, has fundamental implications for the political structure of the United Kingdom as a whole and thus those voting should be very clear about what they may or may not be endorsing and why.

If the Scottish people vote for a parliament to get back at the English, then that is a decision that they are entitled to make, but it is hardly a mature and rational response to the most significant constitutional shake-up in the relationship between the two nations since 1707.[12] Those subscribing to the romantic, English-ravaged view of Scotland's past, which *Braveheart* captured but did not create, would doubtless regard such a response as being true to its 'spirit'. Academic historians, on the other hand, may perhaps despair at seeing recent attempts to develop a more sophisticated, warts-and-all, approach to that past meet the renewed blank wall of public enthusiasm for the old myths. It will not help that Hollywood is rumoured to be making (yet another) film about that evergreen romantic symbol, Mary, Queen of Scots – starring Glenn Close and Meryl Streep.

Again, it could be argued that Scotland is not unique in preferring its old heroes and certainly wishing to present them as enticing bait overseas. However, the patchy teaching of Scottish history in schools particularly has ensured that most Scots do not readily come across alternative histories to the romantic one. This is not because of any great conspiracy to deny the Scottish people their past (as many believe) but because many teachers are hostile to educating students in a subject they themselves know little about: Scottish history has only recently become an established and semi-respectable subject at university, providing a corresponding increase in research and publication and teachers trained in the subject. There is also an understandable belief that Scottish history is not important when laid alongside the world-changing events of the twentieth century, such as Nazi Germany and the Cold War.

Such views should be taken seriously, but equally, access to knowledge through education, particularly about the past, is a powerful tool in raising self-respect and, equally importantly, self-knowledge which is important for any nation. The debate about whether domestic history should be automatically taught is an unusual one since it is generally taken for granted that it should. Scotland's past is no more parochial than that of any other nation, including England and – if it is, it is the fault of the teacher, not the subject.

There is certainly work to be done. Major gaps in the basic factual framework of some periods of Scottish history have only recently been even cursorily filled in, despite a prolific output on Wallace, Bruce *et al.* The existence of an historiography – different traditions, approaches and interpretations of the same events – is still embarrassingly basic for some periods, while Scottish historians have been understandably too preoccupied with the bare bones of the subject to enter into the wider debates about the nature of history itself.

The ability to make a choice comes from knowing what the alternatives are. History provides those alternatives to an audience seeking to know itself and the world around it; equally, writers of history must step back when, having presented their case, those choices are made. *Braveheart* has done wonders for Scotland's profile throughout the world, but it has also provided white supremacists with an example of 'small' people from a distinctive, and implicitly pure, racial group – but who are not Indians or Mexicans – overcoming the tyranny of repressive government. In the end, *Braveheart* has provoked a debate and that can only be a good thing. Those of us who have the opportunity to shape that debate should not give the audience half a history because we believe they cannot cope with more. There *is* no 'us' and 'them' because we all ultimately stand within the same processes of human history and own it equally. On the other hand, there are standards even when – or especially when – dealing with complexity: all interpretations of the past are not equal if they fly in the face of evidence understood in all its shortcomings. History, like nations, changes its points of view and matures in its outlook. *Braveheart* is, essentially, pulp fiction and there is nothing wrong with that, so long as we know it for what it is.

The Author

Fiona Watson is Lecturer in History at the University of Stirling. Her Ph.D will shortly be published as: *Under the Hammer: Edward I and Scotland, 1286-1306.* Other future projects include: a book on the Anglo-Scottish Wars (Addison Wesley Longman); the section 1174-1329 of the new Canongate History of Scotland which is due for 2000 and a *History of the Scottish people in the Middle Ages* (Edinburgh University Press).

References

1   Though, as is well-known, much of it was actually filmed in Ireland.
2   This is the Scots for Hugh.
3   *Cencrastus*, no. 53, Winter 1995/6, p. 2.
4   M. McDiarmid, ed., *Harry's Wallace*, Scottish Text Society publications, Fourth Series, no. 4, Edinburgh, 1968, Introduction.
5   *Daily Telegraph*, 27 March 1996, p. 15.
6   Even the fling with the Princess of Wales was not original, although in the poem she was Edward I's wife.
7   These quotes are taken from the Bravehearters' website which exists specifically to attract comments about the film. The site address is http://www.chs.chico.k12.ca.us/marg/wallace.html.
8   *USA Today*, Wednesday 14 February 1996, p. 7.
9   William Fahey, 'Best Movie of 1995: Braveheart', *Campus*, Volume 7, No. 1, Fall 1995, p. 17.
10 The address of this site is http://www..braveheart.co.uk/macbrave/bhappeal.htm.
11 T. Mico, J. Miller-Monzon & D. Rubel, eds., *Past Imperfect. History according to the Movies*, Cassell, London, 1995, pp. 16, 18, 25, & 11.
12 This is the year in which the Scottish and English parliaments were dissolved to form a single body.

12

The Hungriest Narrative

Devouring Mother Ireland

Kathy Cremin

"Today is a great day for Irish women" said Mary Robinson on the day she was elected President of Ireland by the people of Ireland. An Irish woman now holds pride of place among speaking and heretofore spoken-for subjects. Will speak on behalf of the subjects. An Irish woman now occupies the stronghold of all strongholds: Head of State - titular, symbolic role. But contemporary Irish women know the value of symbols, goddesses or presidents, and we have voted or decided accordingly. Because of this, what has been written "from the beginning of history and before", what I wrote some days ago is now being rewritten.[1]

On 9th November 1990, a truly wonderful thing happened: Ireland became the first country in the world to elect an openly feminist president. On 25th November the following year disaster struck: Field Day published their anthology of Irish writing, and Irish women were appalled to discover the silence that surrounds even the most public and articulate of women. It is through the relationship between these two moments of recent Irish history that I want to approach the *Field Day Anthology of Irish Writing* (1991). This paper argues that *Field Day* consumes submerged gendered narratives of Irish experience to strengthen a dominant (nationalist) history based on long past notions of Irish unity, and in so doing re-enacts historical silences and deep political anxieties surrounding women and the Irish nation.

Under the general editorship of Seamus Deane, twenty-two eloquent, respected, intelligent Irish men produced, in five years, the most wide-ranging, ambitious anthology of Irish writing ever attempted: fifteen centuries, five languages, six hundred authors, four thousand pages.[2] None of these editors were women. Only thirty female authors were included, no

141

section was devoted to women's writing, and where notable developments have occurred in Irish writing – what Eavan Boland describes as the disruption of women changing from passive ornamental objects in poems into authors of poems and demystifying the image of the national feminine – these were ignored.[3] Women poets who were included felt that unrepresentative examples of their work were chosen.[4] And well-established but avowedly feminist writers such as Paula Meehan were not mentioned. Indeed, Declan Kiberd, editing the contemporary poetry section, actually concluded that today's Irish women poets are politically 'reticent'.[5] Yet Irish nationalism has been constructed through feminine icons, and it is hardly credible that in *Field Day*'s dialogue on how historical myths consume us that gendered voices, bodies and experiences – public and private – are not read as political.[6]

Despite this, on publication the editors were shocked by the angry reactions from women. What is really happening when at this level of scholarship Deane offers the barely articulate excuse that the editors simply forgot to include women? Deane is unique among the editors in at least admitting a mistake – he told Nell McCafferty the omissions were 'a prejudice, and a prejudice all the worst for being unconscious'.[7] At a public meeting to discuss the anthology's omissions, Boland said she was ashamed to be included when so many women of note were forgotten.[8] To this, W.J. McCormack replied that *his* hands were clean on the gender issue – he had edited a section on Maria Edgeworth – and he was much more interested and concerned with the representation of Unionists in the anthology. McCormack's attitude distorts what is really at stake in exiling gender from politics – the most disrupting and dissenting politics affecting Southern Ireland issue not from the North, but from domestic and sexual politics. Deane's passing recognition that women's exclusion represents a deeply rooted Irish cultural tension – one so painful it can only be forgotten – might well remind anyone concerned with Irish history that forgetting is a highly political act.

Deane's editorial philosophy provides a vital context for reading the exclusions, for this anthology brought to the fore controversies and dissensions not only about what comprises tradition and Irishness in Irish writing, but also conflicts as to how any proposed tradition might be theorised.[9] Since 1991, it has become somewhat inevitable that critical writing on Irish cultural studies not only gestures towards the anthology as a watershed, but uses the cultural debates surrounding it as a way of articulating a theoretical or political affiliation. Indeed, one of the problems arising from the ease with which the hierarchy of national over gender politics has been re-instated is how frequently an espousal of feminist concern became an excuse to attack the anthology from other political grounds.[10] The initial exclusions of women caused outrage. At least as worrying, and a great deal more surprising, is the reproduction of the anthology's mechanisms of assimilation – rather than differentiation – in the discussions of the anthology's failings.

In some ways the anthology represents a remembered sundering of the possibilities of Irish cultural life: an imagined point where, had diversity been recognized, old dualities would have broken down and life could have been 'different'. Those marginalised within the terms governing Irish tradition continually return to this symbolic loss, so the anthology itself re-enacts the frozen moment of partition *Field Day* sought to dismantle. For Deane proclaimed the anthology as an 'urgent intervention' in critical debates about the dynamics of change and authority in Irish culture:

> It is important to do this now because the political crisis in Ireland, precipitated in 1968, but in gestation for many years before that date, has exposed the absence within the island of any system of cultural consent that would effectively legitimise and secure existing political arrangements.[11]

Simply, Deane believes that two unique, unorthodox features of this anthology will create a more plural, cross-cutting, multi-voiced, post-nationalist dialogue on Irish writing and tradition. Deane suggests that while the anthology does follow wide chronological dictates, other organisational categories sometimes become more important, such as language, genre, autobiography, political writing, historical identification. This structure creates juxtapositions which corrupt received ideas of Irish literary history. Deane actively seeks oppositions and contradictions within received traditions. Secondly, Deane included writing that does not qualify, in the strict sense of the word, as Literature. In preference to the abstract terms 'Literature' and 'History' – which suggest undesirable notions of completeness and continuity – Deane's key terms are writing and narrative: terms which highlight the act of textual construction. Deane attacks historian's version of history as mis-constructing a complete, whole, knowable narrative typical of the post-colonial nation's monologic history. He anxiously stresses that 'unlike historians of limited philosophical resource', the anthologisers do not want to offer a 'true' or 'absolute' version of Irish history. Yet he also states unequivocally that:

> There *is* a story here, a metanarrative, which is, we believe, hospitable to all the micro-narrative that, from time to time, have achieved prominence as the official version of history, political and

literary, of the islands past and present.[12]

How do we reconcile these claims of the anthology as a loose and pliable form, with Deane's assertion of a metanarrative? Such a reconciliation seems vexed and difficult, particularly when Deane insists that the unformed nature of the Irish canon allows us to dismantle the very process of canon-making; yet the anthologisers set themselves the task of reclaiming elements from the English canon. Against Deane's own assertions of dismantling myths and re-figuring the history of the nation stands his introductory attack against revisionism, reiterated in Luke Gibbons' editorial. Deane argues that in the revisionist project, which is in fact remarkably similar to *Field Day*'s own, 'there is often an anxiety to preserve the status quo'. He suggests that revisionists erase their own political difficulties and contradictions by propounding the belief that the process of history is so complicated that:

> At times it seems that there is a link between the impulse to heroicize the past and the consciousness of present political weakness or defeat ... a powerful antidote to criticism and rebellion.

This theoretical philosophy has been extensively explored and critiqued by Edna Longley.[13] I would like, however, to stress again that the moments of Irish cultural history which Deane chooses to remember are those consistent with and integral to a nationalist metanarrative of Irish tradition dominant since the Celtic revivals of the 1880s. Features of this metanarrative include: the famine and a resultant decimation of the Irish language; the consequent and 'never since stemmed' tide of emigration and colonisation as a transformative force upon language, culture and location.

Deane's hazy application of 'metanarrative' is the crux of his introduction, for here colonisation, and therefore partition, are put forward as the centre of Irish intellectual debate. This focuses on the immediate Northern crisis, effectively ignoring the existence of the Republic as a stable and separate political entity. The forces which shape the reality of people's lives – urbanisation, poverty, drugs, class, the effects of an increasingly homogeneous global culture, gendered relations etc. –- remain unanalysed. Instead, the problem of Irish identities are discussed in sectarian terms. *Field Day* abandons social history in favour of a ritualised discussion of dispossession and sacrifice which appropriates women.

It is appropriate here, then, to look at specific exclusions of women, gender and sexuality from the *Field Day* anthology. The inclusion of 'non-literary' writing extends mainly to religious and political writing. There is no attempt to include disruptive writing to flesh out forgotten or neglected Irish experiences: housekeeping diaries, accounts of women's religious life, legal documents, medical records, and so on. Perhaps these absences can be explained by the amount of new research required to collect such material, or by the difficulty of categorising these types of writing. Yet there are other absences which cannot be explained so benignly. Here are some examples.

Firstly, the section on Protestant Oratory has no companion section on Catholic speech-making, presumably because the continuing issues of divorce and abortion would certainly have entailed an uncomfortable negotiation with Irish sexual politics. And because, as Longley frequently argues, in *The Living Stream*, northern nationalists wish to play down the difficulties of church and state.

Secondly, amongst the political writings one may read Ian Paisley, but not President Robinson. Nor can one find writing by any of the women prominent in Ireland's women's movement. None of the material from the long standing campaigns for the reform of abortion, homosexuality and divorce laws, with which President Robinson was involved since the late 1970s is included.

Thirdly, while nineteenth-century topographical writing is included, there is a notable absence where myths of the Irish landscape are concerned. More specifically, the prevalent and forceful theme of Mother Ireland and her feminine body in the landscape (a pervasive feature of nineteenth-century anthropological writing) is not addressed.

Fourthly, the Irish suffragist paper, *Irish Citizen* (1912-20) is listed once in the index, but no citation actually appears on, or indeed near, the listed page. This is particularly interesting, for as the historian Louise Ryan has shown, the *Irish Citizen* was one of the few platforms for discussing the future position of women in whatever kind of state would evolve in a free Ireland.[14] Perhaps this silence is a symptom of the fact that the paper prioritised issues which still concern Irish women today: child abuse, violence and poverty in the home, divorce, abandonment and reproductive issues.

Finally, and similarly, the autobiographical accounts of Irish nationalist women during the first half of this century do not even merit a mention, even though Margaret Ward has anthologised more than thirty accounts concerning the rising, the war of Independence, civil war, experiences of imprisonment and the eventual displacement of women in the free state.[15] De Valera's infamous appeal to women as 'rosy colleens' keeping the hearth aglow *is* however included: weirdly contextualised as an appeal to keep the Irish language alive, and not in terms of article 41.2 of the 1937

Irish constitution (which circumscribed women's citizenship to their role in the home and which, incidentally, remains unreformed to this day).[16]

Siobhan Kilfeather points out that the only political writing which might be termed specifically feminist in William Thompson's *An Appeal on One Half of the Human Race, Women, Against the Pretensions of the Other Half, Men* (1825).[17] This example benefits closer examination. The extract appears in McCormack's section, 'Language, Class and Genre'. McCormack describes Thompson's relationship with fellow philosopher and collaborator, Anna Doyle Wheeler, as follows:

> Thompson's commitment to feminist emancipation resulted from his relationship with Anna Wheeler, the married daughter of an Irish archbishop and god-daughter of Henry Grattan. In this sphere he placed more trust in the ameliorating power of legislation than one might expect from a proto-Marxist theoretician of surplus value, but Mrs. Wheeler's legal difficulties with her vexatious husband deeply affected Thompson's thought in relation to the status of women. Under the pseudonym Vlasta, she contributed to Robert Owen's *Crisis*.[18]

McCormack neglects to give Anna her full double name, describing her instead as a 'married daughter', 'god-daughter', and 'Mrs.' His biography is extremely condescending about Wheeler's effect on Thompson. In fact, his dismissive tone, suggesting some unfortunate love-interest, trivialises Wheeler's intellectual contribution prohibiting any suspicion that the two were drawn together by shared radical intellectual projects. In this way, the gaps in Irish history and literary tradition where women might suddenly become visible are closed. A recent study by philosopher Dolores Dooley establishes Wheeler as co-author of several important documents with Thompson.[19]

Another example of this closing of gaps is that there are many gay and lesbian writers in this anthology whose sexual identities are systematically ignored in their biographies: identities as troublesome for Ulster/Unionist traditions as for Southern/Catholicism.[20] The arrogant editing out of certain Irish identities makes nonsense not only of Deane's original philosophy, but also of the many protestations that the anthology's treatment of gender, and selection of women's writing, simply reflected the state of feminist study in the 1980s. The promised fourth volume devoted to women, scheduled for 1993, has not materialised. But it might yet, for Deane reputedly asked one of his fiercest critics not to give the fourth volume a hard time. Whatever became of the idea of this anthology as a dialogue?

One might dismiss this reticence about sexual politics as peculiarly Irish, were it not that, over the last decade, Irish feminists have helped push Irish politics towards the painful process of separating church and state.[21] In the early 1990s, liberal thinkers and campaigners within Ireland began to achieve recognition, even tolerance and support, from a wider public. From example, on St. Patrick's day 1992, Gay Pride were excluded from the New York city parade. In 1993, their float won the New York competition. The following year, the gay and lesbian float won the Dublin parade. Homosexuality is now decriminalised and Ireland has marginally more liberal laws than England; facts which strongly emphasise how anachronistic *Field Day*'s politics are.

Yet one *Field Day* editor, Paulin, persists in completely dismissing the role of gender and sexuality in the political concerns of the Republic. When Boland argued that the agenda of the anthology was 'symptomatic of a significant shift in Irish writing', Paulin replied:

> Yes, there is the whole question of sexuality and gender – if you look at the way things have developed in Britain and the States, these issues have been aired long long ago, Ireland has begun to catch up. These things get slewed together to make it seem as if there is some kind of conscious conspiracy not to address what are burning issues in the Republic of Ireland. It [the anthology] is not really terribly interested in that obviously. It is for the South of Ireland to do something about itself ... [When asked, as a *Field Day* editor to qualify his disinterest, Paulin said:] I mean, in the minutiae of a rotten hopeless system where you have two political parties, deeply corrupt, based on different sides in the ridiculous civil war they fought seventy years ago. I have no interest in this system whatsoever, its a joke![22]

Paulin markedly desires to idealise the progressive politics of England and America, while trivialising and making inconsequential in cultural terms the political energies and social dynamics of concern in the South. This refusal to acknowledge women's voices in Irish politics is a symptom of the unfailing priority of the 'nation' as a political within *Field Day*'s body of work, which leads to a discourse on power and authority which largely ignores constitutional issues beyond partition. *Field Day*'s own history is consistent with Paulin's display of regressive, nostalgic politics: *Field Day* was formed in 1980 against the background of the H-Blocks. Before their first project was printed, ten hunger strikers had died, and two initial Field Day pamphlets focus on this campaign: a symbolic importance accorded to no other single event. Edna Longley has illustrated how *Field Day* essayist concern themselves with the roots of Irish identities in the early decades of the 1900s, and only with pre-Independence literature or that from the period covered by their own lives.[23] All *Field Day*'s pamphlets focus on the histories of sectarian subjects. *Field Day*'s centre of concern is the North; the South and its politics seem to hold little reality. Consequently, *Field Day* does not engage with social, economic or gender issues as they affect and are affected by, the workings of the state – be that state Irish or British. Less a manifesto for change, the anthology seems more a jaded point of reference for the failure of Irish culture and politics to respond to progressive, democratic forces.

Although great attention has been paid to the anthologist's ways of reading and of defining tradition and history, there has been little or no discussion of what the shift in readings of the anthology might themselves mean. On publication, reviewers were interested in what had been left out and why. Very quickly, the emphasis seemed to change to what is included where and why; questioning the editor's assumptions about the foundation and unity of the modern Irish nation, and notions of belonging. This slippage is from a gendered to a national discourse and reflects interestingly on the anthologists' philosophy, which supposedly emphasises discursive formations over authorship.

I want therefore, to turn to one of the most shocking, dramatic responses to this publication, Mary Crowe's statement that:

> This wound is all the more deep because it is an Irish wound, inflicted from within. The sins of the colonial fathers are being visited on the native sorority by their own brethren. It is an act of cannibalism, of flesh devouring flesh to survive on the bleak mountain tops of a costly liberty.[24]

Crowe's language of wounds, transgressions, sacrifices of flesh and familial betrayal isolates the anthology as a particular moment of epic cultural production definitive of contemporary struggles with Irishness. Crowe's archaic religious terms recalls for women the rhetorics of Catholicism and Nationalism. Yet the image of the cannibal, the West's epitome of otherness, places the furious arguments surrounding the editorial firmly in the thick of contemporary political and literary theory.

Crowe's distinction between civility and barbarianism steals the title of Deane's first pamphlet for *Field Day*, published in 1983, in which Deane analyses the political language used about the hunger strikes. He argues that in Ireland and England, the language applied to Northern politics 'is still dominated by the putative division between barbarism and civilisation'. He says the degraded status that the republican protesters represent with their 'filthy nakedness' is 'vulnerable Irish squalor' warring on 'impersonal English contamination'. Deane argues that the strikers exposure of intimate and taboo dirt represents poverty, filth, overcrowding, lawlessness suggests to the English mind a regressed or primitive mode of life, an 'Irish barbarism based on local kinship, loyalties and sentiments'.[25] Deane abhors the implicit English attitude or righteous and civilised law, which although self-given and self-justifying is imposed on others as if it were authoritative. His argument sketches an approach where political conflict and its resolution are voiced in terms of nation, rather than the political sanctions and authority of the state and civic government.

Deane describes the anthology's stormy reception as 'the vacillation between being-of-the-moment and anachronistic'.[26] Within weeks he responded to feminist critics with a parable by Yeats about how a culture endeavours to overcome political shock. Yeats believed the Irish themselves had destroyed Parnell (by their reaction to his private life) and that faced wit the consequent political loss of their leader, the society's only recourse was to remake Parnell as cultural symbol. Yeats described Parnell's death affecting 1880s Ireland as if:

> We had passed, through an initiation like that of a Tibetan ascetic, who staggers half-dead from a trance where he has seen himself eaten alive and has not yet learned that the eater was himself ... [Deane adds to this] ... Mutilation cannot be erased: it can only be incorporated if there is to be any fulfillment, most especially by a recognition of the fact that the dreadful act was committed not by others but by oneself.[27]

Deane draws an analogy between the moment of cultural loss at Parnell's death and contemporary Irish culture trying to get over the political shock of colonisation by remaking itself in the symbols of the nation. Is Deane offering this parable as a reconciliation to those Field Day have mutilated? For this desire to remake the nation ultimately only serves to increase the knowledge of the cultural losses people have inflicted upon themselves. Deane's cryptic defence of the anthology's silences around women writers neglects to mention either women or their writing. Is his parable a self-justifying warning that only the hungriest, most devouring of narratives can come to the fore in this particular culture?

This disturbing image of a self-devouring culture is a pertinent one. What is at stake in cannibalizing Irish culture and its history? What we learn about the Irish past and present through this particular formulation of Irish national conflict is that Irish critical analysis (as explored here) is overwhelmingly engaged in discussions of nationalism's repression of heterogeneous Irish experiences. Given the current political hopes for change within Northern Ireland, such an analysis is obviously worthwhile. Nevertheless, this critical engagement gravely replays the sacrifice of women's concerns and women's history in the interest of 'bigger' questions of nationality which can be traced from the struggle for Independence and the formation of the state. Yet it is the case that since Independence, every constitutional crisis in the Republic – barring only the charges of gun-running against Charlie Haughey in 1970 and the Beef Tribunals' scandal in 1992 – has been about women, children and the home. Gender politics are then arguably fundamental to any politically and socially informed consideration of Irish culture. Yet there is a marked unwillingness – or perhaps an inability – by many critics to think about such 'real' constitutional politics as explored within contemporary Irish writing. This difficulty is centered, it seems, within the need to deny the relationship between sexual and national identity. Why? Deane has already given us one answer: change, the loss of power and fear of who is devouring whom. Irish women, so often consumed by the famished idealisations of Irish femininity, now fervently consume and reinvent these icons.

Deane and Crowe are not the only critics to describe struggles around Irish culture through an elaborate language of eating and wounding. In a review, Longley described *Field Day*'s anthology as 'engulfing', 'sacrificial', 'a heavy gun emplacement' and 'an elegantly coiled whip'.[28] For Deane, these widespread metaphors of consumption, assimilation and annihilation clearly represent the ambivalence Irish writers feel for the English language, and the fears of both the coloniser and the colonised of who is preying on whom. Deane, in fact, roots Irish fears of 'language cannibalism' in the experience of the famine. But how this fear of being devoured actually works might be seen in Deane's relation of Yeats' parable, which centres on the cultural ambivalence surrounding literature which attempts to symbolically reconcile what it is impossible to reconcile politically: that is, ultimately, the apparent scandal of Parnell's involvement with a married woman was the most acceptable way for nationalists to express their disillusions and feelings that his nationalist politics were corrupted, or polluted.

Here, gender is artificially separated from, and subordinated to, the political. Conversely, within Irish culture, and certainly in recent constitutional politics, gender and more specifically, women's bodies, serve as a symbol of political security and unity. The images of devouring Mother Ireland, sacrificial and starved mother church and the voracious, cannibalistic mother of psychoanalysis, all converge in notions of consumption and assimilation, which are, as we see here, significant critical forms within studies of Irish nationalism, religion and gender. It could be argued that the recurring critical use of starvation and eating metaphors, which Deane seems to suggest is due to atavistic famine memories of language destruction, is more likely an indication that sexual concerns are not just embedded within those of the Irish nation more generally, but that acknowledging an embodied secular voice challenges the structural concerns of the nation-state.

Post-colonialists point out the consistent pattern whereby newly independent countries tend to adopt, virtually wholesale, the state institutions of the colonising power; what Fanon calls the 'sterile formalism' of bourgeois models of representative democracy. Irish democracy, since the foundation of the 'Free State', has arguably prioritised the development of the nation-state over that of civil society. On the grounds that *Field Day* reads Irish culture as a product of colonial crisis, it seems reasonable to ask why all the analysis of Ireland's colonial inheritance has, so far, been of the conception of the nation at the expense of civil concerns. It would be grossly unfair and simplistic to portray Irish society in these terms alone, and writing concerned with gender politics offer another, altogether different history of Ireland during the past fifteen years. Yet this history simultalneouly deals with the politics of culture, the 'structures of feeling' within Irish writing, and the attendant processes of social/political change. The histories of passivity, domesticity, ownership, exile, territory, and exclusion explored through various women's writing from Edgeworth on, might suggest a more complex story of Irishness and difference than we now have. Ultimately, what is at stake in cannabilizing Irish culture through the exclusion of Irish women's contributions is the dangerous privileging of a politics based on ideas of nation and minority rights over the development of an Irish democracy based on the politics of the civil state and civil rights.

The Author

Kathy Cremin is completing her PhD on the cultural politics of contemporary Irish womens' writing at the Centre for Women's Studies, University of York. She founded, and currently chairs, the Women on Ireland Network, a UK-wide organisation for women conducting research on Ireland, Irishness and the Irish Diaspora. The Network supports and promotes research through study days and an annual conference.

References

1   Ailbhe Smyth, November 1990 Postscript to 'Commonplaces, Proper Places,'
    in Penelope Curtis, ed., *Strongholds: New Art from Ireland*, Tate Gallery
    Liverpool, Liverpool, 1991, pp. 45-8, p.48.
2   Volume 1 covers Early and Middle Irish Literature (500 A.D.) through to the
    Intellectual Revival (1830-50); Volume 2, Poetry and Song (1800-90)
    stopping with Prose Fiction (1880-1945) and Volume 3 covers from James
    Joyce (1882-1941) to Contemporary Irish Poetry (1990).
3   Eavan Boland discusses this central concern of her work in several of the
    essays in *Object Lessons: the Life of the Woman and the Poet in Our Time*,
    Vintage, London, 1995.
4   See the article compiled by Eibhear Walshe, 'Women in the Annex? Women
    writers talk about the Field Day Anthology', *Irish Studies Review*, 2, 1992,
    pp. 13-14.
5   Declan Kiberd, ed., 'Contemporary Irish Poetry', in Seamus Deane et al., eds,
    The Field Day Anthology of Irish Writing 3 vols, Field Day Publications,
    Derry, 1991, vol. 3, pp. 1309-16, p. 1316.
6   For a history of Irish nationalism and the feminine icon, see C.L. Innes,
    Woman and Nation in Irish Literature and Society, 1880-1935, Harvester
    Wheatsheaf, Hemel Hempstead, 1993. For an illuminating critical overview
    of the persistence of this iconographic tradition as a site of feminist
    contestation, see Lia Mills, '"I Won't Go Back To It": Irish Women Poets
    and the Iconic Feminine', *Feminist Review*, vol.50, Summer 1995, pp. 69-88.
7   Shortly after the anthology's publication, Deane made this comment during a
    private conversation with the feminist writer Nell McCafferty. McCafferty
    referred to the conversation when taking part in a round table discussion on
    the anthology, chaired by Tariq Ali, 'Bright Through the Tears' for *Rear
    Window*, Channel 4, broadcast on 7 July 1992. The other people taking part
    in the discussion were Eavan Boland, Siobhan Kilfeather, Francis Mulhearn,
    Nell McCafferty and Tom Paulin. See also Deane's 'Silence and Eloquence',
    The Guardian, 12 December 1991, p. 23.
8   Reported by Katie Donovan in 'Absence Stirs Anger Amongst Women: A
    Report on a Public Debate on the *Field Day Anthology*', *The Irish Times*, 21
    February 1992, p. 10. Incidentally, Seamus Deane turned down his invitation
    to this debate.
9   Anthologies always implicitly question notions of belonging and authenticity,
    and the arguments manifest about *Field Day* were familiarly raised about
    other anthologies. Terrence Brown suggests that 'anthology wars' have
    intensified the sense of division between north and south. See Terrence
    Brown, 'Poetry and Partition: A Personal View', *Krino*, 2, 1986, pp. 17-23.
    Or Peter Fallon and Derek Mahon eds., 'Introduction' in *The Penguin Book
    of Contemporary Irish Poetry*, Penguin, Harmondsworth, 1990.
10 For examples of this use of gender see the exchange between Mulhern and
    Luke Gibbons: Francis Mulhern, 'A Nation, Yet Again', *Radical*

Philosophy, 65, 1993, 23-29; Luke Gibbons, 'Dialogue without the Other? A Reply to Francis Mulhern', *Radical Philosophy*, 67, 1994, pp. 28-31.

11 Deane 'Introduction' in *Field Day Anthology,* vol.1, pp. xix-xxvi, p .xx.

12 Deane, *Field Day Anthology*, vol. 1, p. xix.

13 See the introductory chapter in Edna Longley, *The Living Stream*, Bloodaxe, Newcastle, 1994.

14 Louise Ryan, ed., *Irish Feminism and the Vote: An Anthology of the Irish Citizen Newspaper*, Folens Publishers, Dublin, 1996.

15 Margaret Ward, ed., *In Their Own Voice: Women and Irish Nationalism*, Attic Press, Dublin, 1996.

16 Eamon de Valera, 'The Undeserted Village Ireland', in *Field Day Anthology*, vol. 3, pp. 747-50.

17 Siobhan Kilfeather, *London Review of Books*, 9 January 1992, pp. 18-20.

18 W. J. McCormack, 'Language, Class and Genre', *Field Day Anthology*, vol. 1, pp. 1070-1172, bibliographical details, p. 1171.

19 On Wheeler's contribution to this partnership and her co-authorship of a treatise on sexual inequality, see Dolores Dooley, *Equality in Community: Sexual Equality in the Writings of William Thompson and Anna Doyle Wheeler*, Cork University Press, Cork, 1995, particularly Chapter Two.

20 Frequently cited is Forrest Reid. For an exploration of sexual dissidence in Reid's work, and in that of anthologised Kate O'Brien, Molly Keane and Elizabeth Bowen , see Eibhear Walshe, ed., *Sex, Nation and Dissent in Irish Writing*, Cork University Press, Cork, 1996.

21 Cf. Ailbhe Smyth, 'States of Change', *Feminist Review*, 50, 1995, pp. 24-43.

22 Boland used this phrase again with Niel Sammuells, 'An Underground Poet: Eavan Boland Interviewed', *Irish Studies Review*, 4, 1993, pp. 12-13. Tariq Ali, convener of round table discussion on *The Field Day Anthology*, 'Bright Through the Tears, for *Rear Window*, Channel 4, 7 July 1992.

23 Longley, *The Living Stream*, Introduction.

24 Mary Crowe, 'A Constitution for the New Republic?', *Irish Studies Review*, 1, 1992, pp. 18-19.

25 Seamus Deane, *Civilians and Barbarians*, Field Day Publications, Derry, 1983.

26 Seamus Deane, 'Silence and Eloquence', *The Guardian*, 12 December 1991, p. 23.

27 Deane, 'Silence and Eloquence', p. 23.

28 Edna Longley, 'Belfast Diary', *London Review of Books*, 9 January 1992, p. 2.

13

In Search of Englishness; in Search of Votes

Sophie Breese

Consider a thousand years of British history and what it tells us. The first parliament of the world. The industrial revolution ahead of its time. An empire, the largest the world has ever known. The invention of virtually every scientific device in the modern world. Two world wars in which our country was bled dry, in which two generations perished, but which in its defeat of the most evil force ever let loose by man showed the most sustained example of bravery in human history. Our characteristics? Common sense. Standing up for the underdog. Fiercely independent.

The Rt. Hon., Tony Blair MP[1]

... a buccaneering spirit, gritty resolve, give and take, a conviction that everyone is entitled to the same dignity, curtsey [sic] and esteem because of what they are and not who they are. These are some of the values that we all share; that's what makes us a Nation. Down the centuries that have moulded our democracy; it's not a concept of Government copied right across the world simply because it's the oldest. It's because it's the best that it's copied all across the world. We treasure it and that is why we must hold onto it, the Union, Parliament, our voting system.

The Rt. Hon., John Major MP [2]

In 1927 the travel writer, H.V. Morton, while in Palestine, took a vow that he 'would go home in search of England... through the little lanes of England and the little thatched cottages of England... would lean over little English bridges and lie on English grass watching an English sky'.[3] This image of England, politicized by Stanley Baldwin three years previously in his famous address to the Royal Society of St George ('To me England is the country and the country is England')[4] had become, by the 1920s, a key means of representing the nation. It was a story of a unified country centred around an idyllic rural landscape; a cohesive, empowering and inherently conservative story to be told in the face of domestic and imperial instability following the First World War.

This chapter will suggest that, seventy years on, there has been a return to an appeal to a specific notion of Englishness, one that strongly echoes that which was constructed during the inter-war period. It will go on to consider the political utilization of this story in the run up to the 1997 General Election, exploring in particular the rhetoric of the party political conference speeches given in October 1996 by both Tony Blair and John Major in Blackpool and Bournemouth respectively. If, as will be argued, Englishness has been central to the story traditionally told to the nation by the Conservatives, why have Labour begun to make a claim for this story themselves?

An article by Cosmo Landesman in 1995 in the *Sunday Times*, supported by a telling pastiche (including Pulp's Jarvis Cocker, the Union Jack, Shakespeare, and a still from the recent BBC adaptation of Jane Austen's *Pride and Prejudice*), asked why the English have recently 'become so at ease with their Englishness?'[5] While Landesman provides what he considers to be the evidence to ask such a question (citing, for instance, the current popularity of costume dramas), at no point does he explore his choice of the word 'Englishness', as opposed to 'Britishness', even though his examples of Englishness include the successes of Britlit, Britpop and Britart, homogenizing groups which have tended to exclude women.

This problematic idea of Englishness is in evidence more recently, in *GQ*, the 'Gentleman's Quarterly'. The cover of the December 1996 issue announces itself as 'The Great British Issue' and is draped in red, white and blue.[6] Jarvis Cocker stares out through retro specs, surrounded on both sides by names of all the key players (all male) in contemporary 'Cool Britannia'. The first double page is a black and white advertisement, brandishing the purple label 'Ralph Lauren – Made in England'. Already, before the editorial, there has been a shift, without acknowledgement, from Britain to England. The issue creates a particular unease for a female reader, who discovers that 'while', according to Nicholas Lezard, 'it is the height of rudeness to complain about the women who have shagged us and borne our children, there is something about the British male's attitude which suggests that our women leave something to be desired'.[7] Throughout the magazine a whole series of questions are raised and left unanswered. Why is Scotland only addressed by virtue of it having 'rewritten the publishing map' through *Trainspotting* and thus allowing the production of a series of 'Britlit' books all by English men?[8] Why, apart from the editor's recent encounter with Bill Bryson's *Notes From a Small Island* should there be a 'British Issue' at all?[9]

Although *GQ* appears to posit a transgressive notion of Englishness, particularly in its 'inconisation' of Cocker, who broke various social taboos during the Brit Awards in 1996, there is nevertheless a peculiar sense of retrospection that runs through the magazine. The majority of the photographs used are black and white, the fashion pages celebrate the virtues of 'tweed', and the hair feature depicts the 'traditional haircut' performed by a barber, also captured in black and white.[10] For Landesman, 'Englishness' is even more explicitly located in images from the past. Although he argues that this 'revival' of 'pride and pleasure in English culture' is one that celebrates the contemporary, the entire article is imbued with nostalgia, referring back to the time when 'Englishness conjure[d] up names such as... Elgar and Kipling'.[11]

This last reference takes us back to the so-called halcyon days before the Second World War, a period when a notion of 'Englishness', also nostalgic, was prevalent. Between 1918 to the imposition of printing restrictions at the start of the War, the number of texts with the word 'England' in their title more than doubled.[12] In addition to the occasional novel and history book,[13] these texts, and others celebrating a lost England, ranged from armchair guide books or accounts of travel within England such as M.V. Hughes's *About England* and H.V. Morton's *In Search of England*, cited earlier;[14] observations on the English countryside, often with an explicit educational agenda, such as Harry Batsford's *How to See the Countryside* and Dorothy Hartley's *The Countryman's England*;[15] and anthologies eulogizing the threatened national landscape, such as Adrian Bell's *The Open Air: An Anthology of English Countryside* and even the ostensibly left-wing J.B. Priestley's *The Beauty of Britain*.[16]

Each of these texts, which Harry Batsford called 'country writing' books, sought to construct an idyllic, pastoral, natural picture of England.[17] Their rhetoric was 'normalized' by recourse to history, heritage and traditional literary texts (the number of titles alluding to, for instance, 'this sceptr'd isle' was significant); and their story was presented as indisputable. Take, for example, Adrian Bell's introduction to his anthology of English countryside:

> It is something about a countryman that is like the weather, something that, in a word with him on the commonest subject, gives a vista of generations. The spark of true culture is there, which has fed the language, the music and all the arts of English life.[18]

In this celebration of the countryside, the countryman was *fixed* in the landscape as a medium of true culture. He was not intended to evolve and develop but to remain in his position to allow the more articulate – the more cultured – to transcribe his Englishness. This common belief in an essential character of England was articulated by Ernest Barker in *The Character of England* who wrote that the 'English spirit' could 'give to the national mind, a common content or substance which makes for unity'.[19] Similarly, the mission to diffuse this 'English spirit' was evident from the agenda – 'the Englishness of our business' – of the publishing house, Batsford, which published three out of titles referred to above.[20]

The other factor uniting these texts was use of the English countryside as the *site* of the 'English spirit'; a familiar landscape available for the narration of the national myth. Stephen Daniels has explained that 'national identities are co-ordinated, often largely defined, by "legends and landscapes", by stories of golden ages, enduring traditions, heroic deeds and dramatic destinies located in ancient and promised homelands with hallowed sites and scenery'.[21] Likewise, Alan Howkins has argued that 'what our rural image does is present us with a "real England"' and this is precisely the landscape (with its associated legends) that has become central to today's articulation of Britain's national identity, whereby 'Britain' is simply the more politically correct word for 'England'.[22] It can be seen in Major's reworking of George Orwell's vision of old maids and morning mist through to the advertising industry's use of what the journal *Marketing* termed 'A green and pleasant brand' in which 'Burberry's, Laura Ashley, Wedgwood and Dunhill have shrewdly exploited the specious stereotype of Britain as a giant Merchant/Ivory film set'.[23]

Why is there a need, in contemporary Britain, for such a specific story of our national identity to be articulated? Raphael Samuel suggested some reasons in 1990:

> In recent decades the national question has emerged, or re-emerged, as a storm-centre of British politics, most obviously in relationship to New Commonwealth immigration and settlement and Britain's membership of the EEC [sic]. The civil war in Ulster, now in its 23rd year, the recrudescence of Celtic separatism and the Assembly Movement in Scotland, have put the break up of Britain on the agenda of practical politics. Conversely the 'heritage' industry and the commodification of the national past has contrived to make the idea of 'Englishness' aesthetically and visually appealing at the very moment when with the collapse of industry and the withdrawal from

Empire makes it appear politically and economically bankrupt.[24]

To Samuel's list, I would also add Cosmo Landesman's (reactionary) explanation in terms of a backlash against what he calls 'multiculturalism':

> One important factor was the impact of the Salman Rushdie controversy in the 1980s. It was then that many of the old multicultural certainties started to crack. It was pretty hard to worry about being an English racist with so many Muslims calling for Rushdie's blood. And suddenly all those English values such as tolerance, free-speech and fair play – forgotten in our new-found enthusiasm for multiculturalism – were rediscovered and worth defending.[25]

According to Landesman, the gesturing towards an acceptance that there are many differing identities has begun to problematize the whole concept of a Britain as a nation-state, and with it its essentially '*English* values such as tolerance, free-speech and fair play' [my emphasis].

These 'values' were celebrated in both Blair's and Major's addresses to their parties and the nation during their respective conferences in 1996. For the Conservatives this was nothing new and their appeal to a lost England has been much commented on: from key phrases such as 'Victorian Values' and 'Back to Basics', each evoking a former imagined coherent national community, through to a powerful rhetorical mode which naturalizes their own approach and politicizes the ideology of the opposition. By referring back to previous moments of perceived national glory, the language of the Conservatives has constructed a teleology which has been hard to counter, as John Major's address to the Wembley Rally on the eve of the 1992 election indicates:

> Consider the outcome. The walls of this island fortress that appear so strong, undermined from within, the United Kingdom unified, the bonds that generations of our enemies have fought and failed to break, loosened by ourselves. But that is what is at risk on 9th April.[26]

This speech is deeply allusive. It conjures up not only the familiar 'this England' of Shakespeare's *Richard II* and with it ideas of tradition, unity and natural 'bonds', but also the address made by Margaret Thatcher to the Conservative Party rally at Cheltenham racecourse on 3 July 1982 following the conclusion of the Falklands War:

There were those people who would not admit it – even perhaps some here today – people who would have strenuously denied the suggestion but – in their heart of hearts – they too had their secret fears that it was true: that Britain was no longer the nation that had built an Empire and ruled a quarter of the world. Well, they were wrong. The lesson of the Falklands is that Britain has not changed and that this nation still has those sterling qualities that shine through our history.[27]

In this Thatcher is more explicit than Major, empowering her voters with the *memory* of Britain as the Imperial centre and a linear image of history stretching before and beyond, Britain being the bright shining light within. History is, in Conservative discourse, indisputable, and, according to Kenneth Baker, helps us to understand the present day since the 'Conservatives' respect for tradition and sense of history are not quaint antiquarianism but a recognition that the problems of today are not unique'.[28] As such, events can be understood in terms of incidents in the past. In *The Downing Street Years*, Thatcher wrote:

Political recovery followed in the wake of those early signs of improvement with better poll figures in the Spring of 1982. We were about to find ourselves in the Falklands War but we had already won the second Battle of Britain.[29]

Since the first Battle of Britain had already been allocated a place within the discourse of Englishness by, among others, Winston Churchill, Thatcher had no need to explain herself further.[30] And indeed, Thatcher went as far as to define 'Thatcherism' in terms familiar to readers of inter-war 'country writing' in 1987:

We've been working to restore the political system to bring out all that was best in the British character. That's what we've done. It's called Thatcherism... it's about being worthwhile and honourable. And about the family. And about that something which is really unique and enterprising in the British character – it's about how we built an Empire and how we gave sound administration and sound law to large areas of the world.[31]

It would seem, then, that an appeal to Englishness can be read as deeply conservative – if conservative means a respect for tradition and a fear of change. But it is precisely this linguistic slippage between 'conservative' and 'Conservative' that the Tories have been able to mobilize and renegotiate. The Conservative's use of Englishness is actually 'Janus-faced',[32] allowing a familiar rhetoric to inform the dynamic 'modernizing' aspect of Thatcherism, one that promoted the individual, free-enterprise and the gradual withdrawal of state control. Corner and Harvey have observed that 'through a number of different and sometimes conflicting strategies, it [the New Right] has at once challenged, popularized and commodified the values of a more ancient, patrician and rural Conservatism'.[33] As such the discourse of Englishness was able to appeal to the 'working class' (traditionally Labour Party voters) who became a large proportion of Conservative voters.[34] With practical policies such as the encouragement of Council house tenants to purchase their own property alongside Major's continual attempt to instil a sense of the 'class-less' society, Conservatism became meaningful in tangible and rhetorical terms as 'much to the England of ducal estates as to suburban Basildon'.[35] And in the same way that Englishness in the inter-war period was seen to be 'natural' with alternative stories rendered 'unnatural', contemporary (Conservative) constructions of Englishness exclude other stories of England. How then can an alternative story of England invest itself with any meaningful authority?

During the period of Conservative government between 1979 and 1997, Labour's authority to tell a coherent story of Britain – one which locates Labour as the central historical protagonist – was slowly eroded. As Sara Benton observed as far back as 1989:

> The triumph of Thatcherism in the 1980s was that it offered 'Britain' its story of how it came to be and where it could therefore go. Of course, the story is disputed. But a balkanised Left, unable to tell a story of Britain at all because it disputes the existence of a character called Britain, has found it very hard to counter the Thatcherite version.[36]

Instead Labour told several stories simultaneously; stories in which gender, class, ethnicity, age, employment, union involvement and regionality, rather than the nation, were the loci of identity. Greg Philo argues that the loss of the 1992 General Election could be put down to 'Labour's inability to develop an alternative party consciousness'.[37] But, beyond this, or perhaps as a result of this, Labour's overall incoherency and its avoidance of a totalising discourse had long term detrimental effects, even if the positive intentions to celebrate a multicultural community of voters were in place.

It would appear that this has been recognized by Tony Blair in his bid to offer a *New* Labour, following the death of John Smith in May 1995. As he says in his introduction to *New Britain*:

> People want to be proud of Britain, but they have lost confidence. They want us to be strong, but they sense we are losing an old identity without finding or developing a new one. They know in their hearts we cannot do this by looking back.[38]

Blair has moved so far from the attempt to offer smaller local stories to smaller local communities that he has actually taken on not only a coherent story of Britain but, in doing so, has developed a rhetorical mode which is authorised by precisely that which the Conservatives have traditionally depended on. And while he asserts in the words cited above, that a *new* identity must be found, it is clear that despite his claims, a great deal of 'looking back' has been done.

A close comparison of the speeches of the leaders of the two major parties makes this point very clear. Key tropes in both speeches include the family: Major, for example, offers a brief autobiography of his own family ('I was born in the War, my father was 66, my mother was surprised'), broadens his range to include the 'Tory family' one which he grew up in, and finally embraces the whole country in familial terms ('We have given birth to a whole family of nations around the world').[39] Blair describes himself as 'a father, as a leader, as a member of the human family'.[40] His range is different here to Major's since the family is apparently not hierarchical but all inclusive. But this is countered later on when he too returns to the past, to his own autobiography, rendering family values metonymic of national values:

> When I was growing up, the family was strong, the sense of social responsibility was strong. Crime was low. There was a national ethos and spirit that had won the war and stayed with us in peace.[41]

Historical national moments, as the opening quotes indicated, are given a similar weight. Both leaders refer to the Empire, to the Second World War, even to – more radically – football: Labour's theme was 'we are coming home' and Major offered congratulations to both Scotland and England for the football matches they had won that week. Beyond even this is an assumption of shared national characteristics, a process of homogenization and by extension exclusion. For Major, 'building a welfare system we can afford' is one that 'goes with the *grain* of the British nation'; for Blair the 'outstanding British quality is courage'.[42] There are strong echoes, in the language of both leaders, of those inter-war texts which eulogized Englishness.

What is most significant in Blair's speech is the way he wrestles with notions of tradition and heritage, suggesting that despite their claims, the Conservatives have failed to be honest in their construction of national history:

> And we will be envied throughout the world not just because of our castles and palaces and our glorious history, but because we gave the heritage of hope back to the generations, we turned this country round by the will of the people in unity with the party of the people, and we built the Age of Achievement in our lifetime.[43]

Blair is clearly doing something distinct from Major. The biblical tone, reminiscent of Revelations, signals a transcendence of nationhood even in the very invocation of 'Britain Plc'. In doing so he generates a distinction between common humanity and British nationality, but is able to simultaneously appeal to *both*. While celebrating a revival of a meaningful history he is also making promises for the future. The 'New Age' of 'New Labour' will not be one that ruptures history – for he says 'let us call our nation to its destiny' – rather it is the Tories who have been responsible for a diversion from Britain's destiny; Labour will simply get Britain back on course, they will come home.[44]

However, the choice to articulate the story of Labour and thus the story of the nation in such terms is problematic. For one thing it excludes almost as much as it includes, in its positing of an essential notion of nationhood which has been traditionally characterized by white Anglo-Saxon middle class heterosexual males. The football references act as another means of exclusion: the anthem of the Lightning Seeds – 'Football's coming home' – alluded to by Labour, located 'home' as England, a home symbolized not by the Union Jack, but by the St George's Cross painted on the faces of the English fans. This was particularly noticeable in the Scotland–England match of the Euro' '96 Football Championships where England's victory prompted the xenophobic chants of 'Scotland's going home' directed at the fans of the losing side. Similarly, references to football, like the *GQ* issue discussed earlier, arguably exclude a participation on the part of women in the destiny of the nation. England was presented in such gender terms during the inter-war period, as can be seen in the best-selling 1935 book by Dorothy Hartley, *The Countryman's England*, in which Hartley effaces herself from the title and refers to those who experience England in the masculine throughout. The more heterogeneous approaches of old Labour, at least within the last 10 years, may or may not be responsible for their loss of the last few elections but the shift, in rhetoric if not in party policy, is quite spectacular.

There are, however, two positive ways of reading Blair's speech. The first is a claim for the original notions of patriotism, developed by the radicals towards the end of the eighteenth century, partly in response to the French Revolution. The constant reference to Labour being the 'people's party' cues this in. A further appeal to patriotism is made manifest in the imagery now associated with New Labour. The higher profile red rose is one example, with its associations of St George's Day: once again 'England' comes to signal 'Britain', despite the careful use of the word 'Britain' by Blair. Similarly, the bulldog made an appearance as Labour's mascot in party political broadcasts during the election campaign, which, as Robin Young pointed out, was used at least twice by the Conservatives during the 1980s.[45] Once again, Labour are claiming back recently 'Tory-fied' symbols; the historical rupture that Labour are seeking to fix is therefore even larger than might first appear – one of nearly two hundred years.

A second positive way of reading Blair's speech relates closely to the above. As I have argued, over eighteen years the Conservatives rendered any alternative accounts of history (and with that is included a sense of future destiny) as transgressive: the constant recourse to nature and the implicitly conservative construction of Englishness in the inter-war period normalizes the Conservative version of England. Labour appear to have decided that the ideological codes of the Conservative Party are too powerful, too pervasive, to deconstruct. Instead, by signalling a history, heritage and tradition which Labour belongs to, an alternative equally authoritative story could be posited. On 1 May 1997, the voting public were presented with two competing stories with similar themes; the difference between the parties rested (arguably) in policy, not rhetoric.

On the day after the 1997 General Election, in which the Labour Party secured an astounding victory over the Conservatives, Malcolm Bradbury assured the readers of the *Daily Mail*, in a tone reminiscent of H.V. Morton, that

> whatever [their] political persuasion, on one thing everyone must agree: yesterday [1 May], as the sun shone, was a day of exceptional beauty in Britain. The colours acquired a green and pastel freshness that would be hard to match anywhere in the world.[46]

It was a day when the nation was united in the shared act of voting, a day in which Britain was restored to its once infamous supremacy – if only through its natural, rural, beauty. It was a day that would have made H.V. Morton proud.

The Author

Sophie Breese is completing her doctoral thesis on national identity and the contemporary British novel, at St Edmund Hall, Oxford. Forthcoming publications include work on Jane Austen and the heritage industry, and two articles in *Post-War Literatures in English: a Lexicon of Contemporary Authors*. She is also writing her first novel, set in Greece.

References

1   Rt. Hon., Tony Blair MP, Leader of the Labour Party, Speech, Labour Party Annual Conference, Blackpool, 1 October 1996.
2   The Rt. Hon., John Major MP, Prime Minister and Leader of the Conservative Party, Speech, Conservative Party Annual Conference, Bournemouth, 11 October 1996.
3   H.V. Morton, *In Search of England*, London: Methuen and Co., 1927, p. 2.
4   Stanley Baldwin, 'England', in W.L. Hanchart, ed., *England is Here: Selected Speeches and Writings of the Prime Ministers of England 1721–1943*, Bodley Head, London, 1943, p. 227.
5   Cosmo Landesman, 'Pride without the Prejudice', *Sunday Times,* 'Culture', 5 Nov. 1996, p. 8.
6   *GQ*, December 1996.
7   Nicholas Lezard, 'In praise of British Women', *GQ*, p. 173.
8   John Williams, 'Write Fantastic', *GQ*, pp. 94–96.
9   Angus MacKinnon, 'Notes from a Small Desk', *GQ*, p. 23.
10   'Less is more', *GQ*, pp. 242–43; John Morgan, 'At the cutting edge', *GQ*, p. 259.
11   Landesman, 'Pride without the Prejudice', 1996.
12   *Catalogue of English Printed Books*, London, 1914–1951.
13   See, for instance, A.L. Morton, *A People's History of England*, Gollancz, London, 1938; Graham Greene, *England Made Me*, Heinemann, London, 1935.
14   M.V. Hughes, *About England*, J.M. Dent and Sons Ltd., London, 1928; Morton, *In Search of England*.
15   Harry Batsford, *How to See the Countryside*, Batsford, London, 1940; Dorothy Hartley, *The Countryman's England*, Batsford, London, 1935.
16   Adrian Bell, ed., *The Open Air: An Anthology of English Countryside*, Faber

and Faber, London, 1936; and J.B. Priestley, ed., *The Beauty of Britain*, Batsford, London, 1935.

17 Batsford, *How to See the Countryside*, p. 69.

18 Bell, *The Open Air*, p. 9.

19 Ernest Barker, *The Character of England*, Clarendon Press, Oxford, 1947, p. 201.

20 Hector Bolitho, ed., *A Batsford Century: The Record of a Hundred Years of Publishing and Bookselling 1843–1943*, Batsford, London, 1943, p. 55.

21 Stephen Daniels, *Fields of Vision: Landscape Imagery and National Identity in England and the United States*, Polity Press, Cambridge, 1993, p. 5.

22 Alun Howkins, 'The Discovery of Rural England', in Robert Colls and Philip Dodd, eds., *Englishness, Politics and Culture 1880–1920*, Croom Helm, London, 1986, p. 62. For a further analysis of the slip between 'England' and 'Britain' see David Morley, 'Postmodernism: The Highest Stage of Cultural Imperialism', in Mark Perryman, *Altered States: Postmodernism, Politics and Culture*, Lawrence and Wishart, London, 1994, pp. 133–56: 'In that slide, from the "British" to the "English", we also see a process in which not only is Britain equated with England, but the actuality of Britain as a modern industrial country is denied, and the image of English identity is, again and again, a *rural* image, of a country in the imaginary landscape of "Constable country"'. Morley, p. 147.

23 Robert Gray, 'A green and pleasant brand', *Marketing*, 20 July 1995, p. 23.

24 Raphael Samuel, 'Introduction. History, the Nation and the Schools', *History Workshop Journal*, vol. 30, Autumn 1990, p. 77.

25 Landesman, 'Pride without the Prejudice', 1996.

26 Cited in Kenneth Baker, *The Faber Book of Conservatism*, Faber & Faber, London, 1993, p. 37.

27 Cited in Anthony Barnett, *Iron Britannia*, Allison and Busby, London, 1982, p. 150.

28 Baker, *Conservatism*, pp. xix–xx.

29 Margaret Thatcher, *The Downing Street Years*, Harper Collins, London, 1993, p. 155.

30 '[I]t is interesting to note the ways in which Churchill deploys a repertoire of traditional iconography associated with the idea of Englishness – the little man who stands up to the big bully, the idea of "our island home" and the quasi-religious equation of England with the will of God and a manifest destiny.' Judy Giles and Tim Middleton, *Writing Englishness: An Introductory Source Book*, Routledge, London, 1995, p. 112.

31 Margaret Thatcher in an interview with Rodney Tyler, *Campaign: The Selling of the Prime Minister*, Grafton Books, London, 1987, p. 251, quoted in Martin Holmes, *Thatcherism: Scope and Limits, 1983–87*, Macmillan Press, London, 1989, p. 6.

32 Stuart Hall, 'The Question of Cultural Identity', in Stuart Hall, David Held, and Tony McGrew, eds., *Modernity and its Futures*, Polity Press in

Association with the Open University, Cambridge, 1992, p. 295.

33   J. Corner and S. Harvey, eds., *Enterprise and Heritage: Cross Currents of National Culture*, Routledge, London, 1991, p. 14.

34   See Andrew Gamble, 'Loves Labour Lost', in Perryman, *Altered States*, pp. 23–45 for a discussion of changing voting patterns in the 1992 general election.

35   Will Hutton, *The State We're In*, Cape, London, 1995, p. 27.

36   Sarah Benton, 'National Anthems', *New Statesman and Society*, 9 June 1989, p. 22.

37   Greg Philo, 'Politics, Media and Public Belief', in Perryman, *Altered States*, p. 47.

38   Tony Blair, *New Britain: My Vision of a Young Country*, Fourth Estate, London, 1996, p. ix.

39   Major, 11 Oct. 1996.

40   Blair, 1 Oct. 1996.

41   Blair, 1 Oct. 1996.

42   Major, 11 Oct. 1996; Blair, 1 Oct. 1996.

43   Blair, 1 Oct. 1996.

44   Blair, 1 Oct. 1996.

45   Robin Young, 'Blair may find bulldog symbol bites the hand that feeds it', *Times*, 15 April 1997, p. 7.

46   Malcolm Bradbury, 'The darling buds of May', *Daily Mail*, 2 May 1997, p. 12.

14

Stewardship, Sanctimony and Selfishness – A Heritage Paradox

David Lowenthal

A famously sacred cow, heritage none the less needs frequent culling for lunacy. The gulf between good heritage intentions and malign behaviour seems abysmal. Why is so saintly a realm riven with squabbles over possession and control?

It is often taken for granted that heritage stewards are unselfish, disinterested guardians dedicated to protecting and exhibiting the sites and objects in their care. Yet self-serving motives suffuse the whole heritage enterprise. Heritage is mainly sought and treasured as our *own*; we strive to keep it out of the clutches of others we suspect, often with good reason, of aiming to steal it or to spoil it. Indeed, stewardship requires selfishness. The good steward is one who cares intensely about what is in his custody; as in marriage, true devotion *means* excluding others. Whether on behalf of individuals or of empires, stewardship is intrinsically possessive.

But not for one's own sake. The traditional steward is not an owner but an agent, a keeper for another – the guardian of sacred mysteries, the manager of a landed estate. The steward keeps vigil for someone else. For some *one*, not *every*one else – a jealous God against His enemies, a landlord against poachers, a king against rival nobles, a nation against foreign foes. Only those pledged to their clients' exclusive cause can be relied on as stewards. An heir must be sure his trustee acts solely on his behalf, a nation that implacable custodians will yield no part of the domain. Generosity and charity may be laudable traits, but in our chosen stewards they spell betrayal if not treason. Stewards must be fierce watchdogs, not tame poodles.

Dog-in-the-manger zealotry is thus a hallmark of national heritage. Seeing Constable paintings overseas, a British connoisseur exclaims: 'Heritage never means more to us than when we see it inherited by someone else'. Only when the English spoke of shipping ruined Norman abbeys across the Channel did the French rescue them from neglect; only when the Victoria and Albert Museum bought a seventeenth-century Dutch church fitting did the Dutch rally round their legacy; only when Americans were about to ship Tattershall Castle overseas did Parliament act to protect Britain's built heritage.[1] Outrage at J. P. Morgan's transatlantic shipment of a staircase from the Casa de Miranda in Burgos prodded the Spanish into heritage pride.[2] The Tower of London sold off two Hanoverian state crowns in 1836; for decades no one knew or cared where they were. But in 1995 word that this 'purest national heritage of priceless importance' might be sold abroad roused huge dismay.[3] A Brunei prince was found to 'rescue' the crowns for Britain.

Medieval Christendom's most treasured relics were stolen ones; the act of theft attested to their transcendent value. To be sold or given away suggested that a relic had not been prized enough to keep; in order to enhance the fame of their treasures, some even pretended to have stolen what they had in fact bought.[4] Displays of pillaged booty legitimate many a regime. Looted European treasure boosted the egos of Ottoman sultans; Napoleon's conquests of Italy and Egypt culminated in stripping them of their finest works of art and antiquity, which were hauled off to Paris in triumphal pomp.

Heritage that conquerors cannot appropriate is apt to be expunged. As the Romans had done with Carthage, so did the Nazis obliterate old Warsaw as a font of Polish pride. The present decade has seen the archival, archaeological and architectural legacies of Croatia, Bosnia, Rwanda and Rumania deliberately destroyed. As a heritage too eclectic to suit the fancy of Muslim fanatics, almost everything in Afghanistan's National Museum has since 1980 been stolen, sold or smashed.[5]

Heritage rivalry is legion. Ongoing disputes over the Elgin Marbles and the Stone of Scone are the rule, not the exception. Jerusalem is indispensably and indissolubly hybrid, yet Jews, Muslims and Christians heatedly dispute tunnel access to the Wailing Wall and the Via Dolorosa near the Sacred Mount. French potholers dispute government takeover of Stone Age cave paintings in the Ardèche, on a site local peasants also claim as 'the land of our ancestors' for six centuries; potholers and peasants are both bent on keeping some of the fruits of tourism for themselves.[6]

Corporate avarice threatens the American national legacy. A full-page news advertisement on 1 April 1996 advised readers that the fast-food chain Taco Bell had bought sole rights to Philadelphia's Liberty Bell, henceforth to be known as the 'Taco Liberty Bell', though it would 'still be accessible to the American public'. Irate callers jammed National Park Service lines until Taco 'explained' this was an April Fool's joke. But Taco did in fact pay $50,000 for an exclusive parks' facilities franchise – part of a heritage sell-off that included a Coca-Cola concession.[7] Nor has British heritage stayed free from corporate sponsorship. It is hardly surprising to find a nation that privatizes so many national assets likewise marketing its past. British Airways and Walker's Crisps, among other firms, have sponsored signs for street names in some English towns; plans are mooted for the management of Stonehenge under the aegis of Madame Tussaud's.

Only on rare occasions, notably when some beloved national icon is under threat, is public heritage safeguarded from exploitation by personal and commercial interests. Thus a federal Eagle Morgue near Denver, Colorado, protects America's feathered national heritage from Native American predators. In cold storage are hundreds of carcasses of America's endangered national bird, the bald eagle. Twenty years ago, when extinction loomed, eaglet restocking was launched with corporate support. Bald eagle numbers have since soared, but the bird remains at risk owing to burgeoning tribal use and the clandestine collectors' market – a feathered war bonnet can fetch up to $20,000. From the National Eagle Repository, bald and golden eagles hit by cars or downed by electric power lines are sent, packed in five pounds of dry ice, to bona fide customers who have filed a four-page Native American Religious Purposes Permit Application and Shipping Request. But tribal religious resurgence brings three times more requests than there are dead birds; the usual waiting time is now two and a half years. And eagle feathers are needed for initiation and burial rites at short notice.[8]

Heritage angst in Britain now typically focuses on relics held nationally sacred. Patriotic alarm bells rang with the imminent sale of Thomas à Becket's casket to the Getty Museum in Los Angeles. 'Six days from now', thundered a leader in *The Times*, 'this treasure could be lost to the nation.' Yet to a columnist in the same newspaper, Simon Jenkins, the claim of national talisman seemed sheer hypocrisy. 'The casket is not British. The French made it. It attracted no patriotic hordes at the British Museum, where it had been on loan for the past fifteen years.' Yet such was the outcry that the sale was stopped, export rules bent, the casket 'saved for the nation'.[9]

But was it? Measures to save heritage for the public often put it back in private hands; 'for the nation' is all too likely to mean 'on the walls of some country house in Norfolk', seen by only a small fraction of those who could view it in California.[10] (Britain's stewards sometimes seem to prefer foreign products to foreign people: as a cartoon blimp reacts to the headline 'Velasquez Set to Leave Country', "Why did we let the foreigners in here in the first place!") But the tendency to cling to whatever one holds against all claimants, exemplified here in the Elgin Marbles, is anything but uniquely British; 'no' is the habitual response to any request even to share a heritage, as in Spain's recent refusal to lend Picasso's *Guernica* to France.

This is where sanctimony comes in. We become distressed that heritage watch-dogs so often become dogs-in-the-manger because we fail, in my view, to distinguish between venality and self-concern. The term 'selfish' properly applies only to the former. It was first used in the 1640s, when Archbishop John Williams, striving to placate King and Parliament, was besieged in London by Presbyterians bent on root-and-branch reform. His hagiographer relates that Williams reasoned so sweetly the Presbyterians begged him to become their own agent – 'they would buy him, if his Faith had been saleable, at any price, [until] they saw he was not Selfish . . . (a word of their own devising)'.[11] In short, selfishness implied personal corruption, not zealous defence of a cause or a principle, even if undertaken on behalf of oneself or one's family or state. By the same token, those who nowadays immortalize themselves in museum benefactions and academic chairs, like men who formerly endowed churches to save their souls, are at once generous *and* self-concerned.

Unable to divest self-concern from selfishness, heritage stewards eschew the latter for three reasons: it is morally wrong; it is all too likely to boomerang; and it cripples global heritage goals seen as more and more desirable, even essential. I discuss each of these in turn.

First, selfishness is unprincipled; it links us with the covetous and the miserly. Avid accumulators of art or antiquities commodify what should be sacred and debase people into things. Confucian precept in ancient China rebuked the possessive: to amass collections demeaned both object and owner. In a classic caveat, a twelfth-century imperial official tells his wife what to do with his collection as Mongol invasion looms. 'Abandon the household goods first, then the clothes, then the books and scrolls, then the old bronzes – but carry the sacrificial vessels for the ancestral temple yourself; live or die with them; don't give *them* up.'[12] So she learned her own place in the collection: to die gloriously with the sacrificial vessels. Modern collectors are similarly pilloried, notably by archaeologists, as anal-retentive monsters of selfish disregard for all others.[13]

Secondly, selfishness is often self-defeating; rather than promoting it is often a deterrent to stewardship. Buildings listed as historic are allowed to decay or are even razed by their owners on the eve of being legally 'saved' from development. Legacies are often destroyed to prevent anyone else from getting them. New England town chroniclers were foiled by a local hoarder who 'got all the oldest newspapers I could find, took down what I wanted and then burned them. It's all mine now. The history of the Town of Bethel is my own personal business.'[14] The possessor of a unique *incunabulum* is dismayed when a second copy turns up; he at once buys it and then burns it – so his will still be the *only* copy. Ian Fleming's billionaire *Goldfinger* (1959) sought to steal the gold in Fort Knox not to keep but to irradiate it, making his own hoard more valuable by reducing the world supply.[15]

Squabbling over heritage tends to spoil its context and integrity for all claimants. In the centuries-old dispute between England and Scotland, the Stone of Scone was stolen from Westminster by Scottish Nationalists who copied it before returning it, so that no one now knows for sure which is the 'real' Stone; in 1996 it was sundered from its accompanying Coronation chair to be 'returned' to Scotland.[16] Schubert's brother, after the composer's death, snipped his music scores into tiny pieces, giving favourite pupils a few bars each. Rivalry may result in some treasures being withdrawn from view entirely. Forbidden to export a Lucian Freud painting she had bought at auction, an American has locked it away in a London bank vault. 'If Britain's export laws could stop her hanging it in her collection, she would stop Britain's public galleries hanging it in theirs.'[17]

Some legacies are destroyed to save them from abuse. Siegfried Lenz's novel *The Heritage* depicts a Masurian folk art museum subverted by chauvinists, first Russian, then German, then Polish. In the end the despairing curator sets fire to the lot, to 'bring the collected witnesses to the past into a final and irrevocable safety from which they could never again be exploited for this cause or that.' This is no mere literary trope; millions of grave goods returned to Australian aboriginal and Amerindian tribes have been 'purified' by being burnt or reburied.[18]

Thirdly, selfishness stymies global heritage crusades now seen as justified by social equity and by environmental necessity.[19] In the past, heritage was restricted to princes and prelates, merchants and magnates; others had to be content with a legacy of an after-life. The nineteenth and twentieth centuries democratized heritage. The poor inherited few personal goods but increasingly shared national legacies. The end of empire has made heritage a global right. Third-World demands for the return of cultural property, tribal and indigenous demands to restore sacred goods and sites, are accepted in principle, at times even in practise. In the heyday of imperialism, the notion of global heritage was often deployed to rationalize or excuse the aggrandizement of tribal and colonial cultural goods by Western heritage stewards; the great bulk of global heritage still remains in Western collections. But more and more the human global heritage means just that: everyone is entitled to it.

Not only is heritage now seen as a global right, it becomes ever more global in character. When people were fewer and less mobile, cultures were more isolated, heritage diffusion slow and limited; modern communications make such diffusion swift and pervasive. Global heritage is often decried as blandly uniform or spiritually vacuous. But it is also valued for spreading cultures – the arts and skills of classical Greece, of Confucian China, of Enlightenment Europe and of Western science that, whatever its anxious corollaries, has doubled or trebled life-spans and freed millions from incessant toil.

Beyond dispute is the global reach of environmental heritage. The interdependence of the whole world on the legacy of nature is a newly realized but immensely potent concern. Unlike most of our precursors, we have begun to view the living globe as a common resource requiring communal custody. Fresh water and fossil fuels, rain forests and gene pools are seen as legacies common to all – and needing all our care. Even more than culture, nature attracts concerted protection. Antarctica is a reserved continent, global outrage rescued Tasmania's temperate rain forest, global skills and resources combat marine pollution. Few now feel no concern about nuclear decay, global warming, ozone depletion, species loss, eco-diversity.

Yet these and other global agenda time and again succumb to narrow partisan ends. New Zealand museums where Maoris now mount their own displays are assailed by non-Maoris and by Maori women banned from exhibits sacred to Maori men. Aboriginal custodians of Uluru (Ayers Rock) in Australia bar tourists from much of this sacred site. Needs for privacy and secrecy may well justify excluding outsiders. But to proclaim a global heritage cause often inflames local and tribal possessiveness. The disinherited mistrust global pieties that may still mask acquisitive avarice or neocolonial hegemonic bias, consciously or unconsciously pursued. Hence Third-World folk curtail outsider intrusion, denouncing Western fossil hunters, archaeologists and seekers of rare plants and human genes as predators.

The restitution crusade makes states more, not less, retentive. Ex-colonial states that have endured actual or fancied deprivation mistake restitution as a panacea. And Western museums fearing wholesale loss speak of transcendent obligations to conserve and study a dwindling global heritage. Heritage-rich lands ever more jealously cling to their patrimony, forbidding all exports. The less such diktats can be enforced, the more stridently they are voiced.

Every effort to curb private greed for global good aggravates chauvinism. Just as minorities claim sole rights to ritual sites and objects, so each state struts as the sole true steward of its heritage – especially if others contest their claim. As with martyrs' bodies and saints' relics in medieval times, heritage hoarding inflates market demand and promotes looting and smuggling. Classical sites are ransacked, Mayan temples sawn apart to evade export bans. The environment fares no better: Freon, a coolant used in refrigerators but banned from manufacture in the United States to protect the ozone layer, is now smuggled in from Mexico, more lucrative – and deadly – than cocaine.[20]

The best-known example of a heritage uneasily shared between its native begetters and the global community is that of classical Greece. I have elsewhere shown how Greek pride and anxiety alike are bound up in the appreciative purloining of Greek tradition by the rest of the world, leaving modern Greece at once famed and deprived.[21] Global fame inflates Greek pride in the classical legacy but makes it less their own. 'We're glad you all admire our heritage', they say; 'now please give it back.' The Greek story is unique in its antiquity and in the global reach of its consequences. But other legacies are similarly buffeted back and forth among global, national and ethnic claimants.

I conclude with an episode of heritage rivalry unmatched for its complex marriage of stewardship and sanctimony. The Tutankhamen find in 1922 dazzled the world and pitted private and imperial aims against national aspirations at the dawn of Egyptian independence. Archaeologist Howard Carter was the archetype of both personal selfishness and Western arrogance. He loved 'the great days of excavating, [when] anything to which a fancy was taken, from a scarab to an obelisk, was just appropriated, and if there was a difference with a brother excavator, one just laid for him with a gun.'[22] Carter's insistence that he (and his curse-laden patron Lord Carnarvon) 'owned' Tut's tomb stiffened Egyptian resolve to keep it all in Cairo. Western experts strove to distribute the treasure among museums best equipped to look after what, they said, 'belonged not to Egypt alone but to the entire world'. Offended Egyptians rebuffed them. The Tut excavation ended one chapter of cultural imperialism: after Carter, the spoils of archaeology ceased to be automatically Western.

But a half century later, as Melani McAlister has shown,[23] King Tut's triumphal tour through the United States revived Western hegemony cloaked as global heritage. Ostensibly Egypt's gift to America's bicentenary, Tut's three-month visit in fact helped recoup American global stewardship after OPEC's Mideast oil squeeze. The Tut tour was vital to America's Mideast stance. President Nixon warned its major-domo, Metropolitan Museum head Thomas Hoving, that the tour's failure would 'disturb' the government – that is, cost the Met federal grants. Under Hoving, Tut toured the states not as dynastic history but as universal art 'too ennobling and precious to belong to any one people (Arabs) or nation (Egypt)'. Here was 'the common heritage of mankind', owned and operated by the United States in the whole world's interest.

The mania for Tut's gold regalia mirrored obsession with Mideast oil ('black gold'). Indeed, 'the common heritage of mankind' was first a phrase coined in the journal *Foreign Affairs* to refer to Mideast oil. Global oil, like global art, must serve both producers and importers (collectors). Like art, oil needed Western, notably American, know-how. *Our* activity gave *their* resource its value; without Western oil users, Arabs would still be poor desert sheiks; without Western art know-how, Tut would have stayed unsung, underground. Commandeering Tut as universal art stood for regaining control of world oil.

This analogy was undermined, not by Egypt or Arab sheiks, but by Afro-Americans, who highjacked Tut as a symbol of their own heritage. In line with current Afrocentric myths, blacks claimed Tut for themselves. Tut was Egyptian; Egypt was African; Tut was black. When the show came to Los Angeles, the city council under black mayor Tom Bradley made February 12 1978, 'King Tut Day':

> Whereas, each of the rulers of the 28th dynasty was either black, 'negroid', or of black ancestry; and Whereas it is particularly important to focus on positive black male images during Black History Month to instill self-esteem; the Council declares King Tut Day for the increased cultural and historical heritage which has enriched our black community.

Tut was *their* history, not *every*one's art. When museum gurus and art critics sought to reclaim Tut as a universal emblem, blacks denounced this as élite 'whitening'. King Tut had become as integral to black American roots as was Alex Haley's West African *griot* Kunta Kinte.

Steve Martin's comic rendition of King Tut in *Saturday Night Live* signalled further postmodern subversion. Tut now parodied mainstream appropriation of black culture, 'the Blues Brothers [posing as] white guys pretending to be black guys making fun of white guys who pretend to be black guys'. Finally a feminist T-shirt warned all males, black and white, to 'Keep Your Hands Off My Tuts'. What had been sullied as common global heritage was restored first to ethnic and then to inviolable private possession.

Selfishness is crucial to identity – and to cherished difference. We must keep ourselves to ourselves, or we cease to be ourselves. But to cosset our own heritage, need we keep the world so much at bay? Unless we welcome it in we become smug and sterile. While most heritage is private, it is also hybrid in origin. None of it was ever purely native or wholly endemic; and today every heritage is utterly commingled. Purity is a chimera; we are all creoles. Acclaiming the creative commingling of Caribbean cultures, Nobel laureate Derek Walcott refutes purists who despise bricolage as rootless, mongrelized, fragmented.

Break a vase, and the love that reassembles the fragments is stronger than that love which took its symmetry for granted when it was whole. It is such a love that reassembles our African and Asiatic fragments, the cracked heirloom whose restoration shows its white scars. This shipwreck of fragments, these echoes, these shards of a huge tribal vocabulary, these partially remembered customs are not decayed but strong [in the polyglot babel of cities such as Port of Spain].[24]

Stewards should study how sharing can strengthen heritage. The Methodist chapel where Margaret Thatcher's father once preached was dismantled and shipped from Leicestershire to Kansas. Melton Mowbray's planning stewards were at first aghast. But in Sproxton the abandoned chapel had been mouldering; in Baldwin City it is restored to eloquence. A stained glass window above the vestibule carries John Coy's verse commemorating the founder's daughter Mary:

For thou must share if thou wouldst keep
That good thing from above
Ceasing to share we cease to have
Such is the law of love.[25]

A statecraft for sharing calls for law as well as love.

The Author

David Lowenthal is Emeritus Professor of Geography at University College, London. His books include *The Past is a Foreign Country* (1985) and *The Heritage Crusade and the Spoils of History* (1997). He is currently revising his biography of the nineteenth-century American diplomat and polymath George Perkins Marsh (first published in 1958).

References

1   David Lowenthal, *The Past Is a Foreign Country*, Cambridge University Press, Cambridge, 1985, p. 394; on Tattershall Castle, Peter Mandler, *The Fall and Rise of the Stately Home*, Yale University Press, New Haven, pp. 184-88.

2   *New York Times* (1910) quoted in Neil Harris, 'Collective possession: J. Pierpont Morgan and the American imagination', in his *Cultural Excursions*, University of Chicago Press, Chicago, 1990, p. 274.

3   Dalya Alberge, 'Kings' crowns fall into private hands', *The Times*, 4 December 1995.

4   Patrick J. Geary, *Furta Sacra: Thefts of Relics in the Central Middle Ages*, rev. ed., Princeton University Press, Princeton, NJ, 1990, pp. 7-14.

5   Christopher Thomas, 'Lost forever: a nation's heritage looted by its own people', *The Times*, 22 October 1996.

6   Ben Macintyre, 'Potholers lay claim to cave art', *The Times*, 15 November 1996; Marlise Simons, 'Red tape still sealing cave with ancient art', *International Herald Tribune*, 10 December 1996.

7   'Taco Bell buys the Liberty Bell', *New York Times*, 1 April 1996, p. A5; Paul Fahri, 'For whom the Taco Bells toll?', *International Herald Tribune*, 3 April 1996.

8   James Brooke, '"Eagle Morgue" near Denver slowly keeps Indian tribes in fine feather', *International Herald Tribune*, 26 November 1996.

9   *The Times* leader, 29 June 1996; Simon Jenkins, 'Great art knows no borders', *The Times*, 29 June 1996.

10 Quentin Letts, 'Getty boss attacks "bent" British rules', *The Times*, 29 October 1996. One correspondent, however, averred the casket would be safer in Norfolk than in a Los Angeles suburb at risk of forest fire and the earth tremors of the San Andreas fault (Claus Bulow, 'Getty complaint', *The Times*, 5 November 1996).

11 John Hacket, *Srinia Reserata: a Memorial offer'd to the Great Deservings of John Williams, D.D.*, London, 1692, p. 144.

12 Pierre Ryckmans, *The Chinese Attitude towards the Past*, Australian National University, Canberra, 1986, pp. 7-9.

13 I discuss such issues in my *The Heritage Crusade and the Spoils of History*, Viking, London, 1997, pp. 39-43, 245-47.

14 David Lowenthal, 'The bicentennial landscape', *Geographical Review*, vol. 67, 1977, p. 265.

15 Michael O'Malley, 'Fort Knox', in Jean Kempf, *Lieux de mémoire en Etats-Unis*, p. 79.

16 Paul Binski, 'Even more English than Scottish', *Spectator*, 13 July 1996, pp. 11-16.

17 Quoted in Dalya Alberge, 'Buyer frustrates art export laws', *The Times*, 5 March 1996.

18 Siegfried Lenz, *The Heritage*, Hill and Wang, New York, 1981, p. 458.

19 The final chapter in my *Heritage Crusade* deals with these issues in another context.

20 Carey Goldberg, 'Lucrative new contraband', *International Herald Tribune*, 11 November 1996.

21 David Lowenthal, 'Classical antiquities as national and global heritage', *Antiquity*, vol. 62, 1988, pp. 726-735.

22 Brian M. Fagan, *The Rape of the Nile*, Macdonald and Jane's, London, 1977, pp. 92-3.

23 '"Common heritage of mankind": race, nation, and masculinity in the King Tut exhibit', *Representations*, vol. 54, 1996, pp. 80-103.

24 Derek Walcott, *The Antilles: Fragments of Epic Memory*, Faber & Faber, London, 1993, p. 9.

25 James Bone, 'Final resting place', *The Times Magazine*, 26 October 1996, pp. 16-18.

179

THE PROFESSIONAL PAST

15

Sir Charles Peers and After

From Frozen Monuments to Fluid Landscapes

Keith Emerick

There is a great distinction between buildings which are still occupied and buildings which are ruins. Buildings which are in use are still adding to their history; they are alive. Buildings which are in ruin are dead; their history is ended. There is all the difference in the world in their treatment. When a building is a ruin, you must do your best to preserve all that is left of it by every means in your power.[1]

Modern history is separated from ancient by no change of nature, but only by an infinite gradation; the links of the chain are all there, and what was of concern to our forefathers is still of concern to us.[2]

These two comments were made by the same man: Sir Charles Peers, Chief Inspector of Ancient Monuments from 1910 to 1933. He was the second person to hold the post, but was the first Chief Inspector who had to deal with the consolidation of medieval buildings; hitherto the majority of protected ancient monuments were prehistoric features. Before Sir Charles Peers' tenure of office it had been assumed that the repair of medieval buildings would be too expensive an undertaking for the State, quite apart from the frequently made suggestion that State control and protection of medieval buildings was an unwarranted intrusion into the realm of private ownership.[3] Most of our State managed monuments bear his stamp: cleared of all post-medieval deposits, modern accretions, complemented by billiard table lawns and clear building plans. 'Conserve as Found' or 'Treat as Found' was the standard refrain for this period, but this belied the often intense level of structural intervention taken to stabilise the fabric – much of which is invisible to the trained let alone untrained eye. This style became part of the vocabulary of ancient monument presentation; as Ministry of Works practitioners were seconded to different parts of the Empire so one could see examples of the same style from the Middle East Protectorates to India.

In the north of England the treatment of Rievaulx and Whitby Abbeys typified the approach taken by Charles Peers and the Ministry. Rievaulx passed into State care in 1917, and consolidation work commenced almost immediately. With the conclusion of the First World War, work began in earnest: huge mounds of debris were removed from the interior of the building along with large quantities of architectural fragments and structural elements. Many of these pieces were found in the positions where they had lain since the Dissolution, but the method adopted by Peers precluded their re-erection, on the grounds that such reconstruction would be far too speculative.

A post-medieval farmhouse and barns lay across the ecclesiastic east part of the site (Rievaulx is not set out east-west owing to the lack of space): the farmhouse was removed, but the barns remain as they lay outside the area of prime importance. Unfortunately, the clearance at Rievaulx was not conducted in an archaeological manner, although in some instances on some sites, excavation did follow clearance, as at Whitby Abbey, where the excavation of the Anglo-Saxon deposits to the north of the Abbey uncovered the remains of buildings identified as monastic cells.[4]

The approach adopted by Peers presented the monument, and the monument alone, to the public. The drive was to present clear building plans; 'Creative it is not, but rather re-creative...An understanding of what has been is necessary, but imagination must be kept in bounds and not translated into material: repair and not restoration is the essence of the matter'.[5] Figures 1, a and b, have become classic images in the literature of conservation, showing Rievaulx before clearance, circa 1919 and immediately on completion.

Although the finished product bore the same stamp, the process by which it arrived varied from site to site, as was considered necessary. Wall tops were unpicked and the core work replaced with cement and steel; vertical fractures were taken apart, the core excavated out and repacked with cement and horizontally laid rail tracks to stitch the two wall faces together and the face stone replaced in exactly the same position, showing the same fracture. Whole arcades and piers were supported with brick, dismantled and the piers rebuilt around reinforced steel and concrete stanchions (as happened at Furness and Tintern).[6] Earlier, visible repairs were unpicked, all within the 'treat as found' practice. Figure 2, a and b, shows Whitby Abbey before clearance and consolidation (a) and as it appears today (b). Amongst a range of alterations one can note that the supports to the Triforium arcade have been removed and the detail at the top of the windows in the east end has been altered, but what is most striking is the change in ground levels.

Figure 1(a): Rievaulx Abbey from the west end, circa 1919, before clearance.
(Alan East)

Figure 1(b): Rievaulx Abbey from the west end, immediately after completion.
(English Heritage)

Figure 2(a): Whitby Abbey from the south, before clearance.
(Alan East)

Figure 2(b): Whitby Abbey from the south, as it appears today.
(Keith Emerick)

This approach can be understood as something of a reaction to the worst excesses of the re-ordering work undertaken in the preceding century, when architects throughout Europe – with unbounded imagination – sought to give churches, abbeys and castles a stylistic completeness they probably never displayed. With the best intentions therefore, Peers froze time and place.

Today we understand that we create our own past: did Peers? In a way he did: when giving a reply to a question about the rights and wrongs of placing damp course treatments in ancient monuments he said: 'As to damp courses, I took the precaution to say that I did not expect that the repairs we make can be considered permanent.'[7] He knew that he or his successors would have to revisit monuments, but perhaps failed to see that any intervention in fabric would mean that the team of Inspector, Architect and Technician would be faced with choices: leave, repair, replace or sacrifice. Peers faced choices but perhaps did not see them as such. At Scarborough Castle he chose to remove a mid eighteenth-century brick barrack block to reveal the plan of a thirteenth-century Hall. This barrack block had been damaged in the German naval bombardment of the north-east coast in 1914, but not beyond repair or consolidation as found. It is likely – although by no means established fact – that a barracks has less historic merit than a medieval hall, but Peers opted for clarity and chose to unpick the brick re-skinning of the medieval building and display a moment in time rather than the development of a building from high to low – or rather altered status – which is perhaps an issue of particular interest to us today. No monument can be frozen, no monument has a historical full stop in the manner suggested by Peers. So, what if anything has changed?

In some respects nothing has changed; it is possible to see the Peers approach, for want of a better name, as the aberration. Monuments, historic buildings, have always been changed, moved, adapted, dependent upon the political, religious or stylistic demands of popes, potentates and patrons. In some cases in some countries it is or was the accepted practice to sweep away all physical evidence of former dynasties. It is worth noting that the 'treat as found' regime was being practised in England at the same time as large-scale reconstruction projects at both Knossos, Crete and Colonial Williamsburg, Virginia, USA. The Peers approach did have its detractors at the time; in a letter of 26th June 1922, to A.R. Powys, Charles Thompson of The Society for the Protection of Ancient Buildings was to complain:

> Have you heard that HMOW have started in on Whitby to do their damnedest to give us another 'frozen ruin' from the Government cold storage ? Help ![8]

Following Peers' retirement, the new Chief Inspector was instructed to re-erect some elements at Rievaulx (a corner of the Cloister Arcade, which is clearly marked 'reconstruction') because the earlier approach was considered too sterile.[9] And yet, had it not been for Peers, the corpus of monuments we enjoy today might have been much smaller. As an increasing number of monuments was offered to the State for Guardianship (the State taking on the responsibility for maintenance and management, although ownership still resides with the legal owner) in the 1920s, Peers was faced with the gargantuan task of making them all stable and accessible. Before the 1920s, Peers and the Ministry had explored the possibility of creating a National Collection of monuments whereby particular sites would be identified for purchase or Guardianship. The First World War and its aftermath put paid to this scheme as the number of monuments passing into State care became greater than the original wish list; some of the monuments were those which would have been part of a National Collection, others were to find State protection as a home of last resort, when no other authority was willing to take them on.

We have rediscovered the landscape. We realise that we can only understand abbeys, priories, castles, by looking at the evidence from their adjacent and distant economic hinterlands. We see the monument in its landscape, and thus the plan of the monument is no longer as central as it once was. We have become better at identifying the actions of man in the landscape, whether it is a prehistoric ritual landscape in Dorset or the progression from French to Naturalistic landscapes in the eighteenth-century East Riding of Yorkshire. The relevance of landscape and setting has been increasingly enshrined in the international Charters and Conservation Plans which have been written since the Charter of Athens in 1931,[10] beginning with a Bavarian bylaw of 1905,[11] encouraging communes to look to the setting and value of groups of dwellings.

We understand that history has more to offer. Peers, like many historians prior to the 1970s, would not have considered the popular or social historical dimension of the monuments in his care. Perhaps these dimensions could be called the unofficial history of the monument. Large-scale popular movements occur throughout history and are an interesting aspect of the nineteenth century; a good example of which can be identified at Thornton Abbey, North Lincolnshire. The Temperance Society was one such group which could organize mass outings – facilitated by the network of railways in regional areas – and this was to give some monuments a new lease of life. Thornton was particularly popular, and meetings of up to 15,000 people were held on the site, participating in 'rational recreation'. Indeed such was the popularity of Thornton that it had its own theme song:

We will go to Thornton
With speed upon the rail
And there exclaim against strong drink
In spirits wine and ale
Why we will go to Thornton
And there we'll joyful sing
Of liberty from alcohol
The potent, tyrant king ![12]

We have been extremely slow to see the popular dimension of our monuments – a brief glance across the Irish Sea would have recognised the vibrant tradition of pilgrimage.

A second example comes from Scarborough Castle. Cricket has been played at the castle from 1848. In 1868 a touring team of Native Australians played Yorkshire at the Castle, beating them by 10 wickets.[13] The Australian team continued their tour around the country; one member died of TB in London. His gravestone was vandalised and currently the MCC are planning to reinstate a replacement. There are a number of issues connected with both of the examples: many people come to the monuments who have no interest in architectural history or official history, they want to enjoy peace and quiet, let the children run about or whatever. But as can be seen above, the monuments represent more of our (and others') past and culture than we sometimes recognise. They could be made more relevant to a greater number of people than they currently are.

Although it might be inappropriate to present an in-depth analysis of the circumstances and events of the entire Native Australian tour at Scarborough Castle, the tour is of considerable importance to a number of other groups who could be encouraged to enter into partnerships to tell part or all of the story, using Scarborough as one of the venues. This example is particularly fascinating, as one tries to understand how and why such a tour could have been organised, and how the players were received in England and Australia, when one considers the treatment of the native peoples in Australia and Tasmania.

The problem is that because we have not 'done things' to our monuments, we do not 'do things' to our monuments. The situation is beginning to change with Listed Buildings (as opposed to ancient monuments) – redundant churches for example – where alternative use is a possibility. This must be a good thing, putting aside the rights and wrongs of installing, say, a modern style hotel into a church. There are ways of making alternative use possible. Perhaps the central plank of such treatments and attempts is that of 'reversibility': whatever we do must be reversible, it cannot damage the monument or building, or more significantly, alter its narrative. At one extreme of reversibility is the type of work carried out at Fountains. All mortar repointing must fail so that the fabric (stone) survives. If the repointing is harder than the stone then the stone becomes the weak point in the elevation and disintegrates. Thus the perishable element continues to perish and be replaced, whereas the life of the medieval fabric is extended to be enjoyed by future generations. This is a practice not fully understood by the public at large, and the implications of it are quite clear: it costs a large sum of money and will continue to do so. The notion of reversibility can be extended to other aspects of ancient monuments and historic buildings, a wooden roof or floor using existing joist holes being a common option. This can have a conservation benefit, makes the space more understandable to the public and can be achieved with minimal intervention; that is, it can be reversible, and because it uses a different material does not try to convince that it is original. The notion of reversibility might be considered a symptom of a less confident age, but alternatively it may suggest that we have come to terms with and can recognize and accommodate the variety of the past.

The possibility of reuse for many of our ancient monuments is more problematic. There have been attempts to undertake such projects but the majority have foundered for a variety of reasons, usually practical or philosophical rather than financial. In 1946 a group of leading Roman Catholics represented by a committee including the Duke of Norfolk attempted to purchase Fountains Abbey from the Vyner family with the intention of transforming the abbey into a memorial to the English speaking Catholics who died in the Second World War. The Chapel of Nine Altars would have altars to the nations concerned. Fountains Hall would become a monastic Guest House and monks from Buckfast would be installed to carry out any necessary works. The philosophical rights and wrongs of this project were debated in the letters pages of the *Times* and *Telegraph* from August 1946 to final withdrawal of the project in March 1947.[14] Although Fountains was already a Scheduled Ancient Monument, the project fell for various practical and related philosophic reasons; the amount of rebuilding required to make the new chapel structurally feasible would have obliterated the work of Abbot Darnton, to name but one Abbot. It was irreversible. However, one can recognize in the various letters the growing belief that the management of Fountains was a responsibility of national government and therefore public property which could not be sequestered.

Putting the problem of financial resources to one side, the three most pressing and immediate current demands on the fabric of British monuments are: Health and Safety, Disabled Access and Lottery or Millennium bids. Health and Safety demands are becoming more universal, driven to current lengths not so much by genuine regard for safety, but fear of legal repercussions. All organisations have a duty of care once they have invited members of the public onto their property, and it is their responsibility to ensure that the public is protected. For example, when anything over 20cms high can be identified as a tripping hazard, there is then a duty to protect people from that hazard. Most people would find a profusion of barriers on an ancient monument aesthetically unpleasant, but the demands of the legislation have to be met. It may be that site presentation has to be more adventurous to address the demands of Health and Safety requirements rather than adopt the barrier mentality. A particular problem does arise when the monument ceases to be a monument and becomes an element in a cultural landscape. How can one make the landscape safe? Is a rabbit burrow merely a 20cm tripping hazard in reverse – would one be expected to fill in every burrow? The challenge is to temper the gravity of the danger with the likelihood of it happening, whilst avoiding the quick fix barrier mentality.

Universal access to monuments is long overdue. Even if organisations could not bring themselves to undertake access work to buildings, it is still possible to provide discounted entrance fees to those who could not climb stairs to interpretative displays (quite apart from the obvious point of moving displays to somewhere accessible) or see them clearly, or for that matter visit half the site. The situation is much the same as that which applies to Health and Safety. We will have to be more creative, do more to the monuments, and much can be done which does not contravene the prime directives of reversibility and narrative. Thorough research of the consolidation history of particular monuments is likely to reveal that there are more options for change than we currently realise. Again the problem of landscape is relevant: how do we make landscape accessible? Is it feasible to make the entire Hadrian's Wall World Heritage Site accessible to all disabled, aged and pram-bound visitors? Nevertheless it is a duty to make as much as possible accessible to all and intelligently explain that which is not.

Reconstructions and restorations are likely to be near the top of many lottery or millennium bid wish-lists. It appears to be an easy option; in some senses it is easy, but the end product is not always the historically accurate reconstruction that people might have in mind.

A good example of the choices which have to be made is the new roof at Conisborough Castle, South Yorkshire. It made considerable sense from a conservation point of view to replace the roof as the magnesian limestone Keep was suffering from the effects of chemical weathering; the new management group (the Ivanhoe Trust) was keen to see a new roof, to provide protected interior space. However, the roof form which would have been historically accurate would have required the speculative reconstruction of a considerable amount of face stone and internal detailing. The decision was taken to insert a low-pitch roof (historically inaccurate) but leave alone the historically accurate face work. The new roof satisfies a conservation need, has allowed the furnishing of the Keep and is practically invisible to the outside world: a perfect solution? In many ways the 'historically accurate' might come as something of a shock to the public who have become used to their undeveloped monuments (Figure 3).

The new catchword in the vocabulary of conservation is 'partnership'. Shared or matched funding provide the wherewithal; additional partners bring additional ideas. Local authorities may have had an eye on a particular monument for several years, assessing how better display, presentation and preservation may lift surrounding areas or provide a more complete tourist attraction. Members of local societies have the opportunity to see and research the local relevance of their local site, providing information similar to that described for Thornton or Scarborough. Involvement of local groups may completely shift the orientation of some monuments: Scarborough Castle has a long stretch of curtain wall, it stands on a spectacular promontory overlooking the town and rugged coastline, and yet there are no views of the town from the castle – nothing which allows the visitor to see the primary relationship. It should be no contentious issue to build wooden staircases or ramps to provide access to wall walks, or open up 1920s blockings in window apertures to reinstate the connection between castle and town. Much of this talk of partnerships would not be new to an American audience where the relationship and interplay between Federal, State and Local government and local groups is an established and integral part of conservation practice, and much can be gained from a close examination of practice and procedure in other parts of the world.

The key to a flexibility which satisfies the requirements of Health and Safety, Disabled Access and Lottery projects, is good survey, both fabric and documentary. Once one understands the building or landscape, one has a better chance to undertake informed, yet meaningful alterations, adaptations or presentation. It may be that unguarded and steep drops around an opening can be made safe by the reinsertion of missing floor or decking, the position of which can be determined by the evidence in the fabric. Reinsertion of elements can have benefits other than those concerned with Health and Safety or universal access, in that architectural space can be made more understandable to the visiting public. But there should then be a commitment to explain the space, indicating that such and such a floor belongs to a particular phase.

There is nothing to say that all bids or projects will be straightforward, and nobody should doubt that problems of taste, practicality or financial resources lie ahead. However, it is important to realize what can be accomplished, and

Figure 3. An early reconstruction drawing and section of Conisborough Castle.
(English Heritage)

also that monuments have changed in the past and are changing now. Similarly our notions of conservation will change; it may be that a preoccupation with Peers and SPAB is, although not irrelevant, a thing of the past, a debate which has run its course. In considering archaeology, we know that some nineteenth and early twentieth-century excavations were poor in methodological terms, yet we still excavate, because we believe that it is possible to do better. The shortcomings of nineteenth and early twentieth-century restoration seems to have left a more indelible mark, which can be overcome only by a degree of confidence and debate similar to that experienced in the archaeological world. Perhaps the next arena of debate will take place in the historic urban cores of the developing world, areas which are ripe for cultural tourism yet tend to be occupied by the poorest sections of society. As yet conservation has little to offer such people.

The Author

Keith Emerick is Inspector of Ancient Monuments for English Heritage, Historic Properties North, which is based at Helmsley, N. Yorkshire. He is currently reading part-time for a D.Phil at the University of York Archaeology department on the subject of conservation philosophy with particular regard to nineteenth- and twentieth-century repair and use of ancient monuments. The views expressed in this article are those of the author, not English Heritage.

References

1   W.A. Forsyth, 'The Repair of Ancient Buildings', *The Architectural Journal*, Journal of the Royal Institute of British Architects, vol.21, Third Series, 1914, pp.109–37. The comment by Peers is recorded in the discussion section of this paper, p.135.

2   C. Peers, 'The Treatment of Old Buildings', *The Architectural Journal*, vol.38, third series, 1931, pp. 311–20.

3   A. Saunders, 'A Century of Ancient Monuments Legislation', *The Antiquaries Journal*, vol. 63, 1983, pp. 11–34.

4   C. Peers and C. .A. Ralegh Radford, 'The Saxon Monastery of Whitby', *Archaeologia*, vol. 89 ,second series ,vol. 39, 1943,   pp. 27– 88.

5   Peers, 'The Treatment of Old Buildings', p. 312.

6   M. W. Thompson, *Ruins. Their Preservation and Display*, British Museum Publications Ltd., 1981.

7   Peers, 'The Treatment of Old Buildings', p. 325.

8   Letter contained in the Whitby Abbey file, Society for the Protection of Ancient Buildings, Spital Square, London.
9   My thanks to Professor Peter Fergusson, Wellesley College, Mass. USA, for this point. Fergusson is to discuss Peers and Rievaulx in his forthcoming book on Rievaulx, the likely title of which is, *Community and Memory: An Architectural History of Rievaulx Abbey*.
10   C. Erder, *Our Architectural Heritage: From Consciousness to Conservation*, Museums and Monuments XX, UNESCO, Paris, 1986.
11   G. Baldwin Brown, *The Care of Ancient Monuments*, Edinburgh University Press, Edinburgh, 1905.
12   My thanks to Keith Miller, English Heritage, Field Monument Warden, for passing on this piece of his research.
13   My thanks to Bill Neal the English Heritage Custodian for Scarborough Castle, who has begun to research the story of the cricket match.
14   The Fountains Abbey file at the offices of The Society for the Protection of Ancient Buildings, Spital Square, London, contains a comprehensive series of press cuttings chronicling this particular issue.

16

Transports of delight?

Making and Consuming Histories at the National Railway Museum, York

Colin Divall

> A museum of transport! The idea is surely a contradiction in terms, an absurdity. For a museum seems to most of us to be something static – it freezes and preserves things – whereas transport moves, or it is not transport.[1]

Paradoxical institutions or not, transport museums are among the most popular of heritage attractions in Britain. Some 370,000 people visited the National Motor Museum at Beaulieu in 1996, for instance. And while a significant proportion of the public likes to experience travel and movement, the literally static nature of most museum displays does not appear to be too much of a deterrent. In 1995 for example, while some 5.6 million people paid to travel on the country's 101 'heritage' railways (with a further estimated 1.25 million visiting the lines without travelling) only one of these railways managed to attract over 400,000 visitors, a figure commonly met or exceeded annually by the National Railway Museum (NRM) in York – in 1996, the most popular museum outside London for which an entrance charge is made.[1] Clearly transport museums are perceived by many as having something of value to offer.

The question, of course, is what this 'something' is. Since research into the reasons why people visit transport museums is neither particularly extensive nor, for the most part, theoretically and methodologically very sophisticated, we cannot be sure. Nevertheless the general cultural connotations of visiting museums offer some clues. Nick Merriman has argued that the upsurge in popularity of all kinds of museums can be explained partly by understanding them as a means by which upwardly-mobile individuals seek approval from others for their increasingly affluent lifestyles. Briefly, he argues that museums' traditional association with

197

élites means that people who wish to be seen as 'cultured' perceive visiting as a profitable way of spending leisure time.[2] But a person's decision to visit a museum is influenced by her or his cultural competence to gain something from it, and while this capacity is now more widespread thanks to the expansion of educational opportunities, improvements in museum design and practice are equally important. These two developments have 'met halfway to make more people familiar with... [museums'] code and thus make them less intimidating'.[3] Museums with intellectually accessible exhibitions might thus expect to attract not only high numbers of visitors but also a more representative cross-section of the public than displays more closely associated with cultural élites.

Transport museums seem to fit this account well. They presumably enjoy the cultural connotations of being museums, but as institutions commemorating a mundane feature of everyday life they have the advantage of a subject matter which is familiar to many people. Patterns of visiting the NRM are consistent with this supposition; as well as being a very popular museum, the socio-economic profile of visitors is, and has long been, closer to that of the general population than is commonly the case elsewhere in the museum sector.[4] Perhaps Merriman's argument might be pushed a stage further to explain the popularity of the NRM compared with even the most successful of heritage railways with all their kinetic attractions. Do people choose to visit the NRM, in other words, partly because it is perceived as a museum, albeit an 'accessible' one, and heritage railways partly because they are not?

Such questions are no longer of purely academic interest. The simple fact is that the NRM is not as popular as it once was in the 1970s and 1980s and the secular trend of admissions is, at best, static. While many factors have undoubtedly contributed to this decline – increased competition for people's leisure time and changing patterns of tourism in York are just two that come readily to mind – it would clearly be foolish to ignore the effect the style and content of the museum's exhibitions might have on someone's decision to visit the NRM in the first place, perhaps then to return and encourage others to do likewise.[5] Only more and better studies of the way in which people 'consume', and refuse to consume, the railways' past will provide us with reliable answers. But as a prelude to this research we need to understand what – and how and why – the NRM's displays attempt to communicate about the history of Britain's railways. For how else can we judge how well the museum succeeds in its aims, or what needs to be done to improve exhibitions if they prove to be less effective than was hoped?[6]

Making Histories of technology in museums

The tradition of reflecting in a systematic way on the practice of transport museums is not a long one, although railway museums have perhaps been better treated than most.[7] When it comes to analysing the historiography embodied in exhibitions we can, however, take inspiration from studies concerned more generally with displays of industry and technology.[8] Elsewhere I have argued that we may understand many of these exhibitions in terms of two ideal types, namely those drawing upon 'whiggish' or 'social impact' discourses.

Whiggish displays are object-rich and through their 'poetics' – that is, the production of meaning through the overall arrangement of the exhibition's components – connote a narrative of technical progress.[9] By 'technical progress' I mean those improvements in the physical characteristics of artefacts that are defined in terms apparently divorced from human and social goals – such as the achievement of greater efficiency or more physical power. At best, human intentions enter these exhibitions' narratives via the goals of the engineers who designed (but rarely those who built, operated or used) the technologies on display; but even then, these aspirations are often expressed in terms of a technical, instrumental rationality rather than more obviously human goals, such as social power or wealth.

In the usual fashion of whiggish historiographies, the narrative of progress selects from the messy complexity of the past in order to present modern (technical) achievements as the culmination of earlier successes. The criteria against which 'progress' is judged are seen as unproblematic; so too is the movement from one stage of development to the next. But while this initial reading draws visitors' attention away from the social purposes and uses of the displayed artefacts, this very fact may well play an important role in sustaining a more complex and ideologically loaded interpretation of the exhibition. Technical progress can symbolise certain other social processes – for instance, a company or industry's evolution – and do so in a fashion that suggests their unproblematic or even inevitable nature.[10]

By contrast, 'impact' displays comprehend social purpose more explicitly by considering the ways in which technologies shape social, economic, political or environmental change. Usually supplementary forms of interpretation – graphical panels, videos, sound commentaries, and so on – bear the brunt of the interpretive burden in these displays for it is not easy to connote sometimes complex social processes through the arrangement of objects alone; thus there is always a danger that the technologies on show will become mere props for a narrative that is, sometimes literally, written on the wall. Moreover, these exhibitions differ markedly in the weight that they accord technology as a causal agent. At their worst the preferred reading suggests that technologies more or less directly determine certain kinds of social change without the mediation of other – that is, social – factors. When this kind of narrative is combined with an understanding of technical change akin to that found in whiggish exhibitions, the result is a 'hard' technical determinism in which the possibility of the human control of technology and its social effects is discounted.[11]

While the social and industrial organisation of transport differs significantly from that of many other kinds of technology, it does not take a very large leap of the imagination to extend this kind of analysis to museums of transport in general and the NRM in particular.[12] The task of interpreting railway technologies is shouldered at the NRM by exhibitions in two large spaces, the Great (formerly the Main) Hall, the original museum opened in 1975, and the South Hall, opened to the public in 1990 when the Main Hall was closed for major structural repairs and retained when the latter reopened in 1992. With certain important qualifications which I shall detail shortly, the exhibition in the Great Hall tends to be whiggish in character; that in the South Hall inclines more to the social impact approach.

Making Histories at the NRM: the Great Hall

The present exhibition in the Great Hall, entitled 'The Technology of Railways', is broadly similar in concept to that found in the Main Hall during its last three years, from 1987 to 1990. One difference is the setting. The Main Hall was once a locomotive shed, rebuilt in the 1950s, and although naturally it had been adapted and cleaned for the museum's purposes, most informed observers judged that the physical surroundings enhanced visitors' appreciation of the displays of large objects, including engines, that filled the space.[13] To what degree, and in precisely what sense, this was the case we cannot now say, for the rebuilding of 1990–92 was so extensive that very little survives to indicate the original form or use of the structure.[14] Another difference is that one of the two turntables that graced the Main Hall and which formed a focus for the displays has now gone; in its place stands a miscellany of individual exhibits.[15]

In the form that it took from 1987 the exhibition in the Main Hall was more coherent. Heavily informed by over a century's tradition of collecting, restoring and displaying items of railway mechanical engineering, it was dominated by a display of heavily restored locomotives around one of the two turntables, and of passenger coaches – plus the odd wagon – around the other.[16] Both these displays fitted the whiggish category quite well. The locomotives, for example, were placed in roughly chronological order, and although the desire to display different kinds of engine (express passenger, heavy and light goods, and so on), with all their detailed peculiarities of design, meant that there could be no unalloyed demonstration of technical progress, the overall impression was of evolution towards bigger, more powerful, and more efficient motive power.[17]

Figure 1. The Main Hall, 1987. *(NRM)*

Earlier museum displays of railways, including that at the NRM during its first dozen years, had not drawn so clearly upon a whiggish discourse of technical progress – the former Museum of British Transport at Clapham, for example, has been aptly described as 'a gloriously cluttered place'.[18] But policies towards the collection, restoration and, latterly, display of railway technologies have always been informed by their potent symbolism beyond the purely technical. Britain's first railway museum, opened during the mid 1920s in the old station and workshops just inside York's city walls, was conceived by its private owners, the then recently-formed London & North Eastern Railway, partly as means of forging a new corporate identity by celebrating the company's achievements and those of its predecessors. With its heavy emphasis on locomotives, plus some rolling stock, the York collection took progress in mechanical engineering as a symbol of wider corporate success.[19] The nationalisation of the railways in 1948 inevitably implied a shift in the connotations of this kind of collecting – and later, with the opening of the Clapham museum (1961) and others in Swindon (1962) and Glasgow (1964), of display – but it continued nonetheless.[20] Thus although the British Transport Commission's collecting policy of 1951 acknowledged a responsibility towards 'the wider social and cultural heritage' of the railways under its control, in the 1950s and early 1960s the acquisition of locomotives remained at a high priority; engines were collected because they had originally marked a significant technical advance, and the practicability of restoring them to as-original appearance was an important consideration.[21]

Appearances could be deceptive – some of the NRM's locomotives, inherited from the BTC collection, have wooden chimneys. But the application of an original, colourful livery, highly polished to an exhibition finish had important connotations when the engines were put on display.[22] The original exhibition (1975–87) at the NRM gave particular emphasis to engines from the so-called 'Golden Age' of Britain's railways, that is, the Edwardian period when fierce inter-company competition for passengers encouraged the manufacture of elegant steam locomotives and substantial carriages all decorated with fine liveries. [23] It is more than likely that to visitors in the 1970s – who had only recently witnessed the demise under British Railways of an often filthy and decrepit steam railway, and who were not necessarily benefiting themselves from the modernisation of what was left – the dominant connotations of this display were more nostalgic than whiggish.

This tension between nostalgic and progressive meanings remains central to understanding the present exhibition in the Great Hall. It stands squarely within the tradition that values railway artefacts primarily as technical objects but which is also mindful of their wider symbolism. When the Hall reopened in 1992, the display of locomotives around the main turntable was reinstated in a fashion suggestive of a whiggish narrative of technical progress, although this reading has since been compromised by the haphazard removal and substitution of objects. That part of the Hall formerly occupied by the second turntable now includes displays of certain types of engineering that were previously neglected, and the most prominent of these, a 'time line' of railway track and associated vehicles, also connotes a progressive, whiggish narrative.

Figure 2. The Great Hall, mid-1990s. *(NRM)*

But nostalgic meanings are important too. With its miscellany of displays and exhibits, it might be thought fanciful to claim any reading of the main floor of the Great Hall as a whole.[24] This would be a mistake. The sheer bulk and high quality finish of the beautiful pieces of 'engineering sculpture' still make a powerful impact on many visitors, and this is almost certainly more important for the production and communication of historical meaning than the object labels intended to convey technical information.[25] Aesthetic splendour and engineering excellence – 'From Rocket to Eurostar' as a recent photographic essay on the NRM aptly puts it – continue to symbolise and celebrate the triumphs, real or imagined, of Britain's railways. But this, of course, is also the Great Hall's principal weakness: it fails – because it is not intended – to engage casual visitors in a critical way with what is in fact a very particular representation of the railways' past. This is clear, for instance, with the treatment of Mallard, since 1938 the world's fastest steam locomotive and an icon for many casual visitors as well as railway enthusiasts. Restored in the 1960s to its record-breaking condition, the locomotive is undeniably an impressive object: but it is also highly atypical of the struggling railways of the 1930s. The supporting textual and graphic panels celebrate Mallard's technical achievement without giving any clues about the unfavourable business and political circumstances that led the London & North Eastern Railway to try for the record in the first place. The technology of railways might have travelled a long way since Mallard's run, but the same cannot be said of the meaning of its display.

The South Hall

The NRM's South Hall dwells upon the social and economic effects of Britain's railways, understood principally in terms of the movement of passengers and goods although some attention is also paid to the social organisation of railway work. The interpretive style stands in stark contrast to that of the Great Hall, although it is arguable that the preferred meanings are not so different. The interpretation consists chiefly of an arrangement of restored locomotives, passenger coaches and goods wagons into several 'trains' (they are not on the whole typical of historic formations), all set within York's old Goods Station, refurbished to suggest a passenger terminal of some unspecified period in the steam era.[26] Supplementary interpretation is mostly provided by large textual and graphic panels set back from the 'trains' to which they refer in order to minimise visual intrusion; it is likely that the arrangement of the vehicles and their setting contribute even more to visitors' construction of historical meaning than is the case in the Great Hall.

This atmospheric ensemble is undeniably popular with less-specialist visitors, probably more so than the Great Hall.[27] And from the historian's point of view, the recovery of a much greater sense of social context and purpose for the artefacts on show can only be welcomed. Indeed, some recent exhibits, particularly a series of graphic panels on the role of women within the railways' workforce, demonstrate some awareness of the complex and contested nature of history. On the other hand, it is easy – and not unfair – to criticize the exhibition as a whole for its ideologically loaded representation of the railways' social organisation and impact. One recent critic sees in the Hall's very success at the affective level:

> a gestalt effect, in which the arrangement of the objects in relation to one another creates not a representation of the elements of the material culture of the past demanding a thoughtful engagement, but a recreation of the past itself, static and visitable, the spirit of which visitors are invited to partake.[28]

Figure 3. The South Hall, mid-1990s. *(NRM)*

In short, the South Hall offers a nostalgic impression of a mythical Golden Age of Britain's Railways, shorn of encounters with problems like truculent workers, over-bearing managements, or poor service. The casual visitor would be hard-pressed to discover, for example, that for much of the last third of the nineteenth century Britain's railway companies were about as popular as today's utilities. Railway trains, skilfully built and beautifully finished, celebrate past industrial triumphs and thus contribute to the formation of our contemporary national identity.[29]

A recently refurbished exhibition, 'Royal Palaces on Wheels', shows this aspect of the South Hall at its most extreme. The display is a striking and important one, taking perhaps a little under a quarter of the floor area of the Hall – even though the seven coaches on show are only a selection from a much bigger collection of royal vehicles. The refurbishment has very effectively enhanced the display's appeal; a red carpet running throughout the exhibition, a mock triumphal arch, and a sound loop of cheering crowds are intended to imbue visitors with the spirit of a royal visit. Much improved lighting highlights the superb workmanship and luxurious appointments of the carriages, and sound cones, activated when visitors step within their circumference, give potted accounts of each vehicle's history and use. A short video describes the evolution of royal travel by train, and if one follows the preferred route through the display, the arrangement of the vehicles in roughly chronological order does offer some sense of historical change. But the exhibition does not encourage visitors to think of the royal vehicles as anything other than symbols of a national identity that is unproblematic, uncontested, and permanent. Certainly, the opportunity to engage intellectually with a critical view of the role of the railways in the social construction of the British monarchy has largely been missed. Indeed, the assumption of national, social and political harmony that informs the exhibition's representation of the monarchy is mirrored, both here and elsewhere in the museum, by an assumption of industrial order and stability on the railways.[30]

Of course, we only have anecdotal evidence that the NRM's visitors read the displays in the way described. Some will engage critically with what is on show, others ignore it: all will construct their own meanings of their visit. But Bill Wood's small scale study of the East Anglian Railway Museum (EARM) at Chappel and Wakes Colne, Suffolk suggests that relatively few visitors have the level of interest in, or awareness of, historical sources necessary for an informed, critical engagement. Nevertheless, we should be cautious about extrapolating Wood's findings to the NRM as it is not clear that the profile of his visitors was similar to those in York.[31]

Concluding remarks

As someone who has spent a good deal of my professional life teaching at the tertiary level, it has always struck me as a little strange that British museums – institutions which often trade upon their educational credentials – are on the whole so reluctant to test the effectiveness of their major form of communication, exhibitions. For all the faults of university teaching, at least there is feedback in the form of essays, seminar and tutorial discussions, examination papers and so on. Of course, the relationship between a museum's workers and their visitors is nothing like that between a lecturer and student, but these differences do not undermine the desirability of undertaking considerably more systematic research into the way visitors use and understand museum displays. The differences simply mean that we have to develop more appropriate kinds of evaluation.

Quite apart from what I should like to imagine is a demand from all museum professionals that we should be better able to judge our effectiveness as educationalists, there is another, more pragmatic reason why the evaluation of exhibitions should take a much higher place on most museums' agenda. Over the past decade and more, we have witnessed a rising tide of public accountability at all levels of education, a tide that shows no sign of ebbing. Generally speaking this has washed by museums, but with ever-increasing sums of money from the Heritage Lottery Fund (HLF) going to them, in some cases to institutions that have never before received significant amounts of public funding, it seems most unlikely that the status quo will hold for much longer. If museums claim any kind of prospective educational gain from the proposals that they submit to the HLF, then before long some kind of assessment of the effectiveness of the finished projects is going to be required.[32] Surely it would be a good idea for museums to develop their own thoughts on how best to achieve this before the HLF (or its successor) imposes a system which might not be particularly appropriate?

There is, of course, already a good deal of research about visitors' readings of exhibitions, particularly in the USA, and this obviously provides a huge resource for the future.[33] But much of this work focuses on particular displays without much by way of attempts to systematise and generalise.[34] Studies of individual displays will provide us with the kind of tools that we might need to satisfy the HLF in future with regard to one-off grants, but I think there is a strategic dimension that it would be foolish to ignore. The Department for Culture, Media and Sport is taking seriously complaints about the perceived bias of lottery grants towards élite cultural institutions, and this might be seen as both a threat and an opportunity as far as museums are concerned. A threat because of the traditional association of museums with cultural élites, but equally an opportunity because of the sheer variety of museums and their audiences. The scope for systematic, comparative surveys is enormous, both as a means of establishing the background of museum visitors more precisely than Merriman was able to do, but also as a means of discovering just how educationally effective different kinds of museum displays are with regard to particular kinds of visitor.

Transport museums and heritage forms of transport would be a goodplace to start: clearly popular with the public, their – often charitable – status and funding usually depends on some kind of claim to educational purpose. At least with regard to the NRM we have an idea of what it is that transport museums are trying to achieve. We might be surprised at how little – or indeed, how much – of our intended messages get through to visitors. But knowing one way or the other is a necessary first step to creating a better museum.

The Author

Professor Colin Divall holds the only chair for Railway Studies in the country and is Director of the Institute of Railway Studies, a joint initiative of the University of York and the National Railway Museum. He has written widely on transport history and the social implications of technology.

References

1   Jack Simmons, *Transport Museums*, George Allen & Unwin, London, 1970, p. 7.
2   Brian D. Barber, *Association of Railway Preservation Societies Ltd and Association of Independent Railways: 1995 Statistical Survey Report*, n.p. , Publicity Projects/British Steam Railways, 1996, pp. 4, 7. *Visits to Tourist Attractions 1996*, British Tourist Authority/English Tourist Board Research Services, London, 1997.
3   Nick Merriman, *Beyond the Glass Case: The Past, the Heritage and the Public in Britain*, Leicester University Press, Leicester, 1991, pp. 75–95. See also Robert F. Kelly, 'Museums as Status Symbols III: A Speculative Examination of Motives Among Those Who Love Being in Museums, Those Who Go to "Have Been" and Those Who Refuse to Go', *Visitor Studies: Theory Research and Practice*, vol. 4, 1992, pp. 24–31.
4   Nick Merriman, 'Museum Visiting as a Cultural Phenomenon', in Peter Vergo. ed., *The New Museology*, Reaktion Books, London, 1989, pp. 149–71 (at p. 171).
5   In 1996, 25% of visitors to the NRM fell into the AB socio-economic class, 35% into C1, 24% into C2, and 14% into DE. NRM visitors survey, 19–25 August 1996. See also, P. Heady, *Visiting Museums: A Report of a Survey to the Victoria and Albert, Science, and National Railway Museums for the Office of Arts and Libraries*, HMSO, London, 1984, pp. 12–29, 43–104.
6   The experience of previous visits and personal recommendations are the two most important reasons why visitors come to the NRM; currently about half of visitors have been before. (NRM visitors survey).
7   Peter Vergo, 'The Reticent Object', in Vergo, *New Museology*, pp. 41–59, esp. pp. 45–6. Kelly, 'Museums', p. 28.
8   R. Shorland-Ball, ed., *Common Roots, Separate Branches: Railway History and Preservation*, NMSI for the NRM, London, 1994. Neil Cossons, 'An Agenda for the Railway Heritage', in Peter Burman and Michael Stratton, eds, *Conserving the Railway Heritage*, E. & F. N. Spon, London, 1997, pp. 3–17. Richard Sykes, 'Steam Attraction: Railways in Britain's National Heritage', *Journal of Transport History*, vol. 18, 3rd ser., 1997, pp. 156–175.

9   E.g., Alan Morton, 'Tomorrow's Yesterdays: Science Museums and The Future', in Robert Lumley, ed., *The Museum Time-Machine: Putting Cultures on Display*, Routledge, London, 1988, pp. 128–143. Stella Butler, *Science and Technology Museums*, Leicester University Press, Leicester, 1992.

10   For a useful introduction to the poetics of museum displays, see Henrietta Lidchi, 'The Poetics and The Politics of Exhibiting Other Cultures', in Stuart Hall, ed., *Representation: Cultural Representations and Signifying Practices*, Sage, London, 1997, pp. 151–208.

11   Colin Divall, 'Theories and Things: Using the History of Technology in Museums', in Lawrence Fitzgerald and Gaby Porter, eds., *Collecting and Interpreting Domestic Artefacts*, Museum of Science and Industry in Manchester/Science & Industry Curators' Group, Manchester, 1995, pp. 3–11. Lawrence Fitzgerald, 'Hard Men, Hard Facts and Heavy Metal: Making Histories of Technology', in Gaynor Kavanagh, ed., *Making Histories in Museums*, Leicester University Press, Leicester, 1996, pp. 116–130.

12   Divall, 'Theories and Things', pp. 6–8. On technical determinism, see Merritt Roe Smith and Leo Marx, eds, *Does Technology Drive History? The Dilemma of Technological Determinism*, MIT Press, London/Cambidge MA, 1994.

13   See, for example, Colin Divall, 'Changing Routes? The New London Transport Museum', *Technology and Culture*, vol. 36, 1995, pp. 630–35. Idem, 'What Kind of Railway (Engineering) History Should We be Writing?', in Adrian Jarvis, ed., *Approaches to Engineering History*, Merseyside Maritime Museum/Newcomen Society, Liverpool, 1996, pp. 19–27. Lawrence Fitzgerald, 'Travel Bugs', *Museums Journal*, August 1994, pp. 31–34.

14   Neil Cossons, 'The National Railway Museum, York', in Neil Cossons, Allan Patmore and Rob Shorland-Ball, eds, *Perspectives on Railway History and Interpretation*, NRM, York, 1990, pp. 129–135. Handel Kardas, 'Museums, Visitors – and What They Expect', in Cossons et al, *Perspectives*, pp. 136–145. But cf. Shorland-Ball, '"All Change" – New Buildings and Displays at the National Railway Museum, 1988–1992', in Cossons et al, *Perspectives*, p. 154.

15   Shorland-Ball, 'All Change', pp. 146–158.

16   These include a small exhibition on the Channel Tunnel; 'Moving things – the mail', a prototype for a projected redisplay of the Great Hall; items of rolling stock and signalling equipment; and a space given over to temporary exhibitions – currently (summer 1997), 'Toys and Trains'. I have also excluded from consideration the Balcony Gallery, which runs along one side of the hall.

17   Dieter Hopkin, 'A Commentary on Restoration, Conservation and the National Railway Museum collection', in Shorland-Ball, *Common Roots*, pp. 215–21.

18   See, for example, John Coiley, ed., *From Rocket to Eurostar: The National*

Railway Museum in Camera, Atlantic Transport Publishers, Penryn, 1996. Kardas, 'Museums', p. 141.

19   Kardas, 'Museums', p. 139.

20   Dieter Hopkin, 'Railway Preservation in the 1920s and 1930s', in Cossons et al, *Perspectives*, pp. 88–99. Photographic evidence suggests that it might be tendentious to read a whiggish narrative into the cluttered displays at York. See, for example, Peter Williams, *Britain's Railway Museums*, Ian Allan, London, 1974, pp. 9–36. But the meaning of the cavalcade of locomotives and rolling stock organised by the LNER to mark the 1925 centenary of the Stockton and Darlington Railway was much more straightforward: here, progress in mechanical engineering clearly stood for corporate success and pride.

21   It is not easy to discern any single purpose behind the establishment of these museums. The Great Western Railway Museum in Swindon was closest in conception to a company museum, celebrating the corporate and engineering achievements of an organisation that had disappeared in name in 1948 but apparently lived on in the minds of many. Local identities were important as well, for the Swindon of the 1960s was still largely a creation of the GWR; significantly, the museum was, and still is, run by the local authority.

22   'The Preservation of Relics and Records', Report to the British Transport Commission, BTC, 1951, para. 6, quoted in Cossons, 'National Railway Museum', p. 130. Hopkin, 'A Commentary', pp. 217–218.

23   Hopkin, 'A Commentary', p. 218.

24   Cossons, 'National Railway Museum', pp. 132–134. Jack Simmons, *Dandy-Cart to Diesel: The National Railway Museum*, HMSO, London, 1981, pp. 7–34.

25   I am excluding from consideration here two recent displays, 'Moving things – the mail' and 'The Garden'. The former, the prototype for the redisplay of the Great Hall, deserves a more careful consideration than space here permits. Discussion of the latter will be made in my forthcoming book.

26   17 per cent of visitors to the NRM describe themselves as 'very interested' in railways, although a further 25 per cent say they are 'quite interested'. (NRM visitor survey).

27   To one side of the old railway building there is a much smaller, modern space. This is best thought of as an open store, and I shall not consider it further here.

28   Kardas, 'Museums', p. 143; Shorland-Ball, 'All Change', p. 151.

29   Sykes, 'Steam Attraction', pp. 156–175. Sykes's criticism is directed primarily at the 'Great Railway Show', a temporary exhibition put together for the duration of the rebuilding of the Main Hall. The present exhibition in the South Hall is not significantly different, however.

30   Sykes, 'Steam Attraction', pp. 156–175.

31   Sykes, 'Steam Attraction', pp. 156–175.

32   William G. Wood, 'How and Why are Pasts Represented In Museums, and with What Implications for Their Educational Role?', PhD thesis, University

of East Anglia, 1994, pp. 80–128, esp. 123–126. See also, Lois Silverman, 'Making Meaning Together: Lessons from the Field of American History', *Journal of Museum Education*, vol. 18, 1993, pp. 7–11.

33 In the USA, for example, any museum project funded by the National Science Foundation has to include evaluation work, for which 5% of the funding is set aside. I'm grateful to Sandra Bicknell for this information.

34 Kenneth Hudson, *A Social History of Museums: What the Visitors Thought*, Macmillan, London, 1975, pp. 100–122. Sandra Bicknell and Graham Farmelo, eds, *Museum Visitor Studies in the 90s*, Science Museum, London, 1991. Michael Belcher, *Exhibitions in Museums*, Leicester University Press, Leicester, 1991, pp. 197–209. John H. Falk and Lynn D. Dierking, *The Museum Experience*, Whalesback Books, Washington DC, 1992, pp. 1–125.

35 Marilyn G. Hood, 'After 70 Years of Audience Research, What Have We Learned? Who Comes to Museums, Who Does Not, and Why?', *Visitor Studies: Theory, Research and Practice*, vol. 5, 1993, pp. 16–27, esp. pp. 21–23. But cf. Nick Merriman, 'Understanding heritage', *Journal of Material Culture*, vol. 1, 1996, pp. 377–86, esp. p. 384.

17

Issues of National Identity and the School Curriculum in Scotland

Sydney Wood

The readers' letters sections of the Scottish press are frequently peppered with the outraged cries of indignant patriots offended by some fresh instance of English misbehaviour. Within many of these missives lie frequent references to historical events and circumstances, references that convey a Scottish sense of national identity as powerfully dependent on the past. Scotland's nearest approach to a national anthem, 'Flower of Scotland', focuses firmly on a past event: when a Scottish journalist ventured to attack it as dreary and depressing and went on to complain that 'wallowing in 700-year-old battles and making a national profession out of whining and bleating is hardly the mark of a vigorous forward-looking nation', he attracted sharp criticism.[1] The film *Braveheart* provided modern Scots with an intensely emotional opportunity to celebrate national identity. According to a leading Scottish historian:

> Because we are Scots, *Braveheart* is, and for good or ill will remain, one of the major cultural influences of the 1990s. Glasgow songsters now apparently include a new item in their repertoire, "There's only Wan Mel Gibson".[2]

The use of the past to assert national identity, and the enjoyment of stories from the past that bear little relation to historical truth are not, of course, activities that are peculiar to Scots - indeed one late-nineteenth-century French historian observed 'Getting its history wrong is part of being a nation'.[3] Scottish identity today is most obviously publicly proclaimed in ways that owe much to events in the late 18th and early 19th centuries. At the very moment when traditional Highland culture was suffering a post-Culloden onslaught, aspects of it were being adopted as an extended metaphor for Scottish national identity.[4] Whilst Government troops secured a fierce grip on the Highlands, Lowlanders busied themselves in adopting the badges of a mythologised Highlands. Walter Scott's carefully organised reception for George IV's arrival in 1822 in Edinburgh helped to further popularise a version of the kilt and the playing of the bagpipes, thus uniting Lowlander and Borderer with the Gaelic community that they had once regarded with such suspicion.[5]

Such nationally adopted symbols may be useful, the danger lies in confusing myth with reality, in defining identity in terms that combine a romanticised misconception of the past with an intense sense of identity shaped primarily by opposition to England. The school history curriculum should play a crucial part in enabling future citizens to recognise media images of the past for what they are: at present the evidence suggests that it is failing to do this.

The Council of Europe's view that history should occupy a privileged place on the school curriculum indicates its belief that serious study of the past is vital to the development of a realistic sense of national identity and a freedom from bigoted prejudice towards other nations.[6] Across the world innumerable instances can be found of a widespread appreciation of the importance of the school history curriculum and, especially, of what is offered in terms of national history. East European states wrestle with the problem of what to teach now that the Soviet Union's grip on their countries is gone; Japanese society is riven by angry debate over the appearance of a school textbook that suggests that their soldiers committed deeds in the Second World War that were shameful. In England the creation of a national curriculum for history aroused intense interest, and even produced pressures from senior politicians. The Government's Chief Curriculum Adviser, Dr Nicholas Tate, has repeatedly argued for a curriculum designed to build a sense of national identity to counter the fragmenting of society, a curriculum strong on narrative, conveying to children 'a sense of the nation as an entity which stretches back in time, a community of which they are a part'.[7]

In Scottish universities studying the nation's past has grown in popularity in recent years and has led to a major expansion of research and of publications. A sense of unease about the situation in schools led the Scottish Office to set up a Review Group; its report (SCCC 1997) indicated that all is not well and that there is indeed a deficit in terms of Scottish history occupying a worthwhile place on the curriculum. As part of the Review Group's work I carried out research in Spring 1996 into the knowledge of and attitudes towards Scottish history of pupils who were reaching the end of their period of compulsory schooling. Over three thousand questionnaires were completed under supervised conditions by pupils in thirty-five schools from different parts of the country. The questions posed had been evaluated first by three of Scotland's leading historians and the evidence indicated the exercise had been taken seriously – though the occasional pupil, baffled by a question, did attempt what charity suggests was intended as a humorous response. Ramsay MacDonald for example, was described by one pupil as deserving to be remembered for inventing the hamburger.

How important did pupils consider it to be to study their country's past? Responses to a cluster of questions about this issue did not produce the impression that it was seen as of great importance. Faced with the statement 'It does not matter if you are wholly ignorant of Scottish history', more than half were either indifferent (39%) or actually agreed with the assertion (18%). Perhaps these views were not unconnected with their experiences in the classroom, for 20% readily agreed that 'Scottish history is boring' whilst 30% preferred to adopt a neutral stance to this assertion. Within the overall sweep of the country's past, pupils did not strongly maintain the importance of pre-union Scottish history: from a series of broad areas of the Scottish past they (75%) selected studying the First and Second World Wars as being just as important as the development of an independent Scottish kingdom. Well under half of pupils saw much value in studying such topics as Pictish times, the Reformation or the decline of older industries. Around half of responses rated investigating Union with England, or the Jacobites as worthy of attention.

The investigation of where pupils saw such knowledge of Scottish history as they possessed as coming from clearly established the central importance of schoolwork. Three quarters of pupils rated it as of real importance. Pupil's also attributed insights to sources outside school including television (54%), the cinema (53%), spare-time reading (41%) and talking to adults (40%).

The exploration of pupils' actual knowledge and their misconceptions about past people, events and circumstances yielded results that were decidedly bleak. Pupils were asked to select from a range of possible definitions or explanations for each of a list of items. Around half of the pupils were able to recognise the former ship-building identity of Clydebank and that Irish people formed the biggest group of migrants coming to Scotland in the late eighteenth and nineteenth centuries. At the other end of the scale only 13% knew what happened at Flodden and just 15% appreciated the significance of what happened in 685 AD at the Battle of Nechtansmere. When offered reasons as to why Scotland became part of the United Kingdom 37% selected 'because English forces conquered it' and 28% chose 'as the result of a referendum'. This left just 24% as selecting the appropriate answer. The Battle of Culloden was seen as a clash between wholly English and wholly Scottish forces by 41%, just 25% appreciated the heavy Scots involvement on the Hanoverian side. The presence in Scotland of both Protestants and Catholics seemed to 50% of pupils to have been a permanent feature of the country's past, the Disruption was believed to be a split between Catholics and Protestants by 40%; even the origin of the country's name was widely misunderstood with 39% attributing it to the area's very first settlers and 30% agreeing that it was the Romans who had provided the name.

Pupils were also offered a list of dates and asked what of significance to Scotland might have happened then. They did best with 1746 (14%) though the actual recognition level here is dubious since there was a marked tendency to put 'Culloden' next to every date. In fact the preferred response to the other dates was to make no entry at all; around 90% pursued this strategy for such dates as 1320, 1603, 1660 and 1707.

A selection of individual names were set before pupils; they were asked to make a very short statement about the importance of each in Scottish history and a very generous policy was pursued of accepting answers that showed some relevant knowledge. William Wallace and Robert Bruce were recognised by 40%, John Logie Baird by 33% and Flora McDonald by 24%. Nil responses loomed large for the rest, reaching a figure of 90% for Sir Archibald Grant, Adam Smith and Tom Johnston: 1% recognised the first two but not a single pupil could identify the latter. 6% appreciated who St Columba was, whilst 10% thought he had discovered America. 7% recognised John Knox, 13% knew something about Thomas Telford, but only 8% were able to connect James Watt to steam power. The preferred response was that he was in some way associated with electricity, probably as the inventor of the light bulb. Neither Kenneth McAlpin (2% success rate) nor Ramsay MacDonald (3%) aroused any recognition from the overwhelming majority of pupils.

Writing in *The Observer* the Scottish journalist Jan Moir noted the danger to women in the wider world of believing the images projected of Scotland to be the reality:

> Scotland my dears is not full of rippling hunks with biceps like footballs, men who are romantically prepared to die for their country and who will ride their horses right into your bedrooms because they cannot wait one second more to be in your arms ... Scotland is in fact full of wee guys in anoraks wondering what's for the tea tonight. Scotland is full of men with chapped knees and freckles eating deep fried pies and moaning there's nothing good on telly. Scotland is full of blokes who could tell you everything about Ally McCoist but

nothing about Robert the Bruce.[8]

It may be that in education, too, there is a mis-match between the notion of Scottish education as rigorous, traditional, academic, and concerned with knowledge. Certainly it would seem that the country's future citizens are ill prepared to face the crude exploitation of the past to suit current purposes whether those purposes be cultural, economic or political. Yet events in 1965 illustrate Scottish concern to defend its own particular past. In that year the Scottish Office decided it would offer Scottish schools the chance to join English schools in celebrating 750 years since Magna Carta and 700 years since the calling of a Parliament by Simon de Montfort. The suggested school holiday triggered a flood of abusive correspondence to the Scottish Secretary, Willie Ross, as in this example:

> As a prospective teacher I wish to protest at your use of the teaching profession for instilling propaganda tending to assimilate the Scottish people to the English ... I would never have considered becoming a teacher if I had thought that I would be expected by the Scottish Education Department to act as an agent of assimilation by indoctrinating children in the noble myth of England.[9]

In Glasgow the successful campaign to ignore the event was led by the convenor of the school attendance committee: she was equally forthright in rejecting the SNP's campaign to celebrate Bannockburn instead, remarking:

> The gentleman who won Bannockburn was the reverse of democratic ... Historians have described Robert the Bruce as an Anglo Norman bully and history bears this out. It is ridiculous the tripe that children are fed with in history books.[10]

How can such sensitivities be reconciled with the actual state of ignorance that seems to be the result of eleven years of schooling? History does not enjoy the position that it commonly occupies in schools in other European countries either as a distinct and coherently structured subject or as something that all pupils must study till they are sixteen.[11] History became a class subject in 1886 with the history of independent Scotland being confined to Standard III. When History established itself in university courses in 1890 the new departments often recruited their lecturers from England: until the recent past university departments have often been seen as unenthusiastic about Scottish history. History graduates who took up teaching found themselves engaged in an endless struggle for a reasonable place for their subject on the curriculum. During the last thirty years, for the seven years of primary schooling, history has commonly been merged into a myriad of cross-curricular environmental studies projects chosen according to the interests of class and headteachers. The recent *Environmental Studies Guidelines 5-14* neither define a history curriculum nor prescribe a particular time allocation for the subject: a scrappy, minimal, incoherent curriculum remains perfectly possible.[12]

The curriculum in secondary schools is powerfully shaped by a report of twenty years ago which clustered subjects in modes, placing history in a Social Subjects mode along with geography and an amalgam of politics and economics called Modern Studies.[13] In the first two years of secondary schooling pupils experience around an hour a week of history, thereafter they commonly select just one of the three social subject: nearly two thirds of pupils abandon history at this point. Thus a nation intensely aware of its distinct identity treats a subject that is crucial to a proper sense of that identity in remarkably dismissive fashion.

What do teachers choose to include in the little time available to them? During the seventies the Schools Council History course in England led to change seeping into Scotland, a change that stressed the subject's value as a context for skill development rather than knowledge acquisition. Separate and disconnected depth studies served as the vehicle for intellectual exercises strongly focused on source handling. This incoherent curriculum still flourishes today. The absence of detailed prescription for a curriculum may initially seem an enviable contrast with the situation in the rest of the United Kingdom; its consequences are a confusion of topics and real problems over resourcing.

In 1878 a member of the schools inspectorate gloomily reviewed the content of the history curriculum in Scotland as a:

> ghastly line of battles, feuds and deaths that form the salient points
> of Scottish history ... one must question the value of a school history
> that lands a child in the midst of loose laws and looser passions and
> unquestionably helps ... to maintain the sentimental Scotch antipathy
> to England.[14]

Evidence of a curriculum with similar attributes can still be seen today. The reminiscences of one of today's academically successful Scots about the impact on him of school history may serve to illustrate the point:

> School in Aberdeen meant primarily the establishment of my identity
> as a Scotsman ... To this day my knowledge of Scottish history is
> nothing more than a vague chauvinistic haze permeated by hostility
> to England and populated by Bruce, Wallace, Knox, the

Covenanters, Mary Queen of Scots and Bonnie Prince Charlie.[15]

Commonly taught topics include Roman and Viking assaults on north Britain, Wallace and Bruce, the Jacobites and the Highland Clearances. An image of the inhabitants of Scotland as a much abused people is the inevitable consequence of the readily available resources being those produced to serve the English national curriculum, thus perpetuating the 1905 plea about textbooks of the convention of the Royal Burghs of Scotland that:

> a more adequate and accurate presentation be given of the important events in Scottish history, that these events should be presented from an authentic Scottish standpoint ... Scotland receives neither fair nor adequate treatment. It is looked at from a purely English standpoint, its history dealt with in a casual and fragmentary way and is referred to mainly where it affected the history of England.[16]

The result is a sense of identity developed in opposition to England. The Irish journalist Fergal Keane has described a very similar shaping of his attitudes by a school curriculum obsessed with old battles, with suffering and with hostility to England.[17] Pupils in Scotland rarely study many issues crucial to the shaping of Scottish identity. The powerful impact of the Protestant Reformation filtered into and divided Scottish society, turned many from hostility to England to actively seeking English aid and had an impact on Scottish identity still evident today. Yet it is rarely taught. Neither the union of crowns nor the union of Parliaments receive careful attention, the upheavals of the seventeenth century are largely ignored, and the fascinating emergence of a British as well as a Scottish identity is neglected. Nor are the impressive Scottish achievements in science, architecture, medicine, philosophy and literature seriously celebrated.

Scots have had a significant impact on the world beyond their frontiers, not least in Europe. Scots may make fond reference to the auld alliance with France, yet few schools trouble to teach any French history. The involvement of Scots in European affairs from medieval times was so extensive as to cause a leading historian to describe them as:

> a cosmopolitan people exceptionally prone to emigrate in order to seek their fortunes in another country and with a reputation for competence whether their trade was learning, killing buying and selling.[18]

Once given access to the English Empire, Scots become enthusiastic imperialists. The first governor of Canada was a Scot, Warren Hastings gave preference to Scots in the East India Company, Scots missionaries, soldiers, administrators, bankers, merchants, tradesmen, artisans and clerks pushed out the empire's boundaries, developed and managed it and settled in communities whose names indicate their Scottish ancestry. Yet so neglected is this area of study that its leading researcher notes:

> one might be forgiven for thinking that Scotland was more of a colonised rather than a colonising nation.... [H]owever, like it or not, the imperial legacy still pervades Scottish society.... [I]t provided the very substantial economic foundations for Scottish prosperity in the 19th and early 20th centuries and has left us some of the most enduring symbols of Scottish identity.[19]

The education of children in today's Scotland leaves them vulnerable to the images of identity created to attract tourists who have heard of Wallace, Bruce, Mary Queen of Scots and Bonnie Prince Charlie: it leaves them open to persuasion that films like *Braveheart* indeed convey historically accurate accounts of the past: it encourages the glamorising of narrow nationalism rather than self-critical investigation. A rigorous reform of the current situation is highly desirable. Will a new political establishment in Scotland provide it?

The Author

Sydney Wood teaches History at the Northern College, Aberdeen, where he is responsible for the postgraduate certificate course for trainee History teachers. He has been heavily involved in Scottish Office national curricular development work for History in schools. His research work lies in the area of exploring children's understanding of the past and he has published a wide range of books and articles relating to this area, and to aspects of Scotland's past.

References

1   N. Harper, 'Support for Scotland', in *The Press and Journal*, 18.1.1995, p. 8.
2   E. J. Cowan, 'The Wallace Factor in Scottish History', in R. Jackson & S. Wood, eds., *Images of Scotland*, Northern College, Aberdeen, 1997, pp. 5-17 (p. 6).
3   E. J. Hobsbawm, *Nations and Nationalism since 1700*, C.U.P.,

Cambridge,1990, p. 12.

4 J. A. Atkinson, I. Banks & J. O'Sullivan, *Nationalism and Archaeology*, Cruithne Press, Glasgow, 1996.

5 J. Prebble, *The King's Jaunt: George IV in Scotland 1822*, Collins, London 1988.

6 The Council of Europe, *Against Bias and Prejudice: the Council of Europe's work on history teaching and history textbooks*, Strasbourg, 1986.

7 N. Tate, 'The role of History in the formation of national identity', unpublished speech to the Council of Europe conference, York, UK, 18 September 1995.

8 Jan Moir, 'What do *Braveheart* and *Rob Roy* tell you about real Scotsmen?', *The Observer*, 29.10.1995, 'Life' section, p. 4.

9 Scottish Record Office, File, ED48/2094.

10 Scottish Record Office, File, ED48/2094.

11 Sydney Wood, 'The Place of History in the School Curriculum – The European Dimension', in R. Jackson & W. McPhillimy, eds., *Education in the North*, no. 2, Northern College, Aberdeen, 1994, pp. 1-4.

12 Scottish Office Education Department, *Environmental Studies 5-14,* SOED, Edinburgh, 1993.

13 J. Munn, *The Structure of the Curriculum in the 3rd and 4th years of the Scottish Secondary School*, HMSO, Edinburgh, 1977.

14 Quoted in R. D. Anderson, *Education and the Scottish People*, O.U.P. Oxford, 1995, p. 214.

15 David Hay, 'Memories of a Calvinist Childhood', in W. G. Lawrence, ed., *Roots in a Northern Landscape*, Scottish Cultural Press, Edinburgh, 1997, pp. 48-61 (p. 60).

16 The Convention of the Royal Burghs of Scotland, *School History Books*, Edinburgh, 1905.

17 F. Keane, *Letter to Daniel*, Penguin, London, 1996.

18 T.C. Smout, 'The Culture of Migration: Scots as Europeans 1500-1800', in R. Samuel, ed., *History Workshop Journal 40,* O.U.P., Oxford, 1995, pp. 108-117 (p. 116).

19 R.J. Finlay, 'The rise and fall of popular imperialism in Scotland 1850-1950', in C.W.J. Withers, ed., *Scottish Geographical Magazine*, vol. 113, no. 1, March, 1997, pp. 13-21 (p. 13).

18

Contesting the Past, Constructing the Future

History, Identity and Politics in Schools

Robert Phillips

Introduction: postmodernism, consumption and history

The connection between the past and the future has often interested historians and there are good reasons why in the contemporary world this pre-occupation is particularly resonant.[1] In his book *Mythical Past, Elusive Future,* Frank Furedi suggests that 'anxiety about the direction of the future has stimulated a scramble to appropriate the past' and describes attempts by governments and elites throughout the world to reinvent national histories. Furedi also emphasises, however, that history is 'in demand' by a range of competing groups concerned to find identity in a troubled, uncertain world; there is, after all, no longer 'a history with a capital H; there are many competing histories'.[2] This appropriation of the past makes sense only when one considers that history has been subject to the same forces of *consumption* experienced in various aspects of economic, social and cultural life, most commonly associated with the postmodern condition. This reflects itself not only in the consumption of the past through heritage, museums, and local history but also in the ways in which competing forces have attempted to lay claim to *official histories*. One of these official histories – school history – forms the subject of this paper.

Scholars working within the field of educational discourse argue about the radical potential of postmodernism; some stress its sentimental features, whilst others dispute its capacity to challenge 'official knowledge'.[3] Giroux, whose work is considered to be particularly important for this paper, thus refers both to the 'benefits' and the 'ravages' of postmodernism, yet has written at length about its potential radicalism, especially with regard to the construction of what he calls a 'border pedagogy' which not only recognizes, but actively promotes, the recognition of 'other histories'.[4] This chapter is concerned with speculating upon the ways in which contradictory historical discourses influence children in complex ways. I want to do three things:

♦   First, I want to suggest reasons why school history has became politicized in the late twentieth century. History, as we know, has always been political, yet in terms of the professional, public and political interest in the subject in the 1980s and 1990s, the teaching of history was particularly controversial, reflected in the thousands of history-related letters, articles and editorials in the press, and also in the many references to the subject in *Hansard*. I therefore want to speculate about the historical and educational reasons for this political and public consumption of history teaching and then go on to examine the ideological and cultural reasons for this development.

♦   Second, the chapter considers the ways in which both the history teaching profession and pupils themselves have been subject to the complex array of consumptive factors which have influenced education and curriculum in recent years. Whereas it is relatively straightforward to narrate and evaluate the ways in which the history teaching profession has had to respond to the political-public consumption of the past, it is rather more difficult at this point to gauge precisely the ways in which children and young adolescents consume it outside school. Yet these *unofficial histories* may be crucial in the creation of individual and collective identities.

♦   Third, on the basis of the discussion above, the chapter speculates about the future direction of history in schools, about ways in which history and history teaching are consumed in the future by teachers and by children and, perhaps most significantly of all, it considers the imperative of these factors for future notions of identity. Crucial in all of this, of course, is the relationship between the *official* and the *unofficial* consumption of the past by children, a relationship which, it seems to me, has a potentially profound set of implications for the ways in which the nation and the conceptualization of Britishness are imagined in the 21st century.[5]

Public and political consumption of the past: the politicization of school history in the 1980s and 1990s

The relationship between school history and the creation of collective identity partly explains why history became a contested subject within the wider debate over the National Curriculum (NC) established in 1988. I have argued elsewhere that history within the NC in England represented the 'battle for the big prize'.[6] By this I mean that the 'great history debate' was nothing less than a struggle for culture, for identity and for hegemony. Politicians and ideologues of both sides of the political spectrum, within and outside Parliament recognized the ideological and cultural significance of the subject; Margaret Thatcher in particular noticed its potential for influencing future generations. As Kaye has emphasised, governments have traditionally 'feared history' for this reason.[7]

In the 1980s, neo-conservatives within the New Right movement became particularly interested in debates over the teaching of history and English, as they provided opportunities to articulate restorationist visions of culture, heritage and nation.[8] In the process, the New Right cultivated a discourse of derision to attack the historical professional establishment, the innovative teaching and assessment methods used, and the selection of historical content in schools. Above all, the New Right accused history professionals of undermining the cultural heritage of the nation, caused by the 'flight from British history'.[9] When analysed more deeply, the notion of 'British' identity envisaged within this discourse was essentially English. Partington thus denounced the 'systematic denigration of English (later British) history'.[10]

Through this discourse of derision New Right activists were able to influence the debate over history in the important period prior to the establishment of the NC. One of the most effective means was through the use of the press; not only did prominent conservative writers and academics utilize the media to articulate their views, press coverage of the 'great history debate' simplified and polarized highly complex arguments over the subject. Crucially, the debate shifted away from the professional to the political domains: *history teaching had become subject to 'consumption' by the public.*

In the 1980s to the time of writing, therefore, history teaching has been the subject of intense media and public interest. A number of writers have recognized the symbolic ideological significance of the utilization of the press for the cultivation of authoritarian 'common sense' populism.[11] Within these circumstances, the press laid populist 'claims' on the past demanding a return to traditional teaching methods and a more patriotic historical content (*Guardian*: 18.7.89) through the teaching of, for example, the 'nuts and bolts' of history (*Sunday Times*: 13.3.88), 'the great landmarks' (*The Times*: 4.4.90) and the 'great heroes' (*Daily Star*: 5.5.94) of 'Britain's glorious past' (*The Sun*: 5.5.94).

Politicians also seemed to be consumed by the history debate in the 1980s and 1990s. Political involvement ranged from speeches on history teaching made by successive Secretaries of State to direct interventions by politicians to attempt to influence the policy process with regard to history.[12] One of the most publicised interventions came from Kenneth Clarke who, as Secretary of State for Education, decreed that the NC history curriculum in England and Wales should contain only pre-1960s history on the grounds that 'that is the proper subject of the history curriculum, this morning's news on the radio, and current events in the Gulf War, are not'.[13]

Given the degree of direct and indirect political interference outlined above, it seems curious to note that the various working groups established to create history in the NC between 1989 and 1995 did not succumb to it. One of the reasons for this can be found in efforts made by professional organizations such as the Historical Association (HA) in England and the Association of History Teachers in Wales (AHTW) to counter the arguments presented above and to defend the status of the subject. By entering the public and political arenas in the ways that they did, both the HA and the AHTW brought new elements to the notion of the curriculum pressure group. In England, for example, at the time of the NC debate, the HA used the media to run a vigorous and determined campaign to persuade history teachers to support the NC History Working Group's Final Report,[14] (even though school teachers had some reservations about it), on the grounds that politicians – including possibly Mrs Thatcher herself – would replace it with something far worse.[15] At vital points during the crucial period between 1990 and 1991, the HA intervened in the press to counter the arguments of the New Right and also to argue that the compulsory status of history should be preserved. In Wales, the AHTW sent a delegation directly to the House of Lords arguing forcefully for the preservation of the status of the Welsh history statutory orders in 1992 amidst rumours that they were to be reformed.[16]

These actions by the HA and AHTW were efforts made by professional organizations to counter what many teachers perceived to be the propaganda of neo-conservative historical discourse articulated by the New Right in the press. By taking these actions, these curriculum pressure groups were forced to respond to the elevation of the debate over history from the professional to the private and public domains and in the process were forced to embrace many of the strategies of the consuming, populist, market-orientated educational environment of which it is the purpose of this paper to describe. By doing so, however, they were able to influence the NC in ways which mean that the eventual 'official histories' created – and which are now statutory in British schools – are in a number of ways different from the intentions of those who originally conceived the NC. I shall return to the significance of this later in the paper; first, I want to consider the ways in which children consume the past.

Children and the consumption of the past: radicalism and reaction in unofficial histories

An extensive, wide-ranging literature has developed over the past fifty years or so which has sought to evaluate and explain the response of children to official history. Much of this work has been concerned, for example, in applying psychological theory to explain how children learn about the past or how history can properly be assessed. Numerous texts suggest ways in which the subject can most effectively be taught or, to use the language and discourse of the official, how school history is to be 'delivered'. Yet there has been relatively little empirical or theoretical work done to explore the ways in which children conceptualize and are influenced or socialized by those images, histories and pasts which constitute the unofficial. There have been, recently, some welcome exceptions,[17] but the fact remains that the paucity of research in this field means that we know relatively little about the ways children consume the past outside the history classroom; yet the power of the unofficial may in fact be the most crucial influence in shaping the 'idea of an historical education'.[18]

I now want to explore the dimensions and boundaries of the unofficial in greater detail. By considering the symbols, images, versions, texts, institutions and media which bombard children daily with images of the past, I want to consider their potential impact and the ways in which they relate to official versions. Many of my comments are speculative in nature, although I will make reference to some of the recent work which touches upon this issue. Specifically, I want to discuss three unofficial sources of historical consumption: the media (including television and the press), film and museums and heritage sites.

We have already mentioned the role of the press in contributing to the discourse of derision above and its impact upon the polarization of debates over the teaching of history. However, for the purposes of this section, I want to elaborate upon the authoritarian, populist imagery of the press, particularly the images and language it uses in the cultivation of discourses on nationhood and race and their likely impact upon children. Throughout the 1980s and 1990s, the press consistently cultivated a patriotic vision of Britain and Britishness and a sometimes explicit anti-Europeanism, often using historical images in the process. There is no better illustration of this than the anti-German phobia whipped up by the tabloids, often through references to the Second World War, especially at patriotic high points such as international football championships. The precise nature of children's reactions to these images is open to debate but it is likely that they either directly or indirectly contribute to what Billig has called banal nationalism, that is a view of nationhood which is often nostalgic, sometimes xenophobic and cultivated through popular images, for example, through the 'British bull-dog' and other traditional historical images and heroes.[19]

Yet in other aspects of the media, children are bombarded with a range of conflicting messages relating to identity. Television has been increasingly subject to mass globalization caused by consumerism and global telecommunications. These portray images that challenge and run counter to traditional notions of culture or nation, whether through the cult of soap operas or through contradictory post-colonial images. Television has provided a means by which children are transcended into the 'global village'.[20] I am aware of the dangers of over-emphasizing the cultural 'benefits' here: television, of course, has an important reactionary role but the fact remains that it has also played a significant part in breaking down what Connell has called 'parochial tradition'.[21] Nowhere is this better exemplified than in the consumption – through television and radio – of popular music that has transcended traditional cultural boundaries. Contemporary popular music combining more than one cultural form provides one of the most tangible examples of Giroux's cultural 'border crossings'. In so doing, they create alternative possibilities and meanings in relation to what it means to be British.

The growth of interest in the past has been forcefully expressed through the cult of historical or period piece films in recent years. Of course, the historical film or drama has always been a feature of western society but academics now recognize that films have forced historians to 'offer a new relationship to the world of the past' and to 'revolutionize our notions of the past'.[22] Wollen (1991) has argued that the proliferation of films which create idyllic, sentimental visions of the past derive their nostalgic impetus from the uncertainty of a rapidly changing, globalized, post-Fordist, consumerist society. Wollen argues that this 'retrospection holds nationhood exclusively in its sights. Its nostalgia yearns for a nation in which social status is known and kept, and where difference constitutes rather than fragments national unity'.[23] It is possible to speculate about the powerful impact of such images on children, locking them into sentimental 'visions of an old country' long since departed.[24]

Yet this analysis is only part of the picture; it does not fully explain the growth in recent years of a new genre of films and film-making which attempts to re-create, re-interpret and re-invent characters, events and controversies of the past. Some of these films represent a conscious effort by film makers to deconstruct and demystify earlier accounts and myths created by Hollywood: it could be argued that an example here is *Dances with Wolves* (1990) which is a conscious reaction to the thousands of films which portrayed earlier American history from the perspective of white Europeans as opposed to native Americans. Other films, like *Schindler's List* (1993), have attempted to provide shocking images of past events, attempting to 'tell it as it really was' as opposed to 'what we would wish to think it was like'. Others have attempted to provide an alternative (albeit sometimes equally partial) view of crucial events from the past which, crucially for this paper, contrast with official versions. Thus, Rosenstone describes *JFK* (1991) as a work which 'questions the official truths about the past so provocatively that we are forced once again to look to history and consider how events mean to us today' reminding us that, 'it is part of the burden of the historical work to make us rethink how we got to where we are, and to make us question values that we and our leaders and our nation live by'.[25]

Although there may be a tendency here to over-emphasize the beneficial or potentially liberating nature of films such as these, other recent films of the 1990s remind us more obviously of the dangers or 'ravages' of nostalgia, banality and sentimentality outlined by Billig and Wollen above. Films such as *Braveheart* (1995) have given greater impetus to existing nationalist sentiments in Scotland. Moreover, at the time of writing, speculation in the press suggests that Wales is not only preparing to receive home 'the bones of Glyndwr' but is also about to produce its own version of *Braveheart*, charting the history of either Llywelyn the Great or Owain Glyndwr. This reminds us again of the use of myth and history to create the concept of the 'national'.[26]

Museums and heritage sites represent the extremity of the boundary between the official and unofficial, for they 'negotiate a nexus between cultural production and consumption, and between expert and lay knowledge'.[27] Sociologists, anthropologists and cultural analysts have long since recognized the importance of the museum for shaping of public culture, knowledge and national identity.[28] They have also been correct to identify the expansion of museums and the heritage industry as being the most obvious example of the 'consumption' of the past over the past twenty years or so.[29] The heritage industry also provides one of the most obvious illustrations of the contradictions within the postmodern condition, for it represents the representation of the past – heritage – through the market, the consumer and enterprise.[30] By fusing two apparently unnatural bedfellows into one dynamic, museums and the heritage industry have had a major responsibility for the cultivation of sentimentality and nostalgia for the past.

Yet whereas the conservatism of 'the national museum' and the nostalgia of the 'heritage industry' have been recognized, it is also important to emphasize that the effect of marketization and consumption have also forced museums to diversify in a range of extraordinary ways. Museums have thus started to reflect the impact of globalization and have begun to provide means by which different communities and cultures can celebrate and visibly represent the 'politics of difference'.[31] Museums have also diversified in the ways in which they represent the past and have embraced a range of interactive media – visual, technological, dramatic, artistic – for the purposes of public consumption.[32] Thus, it is no longer possible merely to view them as agencies of social control; for the children who visit them, museums now provide 'possibilities and potentialities':

> The increased representation of minority voices in museums - which has been matched in many other cultural spheres - has played a part in shifting the emphasis of social theoretical perspectives on museums from 'control' to 'contest'. This is part of a shift in theoretical emphasis in the social sciences from production to consumption.[33]

The relationship between official and unofficial histories: the growth of a border pedagogy?

I now want to address a central issue in this chapter: what is the relationship between official and unofficial histories? In terms of their effect upon pupils, which is the most influential and dominant? And what are the implications for history teaching and history teachers?

When it was introduced, politicians made no effort to hide the intentions behind the NC. It was national in the sense that it sought to create a set of common values and ideals. Not surprisingly, educationalists have therefore become interested in the children's conceptualization of national identity, particularly their views on 'what it means to be British'.[34] However, only recently has any research work been done on identifying those factors that are dominant in this process of socialization, particularly the relative impact of the official and unofficial. The recent work of Goalen is particularly relevant for the purposes of this paper. In an important piece of exploratory research concerned with evaluating the impact of history teaching upon children's sense of national identity, Goalen found that one of the 'clearest expressions of national affiliation was through sporting allegiance'. He also concluded that television was 'the key influence in the development of children's conception of the political world'.[35] However, when it came to analysing the impact of aspects of the history curriculum which 'made them proud to be British', the most common response in his survey was the history of the Second World War, a typical justification cited by the children being that 'we won'. Yet, crucially, Goalen concluded that:

> There is little evidence from this pilot study that we are in danger of

producing a narrowly nationalistic generation as a result of the centrally imposed history curriculum in England. On the contrary, many pupils are able to draw quite a balanced picture of their country's contribution to the modern world.[36]

Goalen's research revealed, in fact, the dynamic, often contradictory relationship between the official and unofficial and its overall impact upon children. As we have seen, children are subject to a range of contradictory influences: radical/reactionary, enlightening/banal, possibilities/impossibilities, benefits/ravages. Crucial in the process of steering children away from the reactionary, the banal, the impossibilities, the ravages and ideological closure is the role of the teacher; specifically, this involves a commitment on the part of the teacher to what Giroux calls 'border pedagogy' which:

> extends the meaning and importance of demystification as a central pedagogical task...students must be offered opportunities to read texts that both affirm and interrogate the complexity of their own histories... to engage and develop a counter discourse to the established boundaries of knowledge...In this perspective, culture is not viewed as monolithic or unchanging, but as a shifting sphere of multiple and heterogeneous borders where different histories...intermingle...There are no unified subjects here, only students whose multi-layered and often contradictory voices and experiences intermingle with the weight of particular histories that will not fit easily into the master narrative of a monolithic culture.[37]

What is intriguing about aspects of contemporary official school histories in the United Kingdom is that they embrace a commitment to many features of the pedagogy of 'border crossings' outlined above. Whereas it could be argued, of course, that the NC could contain a greater commitment to post-colonial discourse (many history teachers hardly ever contemplate either consciously or sub-consciously the implications of Young's 'white mythologies')[38] nevertheless the NC as a text is essentially 'open' to interpretation, to possibilities and to a plurality of different meanings. There is more than just a touch of irony about the realisation that the history NC as it has eventually been implemented in schools is different in a number of respects to what the original framers of the NC in 1988 intended.[39]

Conclusion: possibilities and impossibilities in the future

Teachers have been encouraged to respond creatively to the possibilities contained in the official school history text.[40] Theoretically, the history NC provides potential opportunities for pedagogical 'border crossings' and for promoting the radical, as opposed to the reactionary elements of the unofficial. The commitment in the NC text to the idea that historical truth, knowledge and certainty can be subject to rigorous analysis does not imply the rejection of historical certainty per se, but implies instead a reconceptualized, more complex view of what 'historical knowledge' is. This has the potential to help children see through the banality of press headlines and may make them fully appreciate the nostalgic or nationalistic imagery in films. It will also allow them to distinguish between popular-memory patriotism and xenophobic nationalism.[41]

The acceptance in the NC text of the reality of heterogeneity, the existence of 'other histories' as opposed to the unquestioning acceptance of a monolithic, homogenous dominant historical narrative, may encourage children to celebrate the 'politics of difference' portrayed in contemporary museums. All this may be cultivating Rorty's notion of the 'ironic re-description' in historical education.[42] This view of the NC as an open as opposed to a closed text, subject by the reader to interpretation, even contestation, may irritate those committed to closure and certainty who see the NC moving in ways which perhaps had not been originally intended.[43] Ultimately, however, research such as Goalen's provides tentative evidence that the unintended consequences of 'official histories' provide scope for the cultivation of a 'border pedagogy' which encourages children to realise the 'benefits' as opposed to the 'ravages' of those dimensions of the 'unofficial' past which they are being encouraged on a daily basis to consume.

The Author

Robert Phillips is Lecturer in History Education in the Department of Education at the University of Wales, Swansea. He has written extensively on history teaching and the connection between history and national identity. His forthcoming book, *History Teaching, Nationhood and the State* (Cassell, 1998), explores the politics of the 'great debate' surrounding the teaching of history in schools in the late twentieth century. A version of this chapter appears in the *British Journal of Educational Studies*, vol. 46 (1998).

References

1   R. Heilbroner, *Visions of the Future: The Distant Past, Yesterday, Today and Tomorrow*, Oxford University Press, Oxford, 1995.

2   F. Furedi, *Mythical Past, Elusive Future: History and Society in an Anxious Age*, Pluto Press, London, 1992, pp. 3 & 8.

3   J. Donald, *Sentimental Education: Schooling, Popular Culture and the Regulation of Liberty*, Verso, London, 1992; M. Apple, 'What Post-modernists Forget: cultural capital and official knowledge', *Curriculum Studies,* vol. 1, 1993, pp. 301–16.

4   H. Giroux, *Border Crossings: Cultural Workers and the Politics of Education*, Routledge, London, 1992; K. Hastrup, ed., *Other Histories*, Routledge, London, 1992.

5   D. McKiernan, 'History in a national curriculum: imagining the nation at the end of the 20th century', *Journal of Curriculum Studies,* vol. 25, 1993, pp. 33–51.

6   R. Phillips, '"The Battle for the Big Prize": the creation of synthesis and the role of a curriculum pressure group: the case of history and the National Curriculum', *The Curriculum Journal*, vol. 3, 1992, pp. 245–60.

7   H. Kaye, *Why do Ruling Classes Fear History and Other Essays*, Macmillan, London, 1996; M. Thatcher, *The Downing Street Years*, Harper Collins, London, 1993.

8   R. Phillips, 'History, Hegemony and the New Right: Implications for History Teacher Education', paper presented at the International Colloquium on Education: British and American Perspectives. Department of Educational Foundations, University of Wisconsin La Crosse, USA, September 29-30, 1992.

9   S. Deuchar, *The New History: A Critique*, Campaign for Real Education, York, 1989.

10 G. Partington, 'History: Re-Written to Ideological Fashion', in D. O'Keeffe, ed., *The Wayward Curriculum: A Case for Parents' Concern?*, London, Social Affairs Unit, London, 1986, pp. 63-81 (at p. 72).

11 S. Hall and M. Jacques, eds., *The Politics of Thatcherism*, Lawrence & Wishart, London, 1983.

12 K. Baker, *The Turbulent Years: My Life in Politics*, Faber & Faber, London, 1993.

13 Parliamentary Debates (Hansard), 185, 12 February 1991, p.722.

14 DES, *National Curriculum History Working Group: Final Report*, London, HMSO, London, 1990.

15 Phillips, 'The Battle for the Big Prize'.

16 R. Phillips, 'Reprieve from "The Sword of Damocles"?', *Welsh Historian*, vol. 19, 1993, pp. 11–15.

17 C. Husbands, *What Is History Teaching?*, Open University Press,

Buckingham, 1996.
18 G. Partington, *The Idea of an Historical Education*, NFER, Slough, 1980.
19 M. Billig, *Banal Nationalism*, Sage, London, 1995. See also the paper by Sophie Breese in this collection.
20 D. Morley and K. Robins, eds., *Spaces of Identity: Global Media, Electronic Landscapes and Cultural Boundaries*, Routledge, London, 1995.
21 R. Connell, *The Child's Construction of Politics*, Melbourne University Press, Melbourne, 1971, p. 128.
22 R. Rosenstone, *Visions of the Past: The Challenge of Film to Our Idea of History*, Harvard University Press, Cambridge MA, 1995, pp.12–13.
23 T. Wollen, 'Over our shoulders: nostalgia screen fictions for the 1980s', in J. Corner and S. Harvey, eds., *Enterprise and Heritage: Crosscurrents of National Culture*, London, Routledge, London, 1991, pp. 178-93 (at p. 181).
24 P. Wright, *On Living in an Old Country: The National Past in Contemporary Britain*, Verso, London, 1985.
25 Rosenstone, *Visions of the Past*, pp.130–31.
26 For wider discussion see R. Phillips, 'History Teaching, Cultural Restorationism and National Identity in England and Wales', *Curriculum Studies,* vol. 4, 1996, pp. 385–99.
27 S. MacDonald, 'Theorizing Museums: An Introduction', in S. Macdonald and G. Fyfe, eds., *Theorizing Museums*, Blackwell, Oxford, 1996, pp. 1-21 (at p. 4).
28 S. Pearce, ed., *Museums and the Appropriation of Culture*, Athlone, London, 1994; E. Hooper-Greenhill, *Museums and the Shaping of Knowledge*, Routledge, London, 1992; F. Kaplan, ed., *Museums and the Making of 'Ourselves': The Role of Objects in National Identity*, Leicester University Press, London, 1994.
29 R. Hewison, *The Heritage Industry*, Methuen, London, 1987.
30 J. Corner and S. Harvey, eds., *Enterprise and Heritage: Crosscurrents on National Culture*, Routledge, London, 1991.
31 M. Prosler, 'Museums and Globalization', in Macdonald and Fyfe, eds., *Theorizing Museums,* pp. 21-45; H. Riegel, 'Into the heart of irony: ethnographic exhibitions and the politics of difference', in Macdonald and Fyfe, eds., *Theorizing Museums,* pp. 83-105.
32 E. Hooper-Greenhill, ed., *Museums, Media, Message,* Routledge, London, 1995.
33 MacDonald, 'Theorizing Museums: An Introduction', p. 10.
34 B. Carrington and G. Short, 'What Makes a Person British? Children's conceptions of their national culture and identity', *Educational Studies*, vol. 21, 1995, pp. 217–38.
35 P. Goalen, *The History Curriculum and national Identity: Exploring children's perceptions of national identity in England*, forthcoming, pp. 5 & 6.
36 Goalen, The History Curriculum and national Identity, p. 10.

37   Giroux, *Border Crossings*, pp. 30–34.
38   R. Young, *White Mythologies: Writing History and the West*, Routledge, London, 1990.
39   K. Jenkins and P. Brickley, 'Always Historicise: Unintended Opportunities in National Curriculum History', *Teaching History*, vol. 62, 1991, pp. 8-14.
40   J. Pankhania, *Liberating the National History Curriculum*, Falmer Press, London, 1994.
41   R. Phillips, 'Thesis and Antithesis in Tate's Views on Nation, Culture and Identity', *Teaching History,* vol. 86, 1997, pp. 30–33.
42   R. Rorty, *Contingency, Irony and Solidarity*, Cambridge University Press, Cambridge, 1989.
43   N. Tate, Speech to the Council of Europe Conference on 'The role of history in the formation of national identity', York, 18 September 1995.

19

Truth, Ethics and Imagination

Thoughts on the Purpose of History

David Andress

At the conference which this volume celebrates, Keith Jenkins presented a paper entitled 'Why Bother With the Past?: The Possible "End" of Professional Historiography'. Although the content of this piece was entirely what one might expect from Jenkins' prior publications, the message, as confirmed to a rather disconcerted audience in questions, was that perhaps, indeed, we should not 'Bother With the Past'. This rather bluntly pessimistic view given by Jenkins of the purpose of history is one that can be seen to underlie his published work, where he has been concerned to break down 'modernist' certainties and to replace them with 'post-modern' individualised perspectives and readings.[1] It is however ironic to discover that what many will have read as a message to students to liberate themselves within their study of history may be underlain by a conviction that the enterprise is futile. In his paper Jenkins effectively enjoined his audience to give up hoping for something to be communicated from the past, and reflected that the 'skills' of history-study could be as fruitfully (or more fruitfully) applied to any more present-centred discipline.

I wish to present an alternative to this view. There is a first, and very practical, reason why those at the theoretical and problematical 'forefront' of historical study should not abandon the past. If we do, we do not leave it bereft of study, but rather we give it into the hands of those who wish it to serve purposes far removed from the delicate reflections of post-modernists. The field of 'history' is vast, a landscape of cultural production ranging from its compulsory teaching in schools (under a heavily politically-pressured curriculum), to its antiquarian and unquestioningly present-affirming amateurs, to its reification in national symbols and monuments, to its endless reiterations in all the modes of popular nationalism. None of this will cease if 'Professional Historiography' gives up the ghost, and though at times the critical historian must feel like a voice crying in the wilderness of crude, blinkered or xenophobic interpretations, it is surely better to light a candle than curse the darkness?

I therefore want to address professional historians' practice in a wide sense – a sense that circulates between writing, researching, speaking and especially teaching. I think all those who are teachers of history would agree in the end that, whatever the purely intellectual demands of research and writing, it is teaching, and teaching well, that is the hardest part of our jobs. Furthermore, I would suggest that there is very little point in conducting complex intellectual debates about our subject if we do not at least try to mediate those debates to a student audience. Unless we can decide what all the current debates about history have to say about our teaching-practices, they will remain sterile disputation, and students, who could be learning to interact with a vastly enriched historical field, will carry on treating history as just so many 'facts', if indeed they are not seduced into conceding its utter uselessness.

The relationship of the discipline of history to an idea of 'the truth' is currently alleged to be in ferment. Although as Beverley Southgate has recently discussed, Plato did not actually win and establish Absolute Truth absolutely all those years ago, you would be forgiven for not noticing this from the pronouncements of many historians.[2] Keith Jenkins has ably summarised many of these views, and shown us scholars as influential as Geoffrey Elton, Arthur Marwick and Edward Thompson staking their claims to this 'truth' in their practice. In the realm of current historical practice those three may not appear to stand out as a particularly diverse group, but as Jenkins is emphasising, on many undergraduate courses, that is as diverse as it gets. Even an historian of Africa and of masculinity like John Tosh becomes very philosophically conservative when he turns his hand to a student primer.[3]

Of course, Jenkins and Southgate are attempting to challenge this habit, but even as they do so, we find Joyce Appleby, Lynn Hunt and Margaret Jacob weighing in to the post-modernism debate with an impassioned defence of 'truth' in historical practice – a rather more politically-correct view of truth than Geoffrey Elton's, no doubt, but philosophically little altered.[4] The tone for much current debate was set in 1991 when Lawrence Stone used the pages of *Past and Present* to curtly denounce post-modernism, post-structuralism and post-anything-else as an iniquitous attack on the idea that the past ever actually happened – an 'ever-narrowing trap' formed by the combination of textual analysis, symbolic anthropology and New Historicism which left history an 'endangered species'.[5]

Stone's remarks were responded to by Patrick Joyce in general terms, and Stone replied at greater length in 1992. Construing the claim that we can only ever access the past textually as a claim that it only ever existed textually, he warned that this would have students lost in a meaningless world of self-referentiality. Stone's apocalyptic interpretation is somewhat undermined by his own remark that: 'My only objection is when they declare not that truth is unknowable, but that there is no reality out there'.[6] Quite where you find 'reality' if you have already abandoned truth is not clear, and in any case, in Jenkins' words, post-modernists do not 'deny the existence of the actuality of the past... only that, logically, that past can entail one and only one evaluation of it'.[7]

Patrick Joyce has also become a central figure in a wide-ranging polemical debate in the pages of *Social History*. Here 'post-ism' is seen as attacking not the sort of empirical historiography Stone defends, but rather the values of a radical, Marxism-centred social history. Here too the central threat is seen as being the devaluation of claims to truth, or to reality in interpretation. This debate, although as it has expanded it has produced some interesting individual viewpoints, has also shown quite clearly what some believe to be at stake – the risk, according to Geoff Eley and Keith Nield, of the complete erasure of thirty years of complex historiography.[8]

These exchanges show some of the dangers of the current course of debate. Joyce has courted controversy with his views, and has obtained it, along with the inevitable accompaniment of a high academic profile. Whether this adds anything to the academic content of the discussion is, however, dubious.[9] The heat-to-light ratio of the debate has been further raised by the recent intervention of Arthur Marwick in the *Journal of Contemporary History*, seeking to rebut the 'presumptuous and ill-informed' criticisms that 'post-modernists' are alleged to make of historians. In the subsequent debate, Marwick's charge that 'post-ism' is a 'menace to serious historical study' is dismissed as 'bizarre and uninformed' by Hayden White, who also succeeds in turning most of Marwick's arguments inside-out.[10]

However, there is a genuine issue here. Although I do not agree that the very existence of historical practice is somehow in danger of being exploded by 'post-ism', all the attacks on this composite phenomenon do have targets. There is a great deal of over-theorised and (perhaps unnecessarily) complex writing produced at the frontiers of history and other disciplines, and one might allege a tendency, carried over from more literary studies, for writers to deploy textual arguments 'for their own sake', a tendency that is as ethically dubious as the 'Eltonist' argument that history ought to be deployed 'for its own sake'. The recent 'Sokal Hoax' in the USA has posed many questions as to the intellectual validity of radical post-modernism, questions that the post-modern advocates have not yet proved very good at answering.[11] If post-modernist historians are to insist in the face of the Stones and Marwicks of the profession that our concerns and methods are valid, we must, in the end, as practitioners of history in the broad sense I began with, ask (and be able to answer convincingly) the question 'what is this for?'

This is a question Keith Jenkins has also encouraged, but as I have noted, his initial willingness to leave it substantially unanswered seems to have mutated into an argument that the subject has no useful purpose. In order to challenge that claim, I turn away here from the debate on 'truth', and to my other themes, ethics and imagination.

The ethical question in one sense underpins a more traditional historians' theme, that of 'objectivity'. Students, and no doubt some practising historians,[12] are all too willing to tie themselves in logical knots explaining how some nirvana-state of positionless, 'unbiased' judgment is to be reached, but in the end any practical definition of it, I would argue, comes down to integrity. Is the historian being honest with him or herself in the use of evidence and its interpretation? Are they satisfied that they can genuinely believe, albeit perhaps provisionally, in their version of events or structures? In this sense, what is traditionally seen as 'objectivity' is in fact a highly subjective judgment (always assuming, of course, that historians do not resort to outright fabrication), and any other usage or judgment concerning the issue is projected into the realm of legitimate debate about conclusions and inferences. Beyond these points, however, a more purely ethical concern can be raised.

There are various complex ways of envisioning the term 'ethics', and it is not my intention to elaborate here any grand theory of an 'ethics of historical practice'.[13] I would posit a simple statement that an ethical approach to history involves the viewing of people in the past as 'ethical subjects' – entitled to the same consideration for their actions and perspectives as we would hope to receive for our own. Edward Thompson has left us with one of the most famous statements of a direct ethical concern in history, within which some essentials of the approach may be seen. To quote the relevant paragraph in full:

> I am seeking to rescue the poor stockinger, the Luddite cropper, the 'obsolete' hand-loom weaver, the 'utopian' artisan, and even the deluded follower of Joanna Southcott, from the enormous condescension of posterity. Their crafts and traditions may have been dying. Their hostility to the new industrialism may have been backward-looking. Their communitarian ideals may have been

fantasies. Their insurrectionary conspiracies may have been foolhardy. But they lived through these times of acute social disturbance, and we did not. Their aspirations were valid in terms of their own experience; and, if they were casualties of history, they remain, condemned in their own lives, as casualties.[14]

Here we see Thompson implicitly accepting the idea of the historical subject as an ethical subject, and deploying what I would see as the two key tenets of an ethical approach: to judge, and to understand. He will not deny the strangeness of past actions to the present, or that by a variety of criteria they could be seen as erroneous, but he will see them as actions by people, people who merit our attention because, in their difference, they are human like us, and perhaps because we are flawed like them, in our own ways. There is of course a somewhat disingenuous component to Thompson's statement, since in 'rescuing' such groups from posterity's condescension he is also seeking to elevate them to supporting roles in his own grand narrative of working-class formation. I do not believe, however, that this devalues the point as it is presented.

Ethics leads us necessarily to imagination, because what is central to the notion that the subjects of history could be taken as ethical subjects is the very idea of the existence of people in the past with real lives, and environments, and decisions to take. We cannot know these people in any absolute sense. We know only textual traces, small surviving fragments of some past that can only be interpreted. Yet Thompson does know the people he writes about, he knows them imaginatively. As Joanna Innes and John Styles have phrased it, the whole agenda of 'history from below' in the last three decades has centred around 'the need to explore and imaginatively to reconstruct the experiences of the dispossessed and inarticulate'.[15]

There is of course a philosophical, 'Collingwoodian' idea of the historian's imagination, of penetrating the intentions of historical actors through what a later generation has adulterated into 'empathy'. This, however, is tied to the modernist perception of the reality of that past actor, and indeed, as Keith Jenkins has again shown, to a general ignorance of historical epistemology.[16] I am concerned with, and indeed arguing for, a more present-centred, and 'practitioner-centred', concept of imagination.

I would suggest that the historian can only function through the deployment of imagination, that the linkages and frameworks of all historical work are fundamentally imaginary. Indeed, it is the failure of imagination in the student which is one of the most decisive flaws in an historical education – one cannot teach someone who cannot imagine the past.

There are problems with this approach. As someone who works with the minutiae of police records from the late eighteenth century, holding in my hand, as I have done often, the crabbed manuscript, signed and corrected by policeman, witness, suspect and secretary, I can scarcely imagine that that paper is not fundamentally about something real. Original sources are a great temptation to literalism, but as the preceding sentence illustrates, imagination is still required even in order to assert a 'literalist' interpretation of evidence. Nonetheless, documentary sources remind us that we do deal with an academic subject that has its limitations. Historical study, as a discipline, has its prohibitions, and if it is *history* we write, we cannot claim something to be so when all the evidence denies it. That is, in part at least, the historian's integrity – one cannot, or perhaps should not, take a philosophical leap as so many other disciplines seem to do, and value the structures of one's thought over and above that to which they refer.

This puts history in a rather awkward position vis-a-vis textuality in general, since that is exactly what one is supposed to be able to do. Yet I think this is where we must define history as not being simply inside the textual game that is part, and only part, of the 'post-modern', albeit not comfortably outside that game either.[17] To write about the past meaningfully it is necessary to define some boundaries that we have to accept, and a central one is to treat the products of our historical research *as if they were real*. I believe it is necessary to do this in order to extract any meaning from our discussion of them, and it is necessary because a central concern of history is ethical.

Putting it bluntly, history is a meaningless study for some at a student level precisely because their imaginations are not exercised sufficiently to see historical participants as ethical subjects. If history is to be invested with meaning it has to contain the potential for ethical identification and ethical judgment. 'Identification' can of course evoke all the worst kinds of historical and national fantasy. It should, however, be the prelude to judgment, the process whereby students attempt to understand historical actors on those actors' own terms, before deciding how appropriate it is to approve or disapprove of them. Thus students should be able to see that, for example, the nineteenth-century bourgeoisie had their own reasons for what they did, and were not simply a collective bogey against whom to parade the glories of organised labour.[18] Of course, there are historical episodes where anything other than total disapproval is unlikely (and undesirable). Nevertheless, historical study should teach that slave-owners or concentration-camp guards were products of their time and place, and not mere manifestations of radical evil. Without a sense of ethical engagement, historical learning can be only either a cardboard-cutout parade of 'facts', or a rote repetition of one's teachers' own prejudices.

Ethics emerges implicitly in the recent polemical debates – Eley and Nield close their argument by affirming that 'we really do resist the evacuation of the imperative to analyse capitalism and its necessary and characteristic inequities.'[19] On one level this is a challenge of the type I have already hinted at: if history is not to 'dematerialise', how can the evidence of capitalist social relations of some description be denied? But is there not, in this choice of words, and in the force with which they put their general argument, another, ethical, dimension? The intensity of polemical energy brought to this debate, notably by Neville Kirk, is remarkable. Is it possible that all this energy is being expended in the cause of 'academic argument', in an abstract sense, or is it because the participants care about the interpretation of their subject-matter in a more personal sense? I leave this question substantially open, but it seems to me to be one of the places where debate about history today ought to start from.[20] A brief debate did surface in *Past and Present* several years ago, as to whether historians were not overly sympathetic to rebels in the past, possibly as some kind of reaction to the troubles of present-day society, but no conclusions were reached, as even the participants agreed.[21]

My own view is that historians, in general, do care about the people who compose their subject-matter, and that they are not wrong to do so, although I would also suggest that one inevitable reason for this care is that those 'historical actors' are the historians' own imaginative creations. As I hope I have made clear, I do not believe that they can be anything else. 'Reality' for all of us is a product of our minds, 'historical reality' all the more so, and no less important for that.

The implications of this sort of statement for research are many, but they have frequently been debated in recent years in one form or another. The issue here is the implications for teaching history. If historical practice is to be reconciled to post-modernism through ethics and imagination, then we must turn our attention in teaching from the materials of history to its practitioners – not merely as Keith Jenkins has done by specifying the nature of history as historiography, but by making students the crucial practitioners.

I believe that teachers of history should begin to ask themselves why it is that students come to them to learn, and why it is that those teachers aim to teach what they do. Some of the answers, especially to the first question, may well be disheartening, but they may serve to provoke re-examination of the second question, and a more fruitful synthesis. Recent writing for students on the basics of historical study has said remarkably little about why it should be done. Mary Abbott in *History Skills* sums up a variety of approaches to history in an introductory chapter, from 'Jane Austen' and Sealed Knot enthusiasms, via a chronological account of major currents, to Catherine Hall's racially-aware critique of Cadbury World and its 'heritage' view of the past. However, the conclusion to this chapter seems to suggest almost that a meaning-centred approach is ruled out by the complexity of the field:

> ...[H]ow does the popular appetite for the past relate to the territory occupied by the professional historian? It is not subject matter or source or approach... but the commitment to interrogate the evidence and interpretations of our sources and to provide readers with the means of checking out our conclusions for themselves that gives us the right to claim the title 'historian'.[22]

Later in the same book, a potentially-interesting point is offered:

> What history offers you is a chance to observe and analyse... the whole gamut of human behaviours, including our species' remarkable capacity for deception. This is a salutary experience and an opportunity to develop valuable transferable skills which you can make use of in the real world.[23]

The second sentence rather devalues the first, suggesting both that moral lessons will be imbibed from history in an automatic fashion, and that in any case they are not as important as learning to present conclusions in a manner satisfactory to a Managing Director. The troubling fact for practising history teachers is that the last point – transferable skills – is precisely how both the students, and the controllers of the Higher Education agenda, see the purpose of the subject. Indeed, history departments and degree-teams across Britain, and doubtless the wider world, sell the subject relentlessly as a general degree suitable for a wide range of career choices. This approach is, in some ways, inevitable. Present socio-economic circumstances demand it, and given that (in my experience anyway) many students approach the degree with no more in mind than that it is 'easy' and has 'no maths', it is at least a device for persuading them to learn.

Beverley Southgate's approach offers the opposite pole from this. His opening paragraph cites Plato's aphorism that the unexamined life is not worth living, and reinforces this with the message that the kind of humdrum daily existence to which most students doubtless aspire 'is to live like pigs, and not as human beings for whom some self-awareness is required'. He then leads into a direct parallel with the practice of history –

'we may be all the happier for declining to confront philosophical challenges that might serve to unsettle our emotional and professional equilibrium' – the message clearly being that this too is porcine, in his view. The book closes with a call for historical study to form the core of a Platonic examination of the life of society, where 'our public problems derive in the end from our personal selves', and these selves are historically constructed in all the multitude of ways current historical practice provides for.[24]

This is an interesting challenge to throw in the face of the historical student body, and in that of the historical profession as a whole, but it is, to say the least, confrontational. There is not an easy path from the anodyne of Abbott to the radical surgery proposed by Southgate. However, this is perhaps the kind of path we have to begin to map out, if the practice of history by its professionals is not to lose touch with the vast majority of its students.

In reflecting on history and ethics, a point of reference for some of what I would aim to say can be found in discussions of the Holocaust. This is one of those episodes of history that is commonly seen – and I take this from the views of my own students – as somehow 'outside' history, an event the fundamental inexplicability of which is only matched by the imperative to regard it with horror. This is not a view confined to undergraduates, as the reception of the recent book *Hitler's Willing Executioners* has shown.[25] What this book aims to show is that some tens of thousands of 'ordinary Germans' were directly involved in the murder-execution of Jews, and took part in these episodes and campaigns not through compulsion or alienation, but through the clear belief that Jews were sub-human vermin whose eradication was justified and necessary.

This book has begun to generate a detailed historical controversy, during which many flaws in it have been highlighted, but such an account nevertheless raises important questions.[26] Few would disagree that in the matter of the Holocaust no dry accounting of facts is sufficient for understanding, though here especially the power of the dry fact to move should not be overlooked. But an historical understanding does require more than a purely emotional response. An emotional response can capture something of the horror of the Jews' experience, but what can it gauge of that of the Germans? Daniel Goldhagen has rather ambiguously tried to put the perpetration of the Holocaust back 'within' the history of Germany, without perhaps allowing for the extent to which it ought also to be put 'within' the history of Europe, and the wider West.

There could perhaps be no greater challenge for the historical profession than to educate students to the point where they could see the Holocaust as a human experience from both sides of the wire, to acknowledge its presence at the end of a long evolution of Western attitudes and behaviours, and to see (to admit?) that we might not be able to put as much distance between ourselves and the perpetrators as we might like. To do so might be to plunge students into a turmoil of ethical uncertainty, but that in itself might be entirely appropriate. Amongst the baggage that a great deal of historiography carries from 'modernism' is the need to be implicitly morally right – whether it be French Revolutionists justifying the Terror, or social historians identifying a shade too closely with the oppressed.

It would be only fair, in an age where modernist certainties are supposed to be passing, if we began to ask ourselves, and our students, just who we think we *are* to so easily claim virtue for ourselves. Becoming less dogmatic about our ethical position might lead to a greater appreciation of the mutability of 'truth', and from there to a better sense of what we can claim as the purpose of history.

The Author

Dr David Andress teaches and researches in the School of Social and Historical Studies at the University of Portsmouth. He is currently writing two books, one a social history of Revolutionary France, the other a study of Parisian political culture and popular politics.

References

1   K. Jenkins, 'Why Bother with the Past?: The possible "end" of professional historiography', Paper presented at 'Consuming the Past', King's Manor, University of York, 29 November-1 December 1996. His published works include *Re-thinking History*, Routledge, London, 1991; and *On 'What is History?' From Carr and Elton to Rorty and White*, Routledge, London, 1995.

2   B. Southgate, *History: What and Why? Ancient, modern and postmodern perspectives*, Routledge, London, 1996.

3   J. Tosh, *The Pursuit of History: Aims, methods and new directions in the study of modern history*, 2nd edition, Longman, Harlow, 1991.

4   J. Appleby, L. Hunt and M. Jacobs, *Telling the Truth about History*, Norton, New York, 1994.

5   L. Stone, 'History and Post-modernism', *Past and Present*, no. 131, 1991, pp. 217-18 (p. 218).

6   L. Stone, 'History and Post-modernism', *Past and Present,* no. 135, 1992, pp.189-94 (p. 193). Response to P. Joyce, 'History and post-modernism',

Past and Present, no. 133, 1991, pp. 204-9.

7   Jenkins, *Re-thinking*, p.74 (ch. 2, n. 8).

8   The latest round of exchanges includes P. Joyce, 'The End of Social History?', *Social History*, vol. 20, 1995, pp. 73-91, and G. Eley and K. Nield, 'Starting Over: The present, the post-modern and the moment of social history', *Social History,* vol. 20, 1995, pp. 355-364. For a slightly earlier round, see N. Kirk, 'History, Language, Ideas and Post-modernism: A materialist view', *Social History*, vol. 19, 1994, pp.221-40.

9   It has recently been argued that Joyce is not, in fact, particularly 'post-modern' in his actual historical work; see J. Thompson, 'After the Fall: Class and political language in Britain, 1780-1900', *Historical Journal*, vol. 39, 1996, pp. 785-806; R. Price, 'Languages of Revisionism: Historians and popular politics in nineteenth-century Britain', *Journal of Social History*, vol. 30, 1996, pp. 229-51.

10   A. Marwick, 'Two Approaches to Historical Study: The metaphysical (including "postmodernism") and the historical', *Journal of Contemporary History* vol. 30, 1995; pp. 5-35 (p. 5); H. White, 'Response to Arthur Marwick', *Ibid.* pp. 233-46 (p. 233); C. Lloyd, 'For Realism and Against the Inadequacies of Common Sense: A response to Arthur Marwick', *Journal of Contemporary History,* vol. 31, 1996, pp. 191-207.

11   See P. Boghossian, 'What the Sokal hoax ought to teach us: The pernicious consequences and internal contradictions of "postmodernist" relativism', *Times Literary Supplement*, 13 December 1996, pp. 14-15.

12   See Tosh, *Pursuit of History*, pp. 130-51.

13   A classic philosophical primer is J.L. Mackie, *Ethics: Inventing right and wrong*, Penguin, Harmondworth, 1977. A more recent, and obscure, survey, is A. Phillips Griffiths, ed., *Ethics*, CUP, Cambridge, for the Royal Institute of Philosophy: Supplement 35, 1993.

14   E.P. Thompson, *The Making of the English Working Class*, reprint of 1968 edition with new preface, Penguin, Harmondsworth, 1980 (original publication 1963); p. 12.

15   J. Innes and J. Styles, 'The Crime Wave: Recent writing on crime and criminal justice in eighteenth-century England', *Journal of British Studies,* vol. 25, 1986, pp.380-435 (p. 382).

16   Jenkins, *Re-thinking*, pp. 39-47.

17   One wonders how far there is a difference between the ties imposed by historical documentation, and those imposed by literary texts – just how far would a Derridean scholar, or a Saidean post-colonialist, go in claiming that Austen's *Pride and Prejudice*, for example, was *not* about property, courtship and marriage?

18   See P. Gay, *The Bourgeois Experience: Victoria to Freud*, 3 vols., *Education of the Senses; The Tender Passion; The Cultivation of Hatred*, W.W. Norton & Co., New York, 1984, 1986, 1993.

19   Eley and Nield, 'Starting Over', p. 364.

20   I would note in passing, having largely in the course of this piece taken a

general definition of 'post-modernism' as read, that critiques such as Kirk's, and those of Eley and Nield, and Price, amongst others, although often starting out from an intransigent position, do succeed in raising important questions about just what sort of 'post-modernism' can fairly be brought to bear on historical study.

21   G. Strauss, 'Viewpoint: The dilemma of popular history', *Past and Present*, no. 132, 1991, pp. 130-49; W. Beik, 'Debate: The dilemma of popular history', *Past and Present*, no. 141, 1993, pp. 207-15; G. Strauss, 'Reply: The dilemma of popular history', *ibid.* pp. 215-19.

22   M. Abbott, *History Skills: A student's handbook*, Routledge, London, 1996, pp. 1-21.

23   *Ibid.*, p. 32.

24   Southgate, *History: What and Why?*, pp. 1 & 137.

25   D.J. Goldhagen, *Hitler's Willing Executioners: Ordinary Germans and the Holocaust*, Little, Brown & Co., London, 1996. Initial newspaper views of the author's thesis ranged from the seminal to the reprehensible; see *The Times*, 24 and 28 March 1996, *The Guardian*, 29 March 1996, *The Observer*, 31 March 1996.

26   See H-U. Wehler, 'The Goldhagen Controversy: Agonizing Problems, Scholarly Failure and the Political Dimension', *German History*, vol. 15, 1997, pp. 80-91; B. Rieger, '"Daniel in the Lions' Den?" The German Debate about Goldhagen's *Hitler's Willing Executioners*', *History Workshop Journal*, no. 43, 1997, pp. 226-33.